COUNTRY,

CONSCIENCE
and
CAVIAR

A Diplomat's Journey
In The Company Of History

Alfred Lesesne Jenkins

BookPartners
Seattle, Washington

Permission to reprint certain photos depicting the author has been granted
by Worldwide Photos.

BookPartners
P.O. Box 19732
Seattle, Washington 98109

Table Of Contents

To Martha,
Sara and Stephen

Prologue

Salishan Hills, Central Oregon Coast. November 1992.

his is the story of a moderately interesting South Georgia boy who went on to lead an immoderately interesting and fulfilling life, dining and sometimes working with kings, queens, presidents, prime ministers and foreign ministers, philosophers, prize fighters and gardeners, living in six countries and visiting 79 more—and having at least a measured hand in momentous events and historic decisions. It is about his growth philosophically, his earnest attempts to serve both his country and his conscience, the ups and downs of four careers, and the profound influence of an extraordinary father.

While much of my adult life has been concerned with Sino-American relations, this is not another scholarly work on China, of which there is no dearth. It is simply a memoir—an account of people, places and events as I remember them, with occasional editorializing whenever I am moved to indulge therein. Grateful for a life of rich variety and psychic rewards, I ponder what I have learned and what I may yet learn, seeking what philosophical and spiritual unity there may be in the diversity of a kaleidoscopic life—a life that, for the most part, has simply happened to me, rather than being sought.

I am temporarily semi-retired, pending a decision as to my next career. I say temporarily, because once, after leaving diplomatic service and lecturing around the world for five years, I proceeded to flunk retirement. I do not wish to invite another such failure. I speak of semi-retirement, because I have learned that writing an autobiography is not to be confused with retirement.

This is only the second time in my long life that I have claimed the luxury of time just to think, free from schooling or career demands. The first was when I spent three summer months tented in deep pine woods, by myself except for my horse, my dog and a foot locker of books from my father's extensive library. That was sixty-two years ago, when I was fifteen. At that time I thought a lot about how I wanted to live my life. This time I am taking stock of how it has been lived—and how it may yet be lived.

I was reared Methodist, but my thought life has undergone fundamental metamorphosis. I was taught as a child to try to think rigorously. While my attention was on matters of international concern, my mind and heart sought answers to questions that philosophers, sages and poets have pondered since consciousness appeared in Earth's human experiment. To me, the inner journey has been as fascinating as the outer one. No, more so.

I am up early this brisk November morning. Since I

may also be in the November of my life (although I hope it is no more than mid-August), I seem to need little sleep. I look out from my home on the Oregon coast, over stately spruce and hemlock trees and across Siletz Bay to the endless Pacific. The ocean is unruly this morning, the aftermath of a beautiful storm late last night. The surf is all froth and smashing waves. I am fascinated by its frenzy. The sun has just appeared, glistening highlights on the ever-changing sameness, the diversity in uniformity, of countless whitecaps stretching wide all the way from shore to horizon. Yesterday's high winds and torrential rain have given way to an almost palpable calm, contrasting with the yet cavorting water.

Last night I slept fitfully as well as briefly. Well after midnight I finished a biography of Henry Alfred Kissinger, with whom I traveled and worked during the United States-China rapprochement in the early Seventies. The book rendered my mind about as turbulent as the Pacific's dance before me, crowding my inner vision with events, people and places, pleasures and pains in my past.

Since the Kissinger biography has directed my mind— and certainly my emotions—to that period, I shall start my story with the first day of my return to China after almost a quarter-century absence, the day when I met Premier Chou En-lai for the first time, and witnessed a China startlingly different from the one I had known.

ONE

In The Great Hall Of The People

Beijing. People's Republic of China, October 1971.

or the first time in my life I am not doing justice to a superb Chinese meal. It has been prepared by master chefs of the Beijing Government Guest House where we are staying. It includes some of my favorite dishes: bamboo shoots and egg-white consomme, a sharkfin concoction, beaten chicken breast bits steamed in cellophane envelopes, a huge, sweet-and-sour seasoned fish, stewed prawns, fried rice with mixed vegetables and pork, and an almond custard dessert. My mind and heart are too full to allow my stomach its accustomed way. I smile in noting that Dr. Kissinger, next to whom I am sitting, is happily more than making up for my negligence.

After lunch we are to go to the Great Hall of the People to be received by Premier Chou En-lai and other Chinese dignitaries. I have never formally met the Premier, although I saw him a few times in the Palais des Nations during the 1954 Geneva Foreign Ministers' Conference on Korea and Indochina. I look forward to meeting him, but that prospect is not what has captured my mind or colored my emotions. At this stage in my career I am not easily awed, and certainly not intimidated, by important personages. Two other things are keeping my attention from lesser matters such as nourishment. First, shock and sadness because the China that I now see is so different from the one I learned to love as a junior Foreign Service Officer more than two decades ago. Second is recognition of the world-altering import of the proceedings that are about to unfold—if they go well.

When Henry finishes eating we all go out into the large foyer and ascend the stately, winding stairs to our second floor quarters. The thoughtful Chinese have scheduled a rest period after lunch. I frown on entering the suite assigned to me, because while my name on the door is correct in English, I do not like the name they have given me in Chinese. It is Chan Chin-ssu, which has no particular meaning, and is certainly not a Chinese-sounding name. My Chinese name, the one I have used for 24 years is Chin Hsi-sheng. It was given to me in 1947 by my favorite tutor, Mr. Chang, a white-haired gentleman of great dignity and avuncular warmth. Since, in his daily visits, I often spurned the prosaic textbook lessons in favor of attempts at philosophical discussion, the old scholar gave me a name that he thought would be appropriate. The surname, Chin, simply means "Gold." The given name, Hsi-sheng, means "aspire to be a sage." Flowery names were the custom, so one was not required to blush. Chinese friends often remarked what a fine name I had been given.

The Chinese Communist authorities have reason to know my true name, certainly from recent Hong Kong news accounts in Chinese, and probably from the Voice of America. We have reports that the Chinese leaders listen regularly to the Voice. I wonder whether having a Chinese sounding name is now viewed by the Communist Chinese as presumptuous on the part of the foreign barbarian.

I explore my heavy and formal, but comfortable and attractive suite. The entrance leads into a large, high-ceilinged living room containing ponderous, overstuffed, dark brown sofa and chairs with lace coverings for arms and back. There is a glassed-in cabinet containing several beautiful and doubtless ancient objects of art, ivory, jade and porcelain pieces of museum quality. On the floor is a beautiful tan carpet of raised design. On the wall is a large bamboo painting. A smaller one on the wall opposite depicts mountains, clouds, a bent pine tree, a waterfall and either an elderly sage or a wine-sotted poet.

The adjoining bedroom contains a large, comfortable bed with a white, handmade, lacy coverlet and huge, square pillows. There are two more overstuffed chairs and a color TV set of Chinese manufacture. A commodious bathroom contains tub and shower, wash basin and commode, and a medicine cabinet filled with toilet articles and lotions, all of which prove to be of Chinese manufacture. As an old China hand, I am impressed. Formerly the toiletries would have been of European manufacture, mainly British. Completing the suite is a balcony off the bedroom overlooking spacious gardens with flowers, shrubs, oaks and weeping willows.

I turn on the TV and prop up in bed to watch the last few minutes of a creditable color cartoon with minimal political content. That is followed by a highly politicized tour of a machine tool plant in Shanghai. While the program would normally be an unfailing soporific, I discover that I cannot sleep. All day I have felt too uncomfortably alien to relax.

I do not like the atmosphere of this city. So far I have not seen one smiling face, even during the half-hour drive from the airport. The crowds of Chinese behind police cordons at every intersection as we were driven through the city to the Guest House were glum, showing no interest in the cavalcade of limousines.

I do not get the feeling today that this is a police state of Stalinist severity, even though at times the authorities have demonstrated a very bloody ruthlessness. In June 1950, for example, only months after establishment of the regime, the Chinese Communists launched a two-year nation-wide program of land redistribution involving expropriation of land and mass executions of millions of landlords and "honorary landlords" who were charismatic local leaders deemed not subject to ready political control. By their own admission, the Chinese Communists disciplined in 1957 some 300,000 so-called rightists by measures ranging from execution to thought reform. This was during the Hundred Flowers Movement, when Mao called for more diversity in intellectual life under the slogan "let a hundred flowers bloom and diverse schools of thought contend." There was such an avalanche of criticism of the regime that the movement had to be brought to an end.

Untold thousands are also reported to have lost their lives in the Great Cultural Revolution beginning in 1966, through gang battles, executions, a rash of suicides and Red Guards excesses (youths licensed by Mao to attack and destroy that which did not represent the new China.)

The Cultural Revolution is still going on while we are visiting China, albeit not as frenetically as in its first three

years. The air still seems to be heavy with weariness, resignation, resentment and fear.

A knock on my door indicates that it is time to join
Kissinger and the rest of his entourage for the drive to the
Great Hall of the People, just as soon, that is, as Julie
Pineau, Kissinger's kittenish secretary, belatedly elects to
descend the grand stairs into the foyer.

We enter the Chinese-built, seven-passenger Red Flag
limousines, reminiscent of the power, comfort and design
of Packards in their heyday. Through the lightly curtained
windows I view a bit of China transformed beyond recognition from the China I had known before. My earlier experience in Peking and what I am now experiencing form
nothing less than a "tale of two cities." The once bustling
dynamism of the street vendors, the smiling faces, the
laughter, the dignity of so many elderly Chinese of *all*
walks of life and levels of society, and the startling beauty
of so many of the young are missing. The faces of the
crowds on the streets lack animation and, judging from the
walk and the stance of most people, their spirits sag. Their
dress is uniform: grey or dark blue trousers and Mao jackets buttoned up to the neck. Men and women are dressed
pretty much alike. Only the children sometimes wear a bit
of color, and often that is discreetly hidden by a somber
outer garment.

As a people, the Chinese have unquestionably stood
up in the world, proud again to be Chinese after their hundred years of semi-colonial ignominy. I am glad of that.
But in individual Chinese, the former serenity and dignity,
the sense of the individual being in possession of himself,
is missing. People on the street are as quiet and as subdued
as in any Eastern European communist capital. To be char-
itable, one might read into their demeanor a grim purpose-
fulness in building a new China, but the whole scene tells

me that to the extent that sentiment exists, it is tempered, even eclipsed, by a pervasive sullenness.

I know from intelligence reports that have crossed my desk that in these days of 1971 the basic necessities of life have been met for virtually all of the nine hundred million Chinese—truly a prodigious achievement. There are reports documenting other impressive accomplishments, from innovative, effective and inexpensive health care to sophisticated manufacturing, Also, even in the few hours I have been here, I have noted with admiration the absence of the obsequiousness formerly shown one's superiors. I suppose it must be difficult to be very deferential while calling another person "comrade."

I know that in coming weeks during which there will be other Kissinger negotiating visits, preparing the way for an eventual presidential visit, I shall considerably refine my first impressions of this ancient city, which, with few interruptions, has been the capital of China for some 700 years. My first impressions, however, are not comforting.

The limos glide down Chang An Chieh past huge, granite, signally unimaginative buildings, seldom evincing any Chinese artistry. I am reminded that for a decade Soviet help was instrumental in building the new China. Finally, we pass in front of the Great Hall of the People, with its eleven huge columns in its entrance. As we round the corner of the colossal structure to proceed down its east side, which abuts Tienanmen Square, we see on our left the south wall, moat and entry gate of the ancient imperial Forbidden City. I recall that most of Peking's walls, moats, palaces and temples were built during the illustrious Ming Dynasty in the 15th century. From above the entry gate and reviewing balcony of the south wall of the Forbidden City an enormous portrait of Chairman Mao Tse-tung looks down upon us. It is a portrait of the chief architect of the New China, revolutionary genius, foremost Chinese Communist theoretician, seldom disputed top Chinese Communist leader since the 1940s, yet not a successful administrator of a country. His renowned charisma is not captured in the portrait. I wonder whether he fears, or has any idea of, the likely effects of a serious "bourgeois bacteria" invasion that will presumably follow an American presence in China—if indeed such a presence results from the efforts we are about to initiate.

The Chinese official in the front seat breaks his silence to inform us that the gigantic Great Hall of the People was built in just eight months. Riding down its lengthy east side I try to focus on the big picture rather than on my personal disappointments. Soon the representatives of two great nations that for more than two decades have been deeply and vociferously antagonistic toward each other—even fighting each other in Korea—will meet. They are to see if common ground can be found on which to build a beginning relationship, leading eventually to full diplomatic relations, accompanied by business, educational, cultural and scientific intercourse. What a transformation that would bring on the world scene! Just now we cannot speculate with much conviction how far the effort may take us. At a minimum, the most influential nation in the world and the most populous nation will each come to understand better what motivates the other, and how each views the parlous state of the contemporary world. If all goes well, there may be established a more stable relationship among the several major powers. After all, China in 1964 entered the growing, hence more ominous, atomic "club."

The limousines silently glide up a ramp on the southern side of the Great Hall, coming to a smooth stop before its entrance. I am guided by Chinese officials along with Dr. Kissinger, John Holdridge, Winston Lord, various advisers, aides and secretaries through the large south entrance. Just inside, Premier Chou En-lai waits to greet us.

I am right behind Kissinger as he and Chou shake hands. They had met on Kissinger's quick, secret trip to Beijing a few weeks earlier. I sense that they greet each other not only as equals, but with mutual respect. I feel for the first time since arrival this morning that we big-nosed, curiously round-eyed foreigners may become reasonably welcome aliens, with promise of fuller acceptance later on.

As my turn approaches to shake the hand of Premier Chou En-lai a cascade of images flow through my mind. I am to greet one whose hands have been incarnadined by ruthless bloodletting in his early revolutionary days. This is the man who has countenanced acts in the name of the revolution that can only be called atrocities. Yet he is the suave, handsome, French-educated gentleman who has been a tower of strength in efforts to preserve a semblance of national stability through the three most chaotic years of the Cultural Revolution horror. He is probably the most widely recognized advocate of sanity and reasonableness in domestic matters, and he also has promoted reason in relations beyond the world of the Middle Kingdom (China).

Close companion to Mao for over 40 years, Chou's loyalty to the Chairman is unquestioned. Like most of the present leadership, Chou is a veteran of the trial known as the Long March, during which Mao became undisputed leader of the Party. Pressed by Chiang Kai-shek's forces, the bulk of the Red Army, including Mao and his pregnant wife, in 1934 abandoned their base in the southeast China province of Kiangsi and made the incredible, torturous 6,000-mile trek over some of the most formidable terrain of western China. They arrived three years later at Yenan in the barren northwest province of Shensi. Mao's headquarters remained there until the Communist victory of 1949.

Since Chou and Kissinger have met before, their greeting is more than perfunctory. For its duration I size up this renowned Long March veteran who has weathered unscathed many a purge of the senior ranks of the Chinese leadership. He unquestionably represents more hope for our purposes of a reconciliation between our two countries than any other Chinese, even though Mao will have the last word.

The Premier is dressed in perfectly tailored light grey trousers and matching Mao jacket of fine woolen material. He wears no decoration or insignia. I am surprised at his small stature, for in pictures he seems to stand tall. Atmospherically, he does now, too, with a self-confidence rendered the more convincing by an all-pervading modesty that validates it. In his reserved, yet warm, enigmatic smile there is a tinge of world-weariness, almost a sadness, along with a distinct promise of humor. The combination makes one want to linger in his presence.

When Henry moves on, I extend my hand to this remarkable man, widely regarded as the most charismatic, the most consummately able diplomat of our time. I find his handshake gentle but firm, and with just enough reserved warmth to make me feel somewhat welcome in the New China. I mutter a simple, "Mr. Premier," as I return his smile and move on.

I pause before greeting other Chinese dignitaries, since Henry has stopped to talk with one of them. I use this moment to sort through the flood of thoughts surging through my mind. I savor in prospect the more peaceful world that may come from this attempt at reconciliation with China. This China, however, is very different from the one that I learned to love in my first assignment in the Foreign Service. I try to focus on the accomplishments of the new China. From that my mind gains satisfaction, but my heart is not happy, and it shifts my mind to fond memories of starting my career in pre-Communist Peking, with my wife, Martha, by my side.

TWO

Student
Life
In China

y first assignment in the Foreign Service was to the State Department's China Language School in Peking. After months of intensive study of the language at the University of Chicago, I could converse with relative ease except on subjects requiring specialized vocabularies and could read Chinese with only moderate recourse to the dictionary. I was eager to further my facility with the language, my knowledge of the country, and my understanding of the remarkable Chinese people.

Martha at first had trepidations about living in China, but after an evening with a lover of life by the name of Tillie Hoffman, a fellow denizen of the Pentagon known to all old China hands, Martha, too, became excited. Tillie had spent years in Peking, and was aching to spend years more. Now that Martha was convinced that life could be beautiful in the other hemisphere, she wanted to learn Chinese. She did so, with her own tutors. I remember walking across Memorial Bridge in Washington one moonlight night soon after we were married and teaching her the first sentence she learned in Chinese: *"Yueh-liang hen p'iao-liang"* (The moon is very beautiful.)

With great expectations, 17 pieces of luggage and seemingly that many inoculations in our hips, one chilly evening in November 1946, we boarded the train in Washington, bound for San Francisco. We had little idea of the momentous events that were soon to take place in China—events that would change the course of history and in the process put our own young lives in some danger. For our first year and a half abroad, however, life was close to idyllic.

Commercial travel to the Far East, as we called East Asia then, was beginning to be reinstated after World War II, but the longest leg of our sea journey to China was to be courtesy of the Navy, on an enormous, all-grey troopship, the *General Mitchell*. It stashed away in its bowels 4,000 Marines, 700 crew, and 250 laborers for Guam. In addition, there were wives of Navy officers permitted to join their husbands in China now that World War II was over, a few young marine officers, a bachelor Foreign Service officer headed for the China Language school, and a Foreign Service wife going to join her husband at the School.

We docked at Pearl Harbor, where the tops of ships the Japanese had sunk poked up out of the water. It was the first tangible evidence I had seen of World War II, since I had spent most of it at the Pentagon. The evident loss of life and of substance seemed insane.

In Hawaii one morning Martha and I were strolling along Waikiki Beach in our swim garb. Martha was stunningly beautiful then. (She improved later.) We passed close by a couple of Chinese boys of college age who were eyeing Martha. One said to the other, not in undertones, for he had no idea I would understand him, *"Pu ts'o, pu ts'o!"* which means "Not bad, not bad!" I turned to him and said, *"Wo wan ch'uan t'ung-i!"* which means "I am in complete agreement!" I'd give a tidy sum for a picture of his expression.

When we docked at Manila, naked lads swam out to the ship and dived deep for coins tossed into the water by the Marines, coming up with them in their mouths. Poverty was severe, and the war damage in the city was hard to believe. Block after block of buildings were gutted and razed by bombing and blackened by fires. An amiable young vice consul from the French Embassy drove us around the city. His stories of Japanese atrocities during the war froze one's blood. They seemed unreal, coming from a presentable young Frenchman speaking drawing-room Oxford English. At other times our transportation was by jeeps turned taxi. They were bumpy, lurching and careening, almost caroming with other vehicles in the crazy traffic, garishly decorated, and life-threateningly fast.

At last Hong Kong, a glitzy British-China of contrasts. The beauty and interest of the bustling harbor was enchanting as seen from The Peak, by day or night, and the mixture of Chinese and British cultures fascinating. I vowed I would return some day.

Our first taste of the real China was when we anchored in Shanghai harbor, which was choked with ships and boats of all sizes, forms, purposes and ports of origin. Why there were not constant collisions was a mystery. There were huge passenger and freighter ships from all over the world. Colorful Chinese junks that served as permanent residences for the occupants. Swarms of little paddle boats with peddlers hawking their misrepresented wares: lacquer boxes, garish scarfs, splotchily embroidered silks with gross stitching in the reddest reds and greenest greens. One boat boasted "beautiful jade carvings" but they were soap-stone.

Our crew turned fire hoses on the peddlers! When I asked why on earth they did so, I was told it was the only way to keep the enlisted men from spending all their money on junk before they went ashore. Even that was unavailing. The doused peddlers came right back for more dousing, laughing as though they enjoyed it. The troops continued to hang out of the portholes, haggling at the price of white silk pillow slips with *MOTHER* embroidered in fire-truck red. Baskets at the end of long bamboo poles collected the dollars and returned the junk. There was lusty yelling on all sides, on water and ashore; there were sharp put-puts from crisscrossing motorboats; there were ear-splitting blasts from great ships, scores of little paddle boats bobbing in their wake; and people——people, people everywhere. Captivating bedlam! Unfettered spontaneity! The noises, the activity, the smells! Already, I liked China more than I could say.

Even in a time of post-war scarcity one could buy almost anything in Shanghai in almost any quantity. Jade and ivory carvings and cloisonné of museum quality. Embroidery so fine it was hard to believe mere mortals produced it.

Finally, 31 days from Washington, we were transported up the Tientsin river in a U.S. Navy landing craft. We arrived at Tientsin at dusk and were driven in a U.S. Consulate General car to the Taladi Hotel, where the lights promptly went out. Stubby candles were $1,000 Chinese each, about $1.40 U.S. at the 1946 exchange rate.

The next morning we took the crowded train to Peking. I was excited to be at last where the Mandarin dialect was indigenous. I roamed through the aisles chatting with everyone who seemed conversationally approachable. To my joy I learned that most Chinese are. Or rather were then; that would too soon change.

Our first time in China was limited to a wondrous year-and-a-half in Peking and a tense year in Tientsin. Those who spoke Chinese called the ancient city Peiping (pronounced Bayping), meaning Northern Peace. At the inception of the Communist regime, when the capital was moved from Nanching, meaning Southern Capital, Peiping became Peiching, (or Beijing) meaning Northern Capital.

Martha and I began our Peiping experience living in San Kuan Miao, a 300 year-old temple compound in the former Legation Quarter that housed the State Department language students. It was near the Hatamen city gate, and opposite the Wagon-Lits Hotel. The famous old hotel was called in Chinese *Liu Kuo Fan-tien,* Six Nations Hotel, a reminder of the allied forces who had put down the Boxer Rebellion of 1900.

The high brick wall around our house had a Chinese-red entrance door with a button that rang a bell in the servants' quarters. The kitchen was part of the servants' quarters and did not adjoin the house. We had been taught never to go to the kitchen, but once when the servants were all occupied with spring cleaning I went out back and took a peek. Unbelievable! Splendid meals, often for twelve and once for twenty, had been produced on one charcoal burner and a jerry-built oven!

For the first few weeks in Peiping we were given only enough coal to heat my tiny study. Since it was winter the rest of the house was useless except for the bedroom when we were in bed. The rail lines were interrupted repeatedly by Communist guerrillas, so coal was expensive.

One bitter day in January the wife of the Consul

General came, with hat and white gloves, to return Martha's formal call on her, made when we first arrived. Normally we would have served her tea and had a nice visit, but she was ushered through two frigid rooms to my warm study, where six language officers in jeans, each unmistakably martini-brightened, were sitting on my desk, on the floor and on two chairs. We were fortifying ourselves to go to a cold theater to see a Chinese play.

Wang went for Martha, who squeezed into the study. The proper Mrs. Myers, rejecting the proffered chair, accepted a stand-up martini instead of the expected sit-down tea. She soon fled the scene, leaving her card with one corner turned up to indicate it was delivered in person. The next day all the language officers had coal enough to heat their entire houses, not toastily, but temperately. When Mrs. Myers learned that to heat her whole house it took a ton of coal a day, she closed down several rooms.

From then on, life was good. The ten to twelve students in residence at any one time were invariably congenial, we were engaged in the common pursuit of learning an exotic language, Peiping was an ancient, historical and very beautiful city, and the Chinese were uncommonly likeable people. Except for times when the Department held us to the unrealistic official exchange rate, things were cheap, and we could live in a princely fashion on a meager vice consul's salary, and even afford a few Chinese objects of art. Life was even better when, after suffering through two disastrous staffs of servants we found ourselves blessed with a staff of whom we simply found no fault.

I don't know what prompted Wang to apply for the job of what was shamefully called our Number One Boy, but he was a Godsend. He had been the favorite steward at the Peking Club. Wang brought with him Hsieh, a wizard of a cook. They were both in their twenties, intelligent, immaculately groomed, and knew all the niceties of serving and protocol. Wang spoke beautiful English and Hsieh's was fair. They always seemed to know what we wanted before we did, and produced it. They seemed to live to make us happy, and they were abundantly successful at it. Furthermore, they appeared to be as happy themselves as anyone I have ever known.

Wang was surprisingly well educated, and had a choice sense of humor. He delighted in making me laugh by mixing slang and literary expressions in the same sentence. In return, Martha and I would sometimes panic the servants by speaking Chinese with an exaggerated American southern accent.

At first Wang tried to be my valet in addition to his other duties. Especially if I were dressing formally for dinner—frequently the case in the Peiping of the 40s—he would not only lay out my clothes, he would hold the bottoms of my tux trousers off the floor while I stuck my legs into them. That was annoying, but I didn't want to hurt his feelings. Finally, I told Wang his management of the household was so impeccable, the floors were as clean as my trousers. His face was saved, as was my independence.

The servants seemed to know everything that went on in the community. One evening we had to go to dinner at the home of a Chinese friend who was a consummate bore. He would say the same thing several different ways, then explain it. He was a teetotaler, and exacted the same restraint from his guests. Martha and I ordinarily welcomed an evening of abstinence, but this particular evening we could have used multiple libations.

We returned home dry and very late, because we were the junior people there and couldn't leave until the seniors left. When we rang the bell at our garden gate (with live-in servants no one carried keys) I thought it strange that there was a little delay in answering. When the coolie opened the door, there stood Wang with a grin on his face and a scotch and soda in each hand. We sat in the garden and revived. We hadn't told the servants where we were dining that evening, nor had we at that time even unpacked our engagement book, but they knew where we were and through what sort of an evening we would suffer.

Wang taught me to understand and like Chinese opera. Whenever I attended one, however, he said I must buy him a ticket in the back row. I should tell the vendors of tea, watermelon seed and peanuts to come to him for payment of my snacks, since it would not be proper for a U.S. Vice Consul to be seen handling money in public. I was about to explain that I had no interest in that sort of face, but quickly realized Wang was thirsting to go to the opera himself, by whatever means available. I therefore submitted to the alleged custom, but felt foolish.

Gradually I came to know what to listen for and what to look for. The music that earlier I had found so objectionable became thrilling. In my ignorance I had mistaken sophisticated subtlety for grating repetition, and the intricacies of makeup and costume and their significance to the story had escaped me. I became addicted.

The audience was noisy. Happily noisy. Vendors of snacks roamed through the audience. Moist, hot cloths were provided to wipe face and hands. It was acceptable to react out loud to villainy or heroics. Chinese opera was meant to be enjoyed without restraint, and decorum gave way to total immersion. More of the Chinese art of living—an art soon destined virtually to die. The Communists would later emasculate, then ban these operas.

o   o   o

Four Chinese tutors came for an hour each to the students' houses five days a week. We were learning to speak Chinese fluently, to read it with facility, and to write it to the extent of individual application. For additional language practice we went to Chinese plays, churches, *hsiang-sheng* productions (a two-man comic act) and Chinese opera, visited in homes of Chinese friends, invited them to our homes, and took week-end trips by train to villages within sixty miles or so. As junior as we were, we met important personages of the day and sometimes entertained them in our homes.

We had language practice in specialized vocabularies by hiring jugglers, tumblers, martial arts performers and magicians to perform in our homes at dinner parties. Their skill was outstanding, their patter amusing, and their charges unbelievably reasonable.

Among my tutors I was devoted to Mr. Chang, my first tutor in the morning. He was a white-haired, dignified, elderly gentleman of the old school, with a rich, deep voice, a quiet sense of humor, a serene, grandfatherly smile and elegant manners. He wore the traditional Chinese gown, silk in summer, padded cotton in winter. He claimed to be impressed by the level of my Chinese after my twelve months of linguistic immersion at the University of Chicago, so we generally gave the lesson of the day short shrift. Instead, we talked of philosophy, psychology, religion, and the benignity of most human frailty. Excitedly, I studied with him the vocabularies involved in speaking of introspection, optimism and paranoia, then had to learn the flat prosaics of the day's lesson mostly on my own. That he got across these meanings to me without any English is evidence of his wizardry and his patience.

Learning Chinese was facilitated by the fact that at that time most Peking Chinese, at least, liked Americans and were allowed to show it. This was especially true of the children. When I walked on the street they would run up, stick their thumbs in the air and, wreathed in smiles, yell, "Hello Joe, *ting hao!*" If I responded in Chinese they would shriek, call others, and follow me down the street, fighting to see who would hold my hand. Just how much the children's devotion to Americans was due to Hershey bars I was never sure. By the time they were in high school they had been exposed to a few -isms and were confused as to what or whom they should admire. By the time they were in college (the small percentage who made it) they had definite political opinions, often unreasoned, but passionately held and loudly propounded.

Even weekends afforded opportunities to polish our Chinese. Many were spent in outlying villages that were still Nationalist-held. We learned to buy third-class tickets on the train for best language practice. The passengers, being jam-packed and uncomfortable, were bonded by a sort of fraternity-in-adversity, like being buck privates in the Army. Once Jerry Stryker and I went by train to Nan K'ou. We engaged a room at a little inn, sleeping on the brick *k'ang,* as the rural Chinese do. We had an incredible Chinese meal at a tiny restaurant—six delectable dishes, tea and hot Hsiao-hsing yellow wine, all for the equivalent of 40 cents each in 1947 U.S. currency. That evening we sprawled on the *k'ang* and talked in Chinese, of philosophy, art, sex, the good life, the future of China and other uplifting, imponderable or degrading topics.

We awoke about 4 o'clock in the morning, both rested and restless, so we called in the innkeeper's son and asked when the next train left for anywhere. Doubtless happy to be rid of lunatics so insensitive to time and space, he dashed down the street and returned with tickets for a place called Ch'ang P'ing Hsien, where we arrived just before a spectacular dawn, to learn that the town proper was some three miles from the station. We deposited our things at the station post office and started out walking. It was a glorious walk, but we learned later that it was a bit dangerous before good light, for the Communists controlled the territory by night and the Nationalists by day, both collecting taxes from the hapless peasants.

Behind purple mountains in the distance the sky gradually shaded from grey to orange. The fall air was bracing, and pungent with the smell of freshly turned fields planted with winter wheat. A few swooping doves graced the scene.

We passed clusters of houses from which radiated the relevant farmlands. Farmers were going into town to sell their wares. Some rode donkeys or walked beside the overladen animals. Some farmers balanced mountainous wares on their own backs. We exchanged pleasantries with everyone who didn't seem to be out of breath.

We arrived in town in time to have a superb Moslem breakfast, surrounded by onlookers ringing our table, listening to our Chinese and telling us how 'perfect' it was. (The polite Chinese do this invariably, even if one's speech limps and contorts.)

In mid-morning we went to a Chinese Christian church. We were early, so we talked for a time with the two ministers about subjects we were used to talking about that also interested them: economics, politics, geography, human relations. They saw we spoke fluent Chinese, so at the end of the 11 o'clock service the minister asked me to give the closing prayer. Oh, God, I knew it had to happen some day. I was not even very comfortable with public, audible prayers in English. I thought Jesus had a point in counseling us to go into a closet and pray in secret. I'm sure the only foreigners these Chinese had known before were missionaries, so Americans were assumed to be eminently practiced in religiosity. Distressingly, I suddenly realized I had no idea what salutary phrase to use in addressing God in Chinese, and more distressingly, I had no idea what the Chinese said in closing a prayer. I had visions of my informing the Deity endlessly about matters of scant interest to Him, since I would be unable to sign off. I considered just saying *wan-le* when I was through, but "finished" sounded a bit flip in speaking to God. I elbowed Jerry as authoritatively as I could, hoping he would jump into the lengthening breach, but he elbowed me with equal authority, laced with unambiguous finality. So I simply had to say, before all those people, that our vocabularies didn't encompass prayer lingo, and we hoped we'd be excused. The congregation, I'm sure, decided we were shameless heathens.

The minute I got home I looked up the Lord's Prayer in my Chinese Bible. It seems the inscrutable Chinese close a prayer by saying "Amen."

THREE

The Inevitable Transition

ntertaining was easy with our excellent staff, and little expense, so we entertained a great deal. In those days if a splendid meal cost more than $1 U.S. per guest, you looked for another cook. On our second wedding anniversary, to Wang's scarcely concealed disapproval, Martha and I had dinner served to the two of us on the floor in front of the fire, dogs by our side. Martha was dressed in a long black satin gown with a pastel lake scene at the bottom, swans and all. I hadn't seen it before. The fire was bright, the food outstanding, Martha exquisite, and I was happy. We went for our engagement book and discovered that it was the first evening in nineteen that we had dinner for just the two of us.

Martha busied herself by forming a kindergarten for the American children and in teaching conversational English to the personnel of a large Chinese bank. The latter connection led to our becoming movie stars. Well, not stars, but we did act in a Chinese movie. The wife of one of the bank men was a very beautiful movie star. Someone told her that Martha had nice Western clothes, so she borrowed several outfits for her role as a daughter of Madame H.H. Kung, one of the three famous Soong sisters. We played the part of foreign guests at a dinner party given by Madame Kung. It was fun to see ourselves and Martha's clothes on the big screen downtown.

In the summer of 1947 the State Department sent me on a five-week trip into Inner Mongolia—Chahar province, to be exact. I traveled by train to Kalgan (Chang Chia K'ou), the capital of the province, taking my bicycle and a dozen crates of U.S. Army 'C' rations. The military guard at the railroad station helped me load my rations onto rickshaws and directed me to the best hotel, calling after me, "It will not be like New York."

I called back, "Who knows, I might be thankful for the novelty." It wasn't, and I wasn't. There was a hole in the floor of my room through which an enormous rat emerged to prance about each night. I didn't object to its presence except for the noise it made running about. I got up at all hours several times and tried to bash it with my bicycle pump, but I was not fleet enough. This went on for a couple of nights, until I put a piece of candy with DDT on it near the hole, and had only one brief disturbance thereafter. I can't imagine why the Consulate put DDT in my effects, but I gave thanks.

The purpose of my trip was to compare conditions under the Communists, who had occupied the territory for an earlier six-month period, with conditions under the Nationalists, who had held sway for the most recent six months. My findings, in nine trips into the countryside by bicycle from Kalgan and further travels for a fortnight by oxcart, horseback, donkeyback, truck and foot, are not of burning import at this writing, so I'll skip them except to say that the peasants claimed thoroughly to dislike the Communists, saying they willfully misrepresented things and held too many meetings. They were not complimentary of the Nationalists, either, except to say that General Fu Tso-yi, the commanding general for northwest China, and a few of his most senior officers were incorruptible and Fu was a military genius. General Fu granted me a long interview and invited me to a banquet a couple of days later. I could scarcely enjoy the splendid fare because of the presence of a pompous young man from the U.S. Economic Cooperation Administration, who had millions to dole out to the Chinese. For a decade after World-War II we did not play the role of top nation with unfailing grace.

I spoke with over 70 peasants about their reactions to the periods of Communist, then Nationalist control, spending time with each of about 30 families, often sitting tailor fashion on their *k'angs* partaking of a simple meal, typically of cone-shaped cornmeal bread and stewed cabbage. I had brought toys for the children of my hosts. All I had to do to get invited to a farm house was to buy fruit on the street speaking Chinese, and a crowd of maybe thirty Chinese would gather. I would get to talking with someone, and half the time end up in homes of the farmers. They were open and friendly, so the associations were enjoyable as well as informative. To be polite, I often had to eat raw vegetable appetizers. I doubtless owe my life to following every mouthful with a swig of *pai gan,* which was invariably offered to guests. No respectable germ would live in that explosive stuff.

General Fu said it would be dangerous for me to go out into the countryside without armed escort, which he would be glad to furnish. That wouldn't do, of course, for it would put a damper on frank talk. I asked the Catholic priest in town if it was really unsafe. He said not very unsafe if I was careful to return to Kalgan before dark. The Communists sporadically ruled the rural areas by night, and they might be very glad to have an American hostage.

I attempted to ride out into the countryside on two of the four roads leading out of the city, but was politely and firmly stopped by guards, who told me it was not safe. The following day I tried the third exit, where the guard happened to be from Peiping. He was so happy to chat with an American speaking the Peiping dialect, I got him to agree that I could go as far as 10 li (a little over three miles) if I would promise to be back well before dark, and not tell anyone in Kalgan that he had permitted it. That wasn't far enough to suit me, so next day I tried a ruse at the fourth and last exit from the city. I rode rapidly past the guard, knowing he would call me back, and hoping he would be rude. He was. He called me back with invectives, a couple of which my tutors had neglected to impart to me. As I had hoped, he took me for a White Russian. Except for Belgian Catholic missionaries, all foreigners in those parts were White Russians. He yelled, "Hey, big nosed one! What do you think you are doing?" He actually pointed his rifle at me. "Come back here. Give me your identification papers!"

I gave him my passport. He seemed to be fairly literate for a Chinese soldier. As he perused it, the blood left his face.

"You are an American?"

"That's right."

"I've never seen an American."

"You're looking at one."

"What is this?" He pointed at the three characters *wai chiao kuan.* I tried to explain what a diplomatic official was. I don't think he grasped the meaning, but the full-page Consulate General chop in red did the trick.

"Please excuse me, sir, I thought ..."

"I know. It's all right. I just want to see something of Chinese rural life. General Fu offered me a military escort, but I didn't want to trouble him."

"You know General Fu Tso-yi?"

"I had lunch with him a couple of days ago."

He put his hand on my arm. "You won't tell him ...?

"Secrets are more certainly kept when each side has one," I observed. "I would like to have a full day in the country, and go as far as I like."

He finally agreed, but only after I promised that if anything untoward happened to me, I would swear that I had slipped out past him, through the fields.

I found crosspaths leading to one of the other roads that led out of the city, so for the following week I covered wide areas of the countryside, first passing through the checkpoint of my friend, with whom I shared reciprocal secrets.

The populace was looking to the United States to help protect them from both the Chinese Communists and the Russians, and that further facilitated friendships and entry into farm homes. From their reports I could understand their dislike of the Russians. Everyone I talked with agreed the brief Soviet occupation at the end of the Japanese war was frightful. The Russians carried away with them machinery, almost everyone's watch, and four-fifths of the sheep, a mainstay of the local livelihood. I later was told that most of the Russian troops that entered China after V-J Day were criminals who had been released from Siberian prisons to stake a claim for the Soviets in the demise of Japanese power in China. The U.S.S.R. had entered the East Asian theater of World War II just before the Japanese surrender.

I sent to the Department a 92-page report on my trip and its findings. Since it was the first report in my diplomatic career, I eagerly awaited word from Washington as to its reception. I was put in my place. The appraisal, written by the "China desk" in the Department, said it attested to my perceptivity and ingenuity, but it was too long for busy people in Washington to read—an appraisal ill designed to encourage a neophyte. I consoled myself by thinking that surely there must be some drone in the bowels of government buildings in Washington who would pounce upon intelligence as to the price of plums in Chang Chia-k'ou on May 12, 1948, to piece out yet another memo destined for oblivion.

Soon after my return home General Fu was transferred to Peiping as commander of all North China. He had been so kind to me in Kalgan that, despite my junior rank, I saw no reason why I shouldn't ask him to dinner. I went by his headquarters and explained to an aide that I knew General Fu was the busiest man in all North China, but he had been so kind to me in Kalgan, I would be most honored if he ever found a free evening and would consent to grace our home at dinner. I then went off to have a leisurely tea with a fellow student at Pei Hai, (Northern Lake). I arrived home at six o'clock to find Martha practically in tears. General Fu's office had just called to say he would be delighted to come to dinner at seven that evening! Martha was trying to arrange for a dinner at the Club. I thought that would not be fitting, and called Wang in. His eyes lit up immediately. Think of the face he would gain if his master entertained General Fu! Wang said for us to get on the phone and corral twenty friends in evening dress, and Hsieh and he would produce the dinner.

General Fu didn't drink, so seven o'clock meant 7:05 dinner. He arrived at 6:59, greeted the sixteen guests who had arrived before him (he had an aide with him, and two of our guests were late), signed our guest book, and we all sat down to a sumptuous five-course dinner with three wines and an exciting dessert. Much of the dinner may have come from the Peking Club's kitchen, but we will never know.

On the latest 'wish list' for the Department, in which one could express a preference as to next assignment, I had elected for Mukden, because the Communists were to attack it first in their expected sweep southward. I was young and stupid enough to want to be where the action was, and Martha was game. I was informed at one point that I had been assigned there, but there were second thoughts, and the Department decided to send only bachelors to that supposedly dangerous post. As it turned out, Mukden fell to the Communists with scarcely more than a little small arms fire in the suburbs. The Department, which we had been schooled to believe was virtually all-knowing, sent Martha and me to the 'safety' of Tientsin—where all hell soon broke loose.

On the train going to Tientsin my ticket, being by seat number, happened to place me next to the Soviet Consul General in Tientsin. We engaged in friendly conversation, but much of it consisted of not so subtle claims that our respective systems of government and economy produced the greatest good for the greatest number. In my innocence I said I hoped he would pay us a visit when we were settled in Tientsin. He replied that while that was an appealing idea, he would not think of endangering me with my FBI by visiting in my home. I laughed. In my inexperience I could not imagine that in my country I could be endangered merely by guilt through association. Such, I naively thought, was un-American. In my mind my loyalty would be unquestioned, simply because I knew it to be unquestionable. Yet later I had to thank him for maintaining his distance. I had no conception of the frightfully un-American, career-destroying Senator McCarthy witch hunt soon to come on the Washington scene.

o   o   o

To our distress, Wang told us that while he and Hsieh would follow us almost anywhere else in the world, they could not go with us to Tientsin. Peiping and Tientsin Chinese at their level of society did not get along well. He and Hsieh would be ostracized, or worse. After our move he twice took the train to Tientsin to see that we were well established. A couple of months later he mailed me a clipping from the Shih Chieh Jih Pao (a Peiping newspaper), without comment:

TSINGTAO WOMEN WITH PERMANENT WAVES FORCED TO CONTRIBUTE MONEY TO COMFORT TROOPS

(Tsingtao, October 30, by our own correspondent) — The Tsingtao Comfort-Troops-And-Do-Acts-Of-Kindness-Committee of Shantung Province passed unanimously a resolution at its session yesterday stipulating that all women with permanent waves in their hair will be requested to contribute $20,000 each to the Comfort-The-Troops Fund. Police corps will patrol the streets of the city to enforce the collection. (complete translation)

o   o   o

The article made me pensive. The troops surely needed their most elementary needs better met. In many units, while the commanding officer enriched himself, the troops turned to begging and stealing to keep from going hungry. An experience that had been seared into my mind during my first week in Peiping came on the screen of my inner vision, as it often did during my first assignment to China:

I was exploring the environs of the Consulate and discovered Central Park. It was just south of the Forbidden City and just west of the Consulate. It formed part of what would become the expansive, and now infamous, Tienanmen Square. It was pleasant in the early afternoon sun, and many Chinese were strolling through the park. Occasionally a young couple would demonstrate a little affection, this being in the time of Nationalist China, before the Communist's puritanical strictures. I found myself wearing a perpetual smile of contentment as I sauntered— until ... all of a sudden I came upon a small crowd watching a Nationalist soldier lying on a bench, obviously dying. His eyes were wide open, but glazed. Occasionally, he took a slow, scarcely perceptible breath. Green flies crawled in and out of his half-open mouth and drank from the corners of his eyes. I stood momentarily transfixed by a sight I could not believe. During those moments several onlookers strolled off, to be replaced by others pausing briefly to stare. In my naivete I suddenly broke into a run to the Consulate, bursting in on Consul Tony Freeman while he had a visitor, and said, "Please excuse my intrusion, but there's a young Nationalist soldier lying on a bench in the park dying, and people are just watching him die. We have to get an ambulance."

"Alfred, if we moved that soldier we would be responsible for him, and would be liable when he dies," Tony explained.

"Then let's get in touch with the proper Chinese authorities."

"Now, Alfred, partly because of the terrible disruptions of the Japanese war, and partly because of the avarice of some Chinese in power, in the military and elsewhere, the neglect is too widespread. It is not surmountable, least of all by us. When you have been here longer, you will understand."

Later, I did. And I still couldn't.

I knew the long Japanese War had left a legacy of chaos, disillusionment, dissolution, fatigue, cynicism and pockets of starvation, due to long military expenditure and graft, and to the resulting inflation overleaping itself. By December 1948 most of North China was in Chinese Communist hands. Peking itself was surrounded by Communist troops. The best of Chiang's forces had been defeated or had defected to the Communist "Liberation Army." All of this chaos and suffering went on while most warlords and some civilian government officials became immensely wealthy.

The plight of that poor soldier forced me to rethink the big picture early in my time in China. In dealing in Chinese affairs in Military Intelligence at the Pentagon and in study of the Chinese language, history and culture at the University of Chicago, I had come to love things Chinese. Now I was being presented with evidence that the China of which I had become fond would not be a happy country for a long time. The neglected, dying boy being taken over by green flies in the sight of curious spectators, with no ambulance, and no superior officer doing anything (there were officers among the spectators) ... I began to limn a picture of inevitable Nationalist defeat. That was sad, for I did not believe that Communism would make China happy in the long run.

Still, what was the alternative to the shaky status quo? My non-communist, patriotic friends were right in saying there was no alternative to the Communists. Many of my Chinese friends at all levels of society came to me and said in effect, "Mr. Jenkins, we know you are concerned about what is about to happen, namely, a Communist take-over. We don't want you to worry. We non-communist patriots are supporting the Communists, because we have to have a new deal and only they can give it. But when they come to power we shall control them, not they us. We are more numerous than the Communists." I tried to tell them that they knew nothing about modern authoritarian methods of societal control, but I was just a very young vice consul from Georgia, and I didn't change history at that point.

Too bad, for I was convinced that at least at the present level of human consciousness attempts at socialism 'on the way to communism' would inevitably end in limited production and in an authoritarian oligarchy with privileges and concentrated power in the hands of the elite few.

At the same time, my reading of Chinese history told me that the Chinese had an innate affinity for that which works. I believed that Communism couldn't work. Therefore, I believed that the talented, perceptive and certainly sinocentric Chinese would not for very many years, at least, adhere to an ideology of alien, Western origin that didn't work. I feared, however, that if a gradual forsaking of it came about, as I would expect, it would take long enough to encompass a great deal of faltering and suffering.

As I had read the writings of the Communists while I was in the Pentagon, particularly of Mao himself (some of them in Chinese that may or may not have been available in English), I came to believe that the Communists fully meant what they said about their ultimate objectives of fashioning a more or less orthodox, if somewhat sinified, Communist society. The moderate and reasonable approach, often used during the Japanese war in large Communist-held agrarian areas between Japanese controlled railroads and cities constituted a showcase era to win over the peasants, was not representative of what was to come later. In other words, I never considered the Communists to be mere agrarian reformers as many Americans, including eminent China specialists, viewed them during World War II.

I further believed that the bitterness stemming from the century of semi-colonialism at the hands of the West made it all the more likely that Communism would at first be widely welcomed in China, partly because of the simplistic view that since Communism was the opposite of the West's 'free enterprise and democracy,' which in many Chinese eyes equated to 'economic exploitation and semi-colonial tyranny,' then Communism must be good. To state it in an oversimplified but basically valid manner, free enterprise and democracy did not mature in China as it had in most of the West, but retained unadmirable features of 19th century, immature capitalism. Being further identified with semi-colonialism, this made capitalism a dirty word to many, perhaps to most, thinking Chinese.

I wanted China to escape the pain and privation of having to learn that communism doesn't work. Yet at the same time I feared it would have to go through that costly process, for complicated historical reasons. Furthermore, at the time the Chinese Communists took over the governance of vast China a strong, centralized control was probably desirable for a time, to bring the war-fragmented country together. At their own pace, the Chinese, I reasoned, were intelligent enough to see that Communism would not meet their needs in coming into the modern world.

Such were my intermittently recurring concerns, even while reveling in the delights of life in the soon-to-die 'old Peiping.'

Cataclysmic changes were not far off. They had been presaged even in my second week in China, when President Truman's special envoy, General George Marshall, departed after an unsuccessful attempt to bring peace between Chiang Kai-shek's Nationalist Government and the Chinese Communists. That meant the civil war would resume in earnest, and the U.S. Marines would soon leave China.

The U.S. Marines, in China post-World War II to help train and advise the Nationalist forces, left Peiping in May 1947. I sampled Chinese opinion concerning their departure. Officialdom decried it. College students mostly applauded it. High school students were undecided. Children and merchants were distraught. I had mixed feelings. We would miss the commissary and some good friends among the Marines, three of whom we had met on the *General Mitchell.* Still, I thought it embarrassing having the Marines in China when the only conflict was a civil one. Besides, not all of them were well behaved. One afternoon I was walking on east Legation Street behind a very drunken Marine when a well-dressed Chinese gentleman was walking toward him. To my horror, the lumbering, stupefied Marine shoved the Chinese off the sidewalk saying, "Get out of my way, you sonofabitch." At least I hoped the Marine thought the Chinese would not understand his insult.

The Chinese gentleman picked himself up, dusted off, and called after the Marine in Harvard English, "My young friend, I believe upon inquiry you would find my genealogy unexceptionable." I imagine the Marine didn't know what the hell the Chinese was talking about, but I still savor the gentleman's aplomb.

I apologized to him, saying, "I am terribly embarrassed by the conduct of my fellow countryman. I wish there were some way I could make amends for his rudeness."

"Please do not be concerned," he said with a smile. "I am sure if that fine-looking young man had been sober, he would have been polite." He accepted my handshake.

The press described General Marshall as 'disillusioned' by the failure of his mission to bring peace between the Nationalists and the Communists. I doubt that such was the case. I think he went knowing that his mission had little, if any, chance of success, but that it was in everyone's interest that he make the effort. I was still at the Pentagon when he left for China, and I was responsible for briefing papers given him before his departure. Needless to say, it was not my place to prejudge the outcome of his mission. However, believing strongly that his mission would have to fail, while applauding the attempt, I would not be surprised if such forbidden editorializing emerged between the lines of my briefing papers. A conversation I later had with General Marshall while I was on home leave, when he was Secretary of State, led me further to suspect that his 'disillusionment' was for public consumption. I told him that I regretted the oral briefing I was scheduled to give him at the Pentagon before he left for China had to be canceled at the last minute, because I would have said things I did not want to put in the briefing papers. He looked at me intently for a moment, then favored me with a masterful survey of the world situation, and the United States place in it. It seemed to be his way of thanking me for the briefing papers I had prepared. I wish I dared paraphrase what he said, but it was too long ago, and I was, I suspect, too overcome by the courtesy of his attention to such a junior officer, that I concentrated on the nature of this remarkable man, more than on what he was saying. I had only the faintest recognition at that time of the pivotal import of his announcement in the Harvard Yard more than two years earlier of the program that came to be known as the Marshall Plan. It was instrumental in putting war-devastated Western Europe on its feet, and signalled that the United States was taking up the burden of leadership of the free world.

What I did recognize in that brief meeting in the Secretary's office was that I was in the presence of a modest and confident man of unshakable integrity—a wise man. I had no trouble characterizing him as a great man. It was written in his calm, his bearing, his vision, above all in his face.

It was one year, minus a week, from General Marshall's departure from China that our eggnog party in Tientsin was punctuated by Communist shells landing nearby.

FOUR

Whispering
Under
The Rugs

n New Year's Day 1949 Martha and I gave a reception for some ninety guests from Chinese officialdom, the consular corps, and the Chinese and foreign business communities of Tientsin, where I had been assigned as political officer. As such it was my responsibility to draft reports to Washington on political and sociological realities and future trends with respect to the host country. In gathering pertinent information for such reports it was useful to get to know well those whom we had invited. Parties such as this therefore involved serious professional interests.

Only a few guests had arrived, when suddenly, WHOOM-BOOM! ... WHOOM-BOOM! ... BOOM! the shelling began quite close by. We knew communist forces were near the city, because they had captured the Tientsin airport three weeks earlier. The Nationalist authorities had then put swarms of coolies to work building a make-shift airport within the city, in order to maintain the flow of munitions and daily necessities coming into Tientsin by air from Tsingtao and Peiping. The Communists disrupted the railroads so often that they were almost useless. Military trucks coming from the new airport had been rumbling by our house on Race Course Road, day and night, for the past two weeks.

At the first ear-splitting reports a group of guests who had just come through the front gate scurried into the house. After greeting them Martha wondered aloud whether many guests would show up, in view of the shelling. We needn't have been concerned. Guests soon streamed in, glad to be off the streets and wanting to be with other people. Doubtless most of them were already en route to our house when the shelling started. At least our house, surrounded by a thick brick wall eight feet high with a solid iron gate, would be as safe as anywhere readily available.

To our surprise and embarrassment several of the Chinese guests brought expensive gifts, hardly expected for a cocktail party. They probably did not want objects of art of any value in their homes when the Communists took over.

It seemed evident that the battle for this prize industrial city was at hand. Questions about the likely shape of the future were on everyone's mind, but thinking about them was more inevitable than profitable. While the outcome of the imminent battle was not a foregone conclusion, almost everyone thought the Communists would win it, because the conviction was now widespread that China simply had to have a new deal. Nationalist morale was at an all time low. The welfare of the troops was grossly neglected and runaway inflation was beginning to make life hopeless for almost everyone. Still, if the Communists should prevail, no one knew what that might mean by way of mass executions, of new and perhaps arbitrary regulations, of physical and emotional suffering almost certain to come in the transition to the new regime, perhaps from pestilence and shortage of food in view of the disruption of the railroads and the huge numbers of refugees in the city. A troublesome unknown was what attitude the Communists would have toward the foreign community.

One of the last guests to arrive on that cold, clear New Year's Day was the dapper Mayor of Tientsin, Steve Tu. He had been at our house for dinner a couple of weeks before and was at that time in high spirits. Today, however, even his inevitable cape failed to convey the usual panache. He dutifully greeted each guest, but seemed to look beyond them. He then promptly stationed himself at the eggnog bowl, which he proceeded uncharacteristically but devotedly to patronize. Indeed everyone seemed to drink and eat more than was customary for diplomatic or consular parties. That morning Martha had thought the servants had prepared too much eggnog, but the guests not only drank more and faster than expected, they stayed, and stayed, and stayed—and drank and ate. Li, our household manager, went out on the streets and miraculously returned with several dozen eggs, a commodity in short supply with the Communists surrounding the city. The cook ran out to purchase more nutmeg and the coolie announced that we would soon have to substitute brandy for bourbon in the eggnog.

The babble of the party exceeded the norm. Perhaps we were trying to drown out the continued shelling, and feigning gaiety to boost our spirits. Yet at times, as though on cue, there would be eerie periods of almost complete silence, simultaneously in reception hall, living room and dining room.

Most of the conversations had to do with considerations of safety during the imminent inner city battle, and with obtaining provisions to last it out. Rumors, too, were passed around generously of Communist locations and strength, of the Chinese employing Japanese technicians and artillerymen, of refugees choking the city with their numbers, of resulting epidemics, of alleged statements by Nationalist military and civilian authorities ranging from bravado to resignation. One could hear anything.

I recalled with discomfort a conversation I had carried on the previous week with a bright young major in the Nationalist Garrison Headquarters. I mentioned to him the report we had received that Chairman Mao's Communist forces had taken Mukden with scant resistance on the part of Chiang Kai-shek's Nationalist forces. I said if that was going to be a pattern, China was in for changes of a magnitude difficult to imagine. He said he didn't think the Mukden debacle would be a pattern, even though he admitted hearing that the Communists had taken over huge quantities of arms from the Japanese, courtesy of the Soviets, who had received the Japanese surrender in that area at the end of World War II. "Anyway," he added, "no matter what, the great United States would never permit a Communist takeover of China. You know that." I said I knew nothing of the sort. I said the "great United States" would be very concerned if that should happen, but it was unlikely that any outside power could swing the balance if the Nationalist forces were as neglected and demoralized as a great many of them were known to be, and if they did not have the support of the populace, which I believed to be lacking. I related this conversation to a group of the guests, and the consensus was that many Nationalist military leaders had long been complacent in the knowledge they had a strong—some thought invincible—friend in the United States (witness The Bomb) and consequently tended to bend their energies toward filling their pockets rather than their troops' stomachs.

My boss, the U.S. Consul General, Bob Smyth, of renowned but unconvincing irascibility, and Al Wellborn, the Consulate's able and earnest administrative officer, arrived late. They informed us that the shells we heard exploding were an attempt by the Communists to disrupt air traffic at the new make-shift airport. They knew whereof they spoke, for their houses bordered on that airport, as did a third, also owned by the Consulate and occupied by three female secretaries. Planes often flew low over their roofs in taking off or landing, and it was those planes the Communists were attempting to blast out of the sky. They were also attempting to make the runways unusable.

The residents of the three houses were understandably reluctant to remain in them. Al Wellborn soon left the party to collect a few essentials at his house, then he and his wife, Carol, with their 19 month-old daughter, moved in with us. Carol, a proper and likeable New Englander, would be a great comfort to Martha during the perilous time ahead. Most of the guests finally took their leave, since the shelling at the airport had ceased for a while. The director of the Tientsin Foreign Affairs Bureau stopped by when only a half-dozen guests remained. He had merely come to apologize for being too preoccupied to attend the party. He was a thoughtful, gentle man who had always been kind and helpful to us. Unfortunately, he happened to be on the losing side of the civil war, and in a vulnerable official position. According to a letter we received later from a missionary friend, both the Foreign Affairs Director and Mayor Tu were among those executed by the Communists soon after the city fell. As Chairman Mao once understated, "A revolution is not a dinner party."

When the last guest finally left, Martha and I collapsed on a sofa in the living room and did a post-mortem on the strange party. Then Martha went upstairs to help Carol Wellborn get settled and I sprawled on the floor, reflecting on Martha's and my brief time in the Foreign Service, and on our happy circumstance so far.

Being weary, we retired early, but sleep did not come to me. I arose, went downstairs and attempted to read, but on the pages of the book I still saw the prescient, sober finality written on Mayor Tu's face at the party.

Many foreign business people as well as wealthy Chinese had left China prior to the expected Communist southward sweep. Several of our Consulate General colleagues had also returned to the States. I thought of doing so, because we had received a report that the Chinese thought I was a member of the Central Intelligence Agency, which was not true. If the Communists believed that when they took over, my fate could be problematical. I discussed this with Martha, and, being innocent, we decided to remain. The Consulate General was left with a skeleton staff all prepared to remain, come what may.

We did not have long to wait to find out what that would be. We knew we were crossing a watershed between the old and a new China, but we had no idea what a definitive watershed it would turn out to be. What was about to transpire would constitute perhaps the most thoroughgoing and rapid social, economic and political transformation of a large society in all of history. It would be brought about to the accompaniment of an untold amount of bloodshed, not only in civil war, but in regime or regime-induced executions, especially in the ruthless land reform movement of the first two years of the regime, when a great many landlords were executed. A very arbitrary judicial system claimed many other lives in the years to come.

Given a Communist takeover, I could not then imagine what would happen to ancient, troubled, fragmented, Japanese-and-civil-war-torn, inflation-smitten, ever-lovable China. Communism come to China? Proud China adopt a Western political, social and economic scheme like Communism? It seemed bizarre.

The cook happened to see the light on in the living room in the small hours of the morning and brought me an unsolicited coffee and brandy. I put aside the book and fell again to thinking about just what was happening to China—and what might happen to us.

The civil war between the forces of the Nationalist Government under President Chiang Kai-shek and the Chinese Communist forces under the leadership of Chairman Mao Tse-tung was but the continuation of a century-old struggle by China to create a workable national authority and to come into the modern world. For more than three thousand years the Chinese had developed their remarkable culture largely untouched by outside influence. The Middle Kingdom somehow managed to absorb its invaders, who adapted to the superior Chinese civilization. For centuries China had the most advanced culture on earth, technologically, artistically and in political organization. It was natural that the Chinese came to view themselves as the center of the world—as the unique, the highest expression of civilized humankind.

In the middle of the last century, however, China's self-esteem in its presumed centrality was shattered by the military and economic insistencies of the recently industrialized West. The cornucopia of the Industrial Revolution required expanded markets for an avalanche of products, as well as new sources of raw materials. China appeared to be a promising answer to both needs, and the Western erosion of the ancient Confucian society began—battleships, Bibles and opium all being prominent in the onslaught. For more than a century, then, the deliberate destruction of that ancient Confucian social, moral, political and economic order by the Chinese themselves, aided by an avaricious, nominally Christian, proselytizing West, brought about repeated crises of national authority. I tried to ask myself just how I felt about what was now happening, since it was in part a result of the last century of East-West relations. I think my chief impression was "you reap what you sow." The West had not sown in the East with impressive pre-science.

o   o   o

For the next two weeks the shelling became progressively heavy around the outskirts of the city. Quite a number of the villages on the periphery were burned down by the Nationalists so their range would be clear to fire on the Communists, and to form a no-man's land that the Communists could not cross with impunity. Some of the villagers had only a few minutes' notice to clear out. It was heart-rending to see the swarms of refugees straggling into the already overcrowded city, a few possessions on their backs, not knowing where to go or how they would exist, except for those who had relatives in the city. All Chinese schools had closed down to house Nationalist troops. The missionary schools were turned over to the refugees, but they could care for only a pitiful fraction of them.

Both the incoming and the outgoing shelling increased each day. Surprisingly, the Nationalist troops were making a serious attempt to defend the city. Most people had thought they would not do so, since they were so demoralized. Previously they had accepted their own propaganda that the Communists were poorly armed 'bandits' who could not prevail over the Nationalists' preponderant fire-power. As they grasped the import of the Communists taking over Japanese armament in Manchuria and the rapid fall of Mukden, however, a do-or-die attitude in defending Tientsin was engendered.

The day that the battle and its frightening destruction reached downtown Tientsin in earnest, and while we at the office were preoccupied with plans for our very survival, Martha phoned me to say she had heard of a factory selling beautiful oriental rugs at give-away prices. The river traffic had been cut off and the rugs could not be shipped. Would I agree to her picking up a couple? I couldn't believe what I was hearing. Shaking my head, I tried to dissuade her. When she persisted, I reluctantly said, "If you must," since I did not have time to launch a promising protest. I knew that to be effective it would tax my argumentative abilities beyond the resources of the moment. "Women! Bargain-hunting for rugs at a time like this!" However, shortly thereafter, the purchase turned out to be an absolute Godsend, and we all warmly thanked Martha in our hearts for her folly.

Suddenly, just after noon on that clear, cold day in mid-January, an exceptionally loud report was heard very near the office. Several of us took the elevator up to the apartment of Gordon Tullock, a bespectacled young vice consul with a sort of bewildered efficiency, an elfish sense of humor and a knack for numbers, who was the commercial officer. He lived on the top floor of the twelve-story Leopold Building which housed the American Consulate General on the ground floor.

We arrived at Gordon's apartment just in time to see from his living room window, which took up one whole side of the room, a second shell land on a warehouse just across the river, a scant 400 yards from the Consulate.

Chinese were scurrying away from the site in all directions, faster than normal human capacity. We wanted to continue watching the battle from that vantage point, but Bob Smyth, having just discovered a bullet hole through the top of the large window by which we were standing, had us all return to the office quarters immediately. On arrival at my office I was relieved to find that Martha had just returned from her shopping audacity.

One hundred and five mm. shells were whizzing by the Leopold Building. We prayed they were not just missing the mark, with the mark being us. We soon decided they were aiming at the Garrison Headquarters, which was behind our building. Nevertheless, we took a couple of phones into the hallway, where we all sat on the floor, after blocking the doorways with steel safes to keep out stray bullets or shrapnel. The Consulate's radio was still operating, so occasionally one or two of us would go to Gordon's apartment to watch the progress of the battle so as to report to the Department. At those times Gordon graciously permitted us to raid his refrigerator, our only source of food for two days. He had just bought a turkey. We had turkey sandwiches until the bread gave out. Then we had turkey.

Some American newswoman still in Tientsin kept phoning me to describe how honest the People's Liberation Army soldiers were, how compassionate and thoughtful of the citizenry, how polite, how well-dressed even in battle, etc., etc. She told one story of a soldier crossing a street peppered with bullets to carry a jar of cold water to an old lady. It sounded straight out of Luke or The Acts.

That was all very well, but my concern was for Martha, two miles away at our house. I wondered whether the battle was raging in that part of town as it was downtown.

My estimation of the Consulate General's Chinese employees, already high, skyrocketed during this tense time. They were calm, courageous, thoughtful and thoroughly good companions in adversity. One act was impressive. I happened to mention to Gordon that I would give anything to be able to know that Martha was safe. Our young telephone operator overheard me. Without my noticing, (I would not have permitted it if I had) she slipped out of the hall, crept along the baseboard to the other side of the large first floor room that was all glass on two sides, reached up to plug in our line to the Marine field phone at the house, and gave it a crank. She crept back along the baseboard, with all sorts of armament being loudly expended outside, and told me to answer the Marine phone in the hall.

Martha was on the line. We each confirmed our safety and, since there was no way for us to ring each other with the switchboard line permanently plugged in, we agreed to come to the phone every even hour on the hour and say 'hello' until the other one did. That way we had contact every two hours throughout the battle, except for one time when Martha would not leave the furnace room because machine guns were spraying bullets into our garden.

Later Martha wrote to her mother of her experiences during the battle. I quote from it just as it was written. She did not paragraph in order to save weight in a long letter, but in that form it adds breathlessness to the relating, which is appropriate.

"After we had bought the rugs we started back to the office, despite the misgivings of the driver. We found Alfred in a state of what for him would qualify as agitation. Just then another shell fell nearby and the building shook. Alfred's office on one side is all windows, and they rattled so I thought they would shatter. He said I should leave immediately, so I reluctantly went with Jane Smyth to their temporary apartment in the National City Bank. The men came to the apartment about an hour later and we had lunch. The shells were still falling nearby when the men went back to the office. About seven o'clock Alfred came with Al Wellborn and with some trepidation we drove the two miles home. There had been a six o'clock curfew, so Alfred had to explain our way through three check points. Carol was so glad to see us. She thought she may have to spend the night alone, which would have been no fun, since she couldn't speak Chinese. Our Number One Boy was sick that day and the substitute was deaf as well as stupid, and knew no English. Friday morning there was a lull in the shelling and we got the baby ready to go out. The baby's amah was not here because Monday afternoon she came running in to me and said, 'Please tell my mistress (Carol) that I must leave right away. My brother came here and said our parents' house has been hit by a shell and they may all be dead.' She was sobbing so much I could hardly understand her. Just after she left we heard a loud siren alarm. We got the baby inside immediately. We had been in about ten minutes when the most awful blast I ever heard sounded. Our French doors in the dining room leading to the terrace were locked for the winter—and in the Chinese fashion to keep out the cold, cotton had been stuffed in the cracks and white paper pasted over all that. The blast blew open the locked doors and blew all the cotton out of them and out of all the windows on that side of the house. We later learned the explosion involved a huge aviation fuel tank some *three miles* from the house! The water went off at this time and about a half hour later the electricity went off. Both came on again late that night, so we filled the tubs and a number of pots. We called the men at the office to tell them what happened, and they said that was mild compared to what was happening downtown. They were too busy to talk, getting telegrams off to the Department. They just had time to say they couldn't get home that night, because in addition to 105 mm. shells whizzing right past the building, small arms firing had begun in the streets, and grenades were exploding. They would have to sleep at the Consulate—not a joyful prospect. There was no electricity, which meant there was no heat. And my Alfred still with Georgia blood in his veins! (Tientsin has something like Boston's climate.) So the five Americans and four Chinese who had not been sent home earlier gratefully slept under the four rugs I had bought. They slept in a little room in the basement with one small window. To get there they first had to go outside, and they scurried because the atmosphere was not healthy. Well, here we were, two women with an infant and five servants. Our cellar is only a furnace room with an adjoining room filled with coal, but I decided we would spend the night there. We dismantled the baby's bed and took it to the furnace room, then a double bed from the guest room. We went to the cellar and crawled in bed with all our clothes on. Carol kept waking up, asking if I thought the furnace would explode. We were not used to tending it, and regulation of the steam pipes was a mystery. It was a night not easily forgotten. The next morning we got up about seven, the servants brought us breakfast, and since the shelling had died down we went upstairs to raise our spirits by listening to some music while we still had electricity. Carol was on her way upstairs to get one of her coats when Wang, the coolie, came dashing in and said, 'Mistress, go to the cellar.' He fairly snatched up the baby, Carol's fur coat, her purse, a small suitcase, and ran to the cellar. We were on his heels. We sat there for about ten minutes when a lot of machine gun firing started. Just then we heard footsteps coming down the cellar steps and four men servants and the wash amah ran down and sat on the bed with us. Wang said, 'Someone is pounding on the front gate. I think it is soldiers.' Then we heard machine gun firing very close, as though it were right in front and we thought they were trying to shoot the lock in order to get in. Our wall all around the property is not easily scaled. Right across the street is a large school in which Nationalist troops were stationed, so that was probably the actual target. Rifle fire sounded very close, too. Then we heard a machine gun right in our garden. We wondered if they would give us a chance to identify ourselves when they entered the cellar, or whether we would just be mowed down! We had carried a spoon to the cellar with which to dig in dirt. We wrapped our rings in Kleenex and buried them in a flower pot. Pretty soon the servants thought they heard someone walking around upstairs and they thought it would be better to let them know where we were, lest they simply toss grenades into the cellar to clear out any Nationalist soldiers who might be hiding there. The men at the office in one phone conversation said they had talked to the Italian Consul General, who had retreated to his large cellar that was divided in half by a cement wall. The communist soldiers tossed a grenade into one side—fortunately the side where he was not. He had presence of mind enough to dash over to that side, reasoning they would also try to clear out the side he had been on. They did. He then wasn't sure what to do, so he burst into the open, screaming in Italian, 'I am the Italian Consul General, don't shoot!' Of course they didn't understand Italian, but they understood it was not Chinese, and they were only after soldiers. Eleven o'clock to one o'clock was torture. Machine gun bullets were ricocheting off our garden walls, whether from the inside or the outside we weren't sure, but it sounded like both. We were sure, however, that rifle fire came over our walls, doubtless from the second story of the school across the street. In the midst of all I was trying to phrase just what I would say to the People's Liberation Army soldiers if they burst in, but I wasn't very good at thinking even in English just then, much less in Chinese. I really thought I would never see my husband again. In the midst of all the bullets ricocheting off our walls, the cook crossed the yard from the guest house to our kitchen and prepared lunch for us and the baby! I don't know whether that should be labeled courage or foolhardiness, but it could safely be called loyalty. When he appeared in the cellar with hot food I didn't know whether to embrace him or scold him. We ate there, on our suitcases, not at all hungry, but we couldn't hurt Chu's feelings after he had gone to trouble and danger for us. The city phones had been knocked out, but a U.S. Marine field phone had been run out to the house from the

office for just such emergencies. At one point Wang
went upstairs and talked with Alfred on it. He
returned, flashing his solar-effect smile, saying
things would soon be all right. The Italian Consul
had already been 'liberated' and they would soon
arrive at the American Consulate. Alfred had said
we should stay where we were, for it looked like
our section of the city would be the last to be 'liberated.' It was hard to keep the baby happy, and we
weren't what you would call uncontrollably merry,
ourselves. The lights had gone out ten minutes after
we went down there and we didn't want to burn a
candle. So Louise played in the coal dust, getting it
all over us in the process, but in the dark we weren't
aware of it. With puzzling suddenness things
became quiet about a quarter to four, so I ventured
to stick my head out and go upstairs to make the
four o'clock phone engagement with Alfred. (He
will probably write you how we could use the
Marine phone, though we couldn't ring each other.)
Alfred said things were all right there except for
window damage. All were safe. He had already
talked to a Communist soldier. We could come out
of the cellar. As I was washing my hands at the
downstairs sink Carol came running to me saying
there were two Communists in the kitchen. The
cook was grinning, offering the soldiers tea, and
Wang explained, 'This is my mistress, Chin Tai-
tai.' The soldiers were small of stature, very well
dressed, and heavily armed. They said they would
have to look around. They went to the cellar and
returned to the kitchen where we still were. One
said, 'You were afraid? No need to be afraid any
longer. It is all over.' They were polite, but that is

all. They left and about five minutes later two more came, this time through the front door. They said they wanted to go upstairs, so I said go ahead, but they then decided not to. A little later Wang told me there were five soldiers at the front gate, but when he told them this was an American vice consul's house they didn't come in. Well, Alfred called at five and said they couldn't come home because they had to go to a meeting with the ECA head (Economic Cooperation Administration) who was being questioned by Communist officials. By the time the meeting ended it was almost seven, and the curfew had become absolutely strict, so they couldn't get home again! They did go to the Smyth's apartment in the bank, had a good meal, a bath and went to bed. Al Wellborn came home about eleven the next morning. Alfred was still in meetings with Communist officials, but got home briefly for lunch. He hadn't shaved for three days and had one of Bob Smyth's shirts on that was several sizes too big for him, but he looked wonderful to me. He had to go back to the office that afternoon, but returned for late dinner.

So that is how I spent the time during the battle, mother. I would never want to go through it again, but I'm so glad I didn't elect to return to the States without Alfred, because the agony here, though intense, was relatively short, and it would be worse to be separated for a year or so. All love,
Martha"

I don't remember how many hours we all sat in the hallway while the battle raged, but it seemed like days. The electricity went off in the late afternoon, and we began to get cold. We didn't talk much, so there was time just to think—and to listen to battle sounds. I had seen the results of warfare at Pearl Harbor and in Manila, but this was the first time I had been in the midst of warfare. It seemed like a simply unreal waste. I had to believe that humans had not been out of the muck in their evolution long enough to find means of avoiding such stupidity as was going on. I wished I might be alive a hundred years from then, or X-hundred years, however many it would take, when human consciousness would have matured and there would not be the greed, the hatred, the thirst for power and the dedication to dogmas, secular or religious, to produce such costly idiocy.

That bitter January night, since there was no heat, with inexpressible gratitude for Martha's folly, we slept in the basement under the rugs that Martha had just bought. I was next to a young Chinese interpreter employee named Li, my best friend among the local Consulate General employees. He had been in our home a good deal. We were keyed up, and talked most of the night. Others whispered or murmured, too. Apparently no one could sleep. Certainly I was too shivering cold and hungry to get to sleep, and the darkness was so absolute it was eerie. I couldn't see even a suggestion of Li's face, just inches away. We talked about some good times we had enjoyed together and wondered if visits in my home would be permitted now, or if permitted, whether it would be prudent, considering the Communists' view of Americans. Mostly we talked about what was happening to this country we both loved. Li confessed he had little idea what the future held in store, but he proved to be prescient on at least two counts. First, he said the new regime would be pretty successful in its certain attempts to stamp out the 'tattered remnants' of Confucianism. And second, he feared that he, as an intellectual, would have a difficult time under the new regime.

Confucianism was the predominant philosophical force

in Chinese society for over 2,000 years. Founded by Confucius (551-479 BC), this secular faith advocated the "three bonds" that held Chinese society together: the subordination of children to parents, of wives to husbands and of subjects to rulers. Confucian temples were built in every one of the 2,000 counties throughout the country. Confucianism became synonymous with learning, and study of the Confucian classics the way through examination to official position. The end of imperial rule undermined the institutional aspects of Confucianism, and in the early part of this century scholars such as Hu Shih cracked and shed the Confucian carapace that had so long restricted philosophical thought, attacking Confucian teachings and rites as standing in the way of China's modernization. In the late 1940s I witnessed some of the "tattered remains" of Confucianism, when Chinese friends invited me to their homes to witness Confucian family customs at the time of the Chinese New Year, such as kowtowing to one's superiors. The forms were gone through with obvious lack of seriousness, amid much giggling.

I thought Li was absolutely correct that the Communists would scuttle the quasi-religion of Confucianism, for there would be no place for it in opposition to the quasi-religion of Communism that Mao would impose.

I cannot express the grief I feel today for my friend when I reflect on how right he was in his second prediction, concerning the fate of intellectuals under the Communists. When Martha and I returned to Tientsin 23 years later, after the United States and China had finally resumed relations, we were walking in a park near the Leopold Building when an elderly and very broken man came up to me and said in English, "Aren't you Mr. Jenkins?" I said I was. He said he recognized Mrs. Jenkins, broke into tears, then resigned to

quaking sobs. When he tried to speak at all, he spoke so
softly, indistinctly and incoherently, with his face so contorted from crying, I could not get much out of him. I
thought we could communicate better in Chinese, but he
still tried to speak his 'rusty' English, probably because he
didn't want the children crowding around the two foreigners to understand. We got that he was an old employee of
the American Consulate General, but we never got a distinct name out of him, he was so broken up. And again,
possibly he did not want to say his name in view of the
crowd that had gathered, a few of whom were adults.
Never mind. He had to be Li. I could see a faint resem-
blance through the toll of the years, the obvious suffering,
and the contortion of his face in crying. He continued to
quake silently for a while. Finally we just looked at each
other for a long time, in silence and in a sort of questioning
affection. The face was that of a very old man. His hands
trembled. I thought of his vibrancy, his lively intelligence,
his happy self-confidence of a mere 23 years earlier, of his
inheriting our beloved Alsatian. Those years, and doubtless
the authorities had treated him very badly indeed.

We hesitated to hug him on departure, lest it be a disservice to him in the climate of the time, but somehow we
had to, and did. Then we crossed the street in deep gloom
to the ever gloomy old Taladi Hotel, where each of us
dreamed a while about old times in China that could never
be again. Of course I do not know what has happened to
him since, but Li did not deserve the heart-rending condition of his young old age.

After the colleague on the other side loudly cleared his
throat a second time Li and I became silent. That is, our
voices did. My mind did not. I wondered why my friend
was so sure he would meet with trying times personally
under a Communist regime. Only later did I gain some

conception of what he seemed instinctively to know, and probably could not himself at that time articulate. He was an intellectual, by Chinese definition of that era, and intellectuals are habituated to thinking and reasoning, even questioning. Communism, as has often been pointed out, is a religion—a secular, non-theocentric religion. Like all religions, it is based not primarily on reason, but on articles of faith to be unquestioningly embraced by the faithful. A creed, to be accepted *verbatim* and repeated by rote, states what is alleged to be eternal truth, and that is to be valid for all time. One is told what to think, and thus thinking is discouraged. That is obviously anathema to any self-respecting individual.

Therefore, in the early, emotional, orthodox stages of a new religion, whether secular or sacred, the authorities usually must impose some sort of inquisition on its thinkers— i.e., heretics, apostates, renegades, perverse deviants from the Establishment's truth. This is especially true of a secular religion, for it not only embraces moral and spiritual 'truth,' it exercises political and economic authority as well. The Chinese Communist religion during the height of the Cultural Revolution almost lost its claim to the secular nature of its 'eternal truths' because of the virtual deification of Chairman Mao and the 'canonization' of the famous Little Red Book of Mao sayings that was waved aloft from every fist at rallies.

My friend was doubtless the victim of an inquisition, as were many, many thousands during the Cultural Revolution, when China went mad. That curious, self-destructive phenomenon, in addition to ruining untold numbers of lives and snuffing out a great many, for a decade made a shambles of the educational system and destroyed priceless national treasures. It was perpetrated by the Chinese, on the Chinese, largely in frustration with a system that was supposed to be the quintessence of truth but simply did not work very well—yet to which the leadership had a lifelong, more than quasi-religious dedication.

The regime's see-sawing experimentation has been in the vain attempt to find the optimum balance between 'redness' (Communist orthodoxy) and 'expertness' (that which works)—vain, because the two concepts are basically so antithetical there *is* no optimum balance.

The Chinese attempt, so frequently frenetic, to make a secular-religious-political-economic-social system work when it cannot, has produced empathetic frustration on the part of the world-wide sinophilic fraternity, for the uncertain, swerving path taken by the Communists has been immensely costly in lives, substance and personal dignity. We were witnessing the fact that there were places on the planet so goaded by hopelessness that the people would risk readjusting heaven and earth in experimenting with the unknown, because the known was intolerable.

The old China will never be again. Much of it should not be. The venality and nepotism in high places, the excessive loyalty to family and clan at the expense of society as a whole, the tolerance of enormous differences in rich and poor and the related callousness toward the underprivileged and even toward life itself, the greed that contributed (together with the Japanese war) to runaway inflation, the widespread use of opium, the long term belief that China was the 'biggest and best' leading to complacency and lethargy, the related admiration-fear-hatred of foreigners, the lack of institutionalized forms of justice, all contributed to the decline of the pre-Communist society.

On the other hand, it surely had its values and its charms. The average Chinese made an art of living to a degree that I have never seen excelled. The sounds in the evening, the bells, drums, cries, quietly offering services and wares from massages to mooncakes bespoke a civilization of incomparable appeal. There was a dignity, a serenity, a semi-detached watching of the parade of life, an acceptance of that which is, and a tendency for moderation in all things. Of course, there were those who tasted of life to excess in various forms, but nothing to compare with the self-indulgence and frenzy of much Western life. I remember an observation of the Chinese author, Lin Yu-tang. In speaking of the syndicated novelettes offered a chapter at a time in the daily papers before the advent of TV soaps, he said if a paper in the United States suddenly stopped printing in the middle of the story it would cause nation-wide panic in the readership. In China, it would scarcely matter at all—simply because it would scarcely matter at all.

As I lay awake—almost all night—while the battle for Tientsin raged, itself a key symbol of the watershed between the old and the new China, I gave silent thanks for our privilege in experiencing the charm of the twilight days of the old China, and offered a deeply felt prayer for the new.

The cold, the darkness, the fright of battle, the not knowing what was coming, the separation from Martha, to say nothing of the separation from Georgia, family and old friends, all combined to provide an uneasiness unique in my experience. I wondered if what was going on formed a watershed in my own life, but I had no idea what that would mean. If both Martha and I came through the battle safely, would we be safe as Americans under the Communist regime? Would we have to leave China? Indeed would we be allowed to leave China, when and if we wanted to? Would my years of preparation for service in Chinese affairs go for naught? I felt ungrounded for the first time in my life. My childhood had been so safe, warm and loving, and my youth happy and fulfilling. Even my college circumstance seemingly had been tailor-made to serve my intellectual, emotional, spiritual and leadership needs. As I sank into drowsiness, gratitude for my life so far supplanted the chaos that my mind had entertained moments before. Finally, I slept soundly, if briefly.

FIVE

Chickens Are Raised

y mother died at my birth. I was born in a Caesarean delivery in the early hours of September 14, 1916 at my maternal grandparents' home in Manchester, Georgia. Doctor White later confessed that by persisting almost beyond reason, at my mother's urging, in his efforts to get me to breathe, he neglected to tidy up something before suturing my mother's incision. She died from his mistake, but in those days no one would think of suing the revered family physician. One simply grieved and accepted honest intent.

I have been told there was earnest but brief discussion as to who would take care of me, pending my dad's remarriage. Earnest, because Grandmother, having lost a favorite daughter, wanted to keep me to fill the terrible void. Briefly, because my natural father, Elliot, whom I refer to as Dad, had already decided to entrust me to his much older brother, Charles, whom I call Father, and his wife, Beulah, who became my mother. They were summoned from Macon, where Father was then President of Wesleyan College. They took me home with them on the train when I was five days old. Since that day they have been my parents. Dad did remarry, but before he could take me back he discovered he had tuberculosis. He died in Albuquerque when I was six. Apparently he was a charmer. He is said to have had an imposing height, an irrepressible wit, a lively intelligence, a boyish but deceptive naivete, brown eyes that melted all females in range, and large, protruding ears. I inherited the ears.

When I was four, Dad came east to say goodbye, and to arrange for Father and Mother to adopt me legally. He did not expect to live much longer. I loved Dad immediately, because he was full of fun. I was inconsolable and left the table when he would not eat with my little child's set of silverware that I proffered him. His refusal was due to his illness, of course, but I knew nothing of that. It must have been a painfully moving visit for my dad and my father, for they were close brothers. My father had been the primary provider in sending my dad through Emory College, and he and Mother had housed my dad for a while after his graduation.

Father was by far the greatest influence on me in my childhood and probably the single greatest influence in my entire life. I often think of him with some biblical or religious connection, for he was a Methodist minister. He never overwhelmed me with religious dogma. He was more interested in instilling in me Christian precepts, and that more by example than by teaching. I'll never forget how he especially tried to make me see the importance of accepting personal responsibility.

One Sunday when I was nine I announced at the dinner table, "My Sunday School teacher is a liar."

"How's that?" Father asked, less disturbed than I had hoped.

"She said a whale swallowed Jonah and three days later coughed him up on dry land, good as new."

Father smiled. "What do you think?"

"I think I won't go back to Sunday School."

"That's up to you, son. But if you read the story, you'll learn that Jonah was running away from responsibility. His duty was to go to Nineveh to do something he didn't want to do. Every time I have shirked responsibility a 'whale' of some sort has swallowed me. That is, something bigger than I am has caught me up, cut short my lesser purposes, and after some big or little ordeal has deposited me on firmer ground than where I stood before. I don't like being swallowed by a 'whale,' so I have developed respect for accepting responsibility. Think about it a bit."

I did. Quite a lot. This conversation was typical of many I had with Father. He had a way of defending his faith in an intellectually respectable fashion—usually. That is the chief reason why I have at least remnants of the traditional Christian faith left to me, and also why I have felt unfettered in gradually developing a less than traditional credo that better sustains me today.

In the course of the next decade and beyond I was assailed by those questions that every thinking youth asks: what is my purpose in being here? What is success? What is of lasting value? Is there absolute truth? Is there a God, and if so, what is He, She or It like? These questions demanded answers that no prefabricated casuistry that I knew of, secular or religious, could satisfy.

In pondering these core questions I wondered why I happened to be a Methodist. Pixy Aunt Annie, my chief, if dubious, source of ancestral lore, once tried to explain—I should think with tongue prominently in cheek—why I was a Methodist. She said by long Jenkins momentum I should have been born comfortably Episcopalian, but in the Civil War the Jenkinses lost their South Carolina plantations. They were then of course too poor to be Episcopalians and not quite poor enough to be Southern Baptists of that era, so *faute de mieux* I was born Methodist. Following her musical laughter she added, "Maybe you are really a closet Unitarian." I was for some years while remaining nominally a Methodist out of deference to my father.

Aunt Annie, being an astute observer of human nature as well as a peculiarly accomplished embodiment of it, reported that through the years the family tended to be devout in inverse ratio to the fertility of the soil they tilled. After the Civil War Grandfather Jenkins had to move his ample brood to a rocky farm in Harris County, Georgia, where the family became so extravagantly devout all six sons became Methodist ministers. So much for Harris County soil.

It was the oldest son, my Uncle John, who had taken to wife Aunt Annie. At a neighbor's party he met that beautiful, vivacious and reportedly unattainable siren from out of town. Later that very night he awoke Father, to announce "Veni, vidi, vici!" ("I came, I saw, I conquered!") I am very glad, for Aunt Annie's irrepressible and invariably kindly sense of humor leavened the earnestness of the sometimes dour preacher sextet.

My mother was a sweet, dear woman who never raised her voice at me, though I gave her ample provocation. I loved her very much, but considered she was hopelessly pedestrian. Still, she was in most ways an ideal Methodist minister's wife. She learned at Brenau College for women to paint china, to play the piano, never to cross her knees, and to refer to her legs, if reference ever simply had to be made, as her 'limbs.' Somewhere she must also have learned to accept and nurture, without writhing, whatever religious dogma marriage offered her. Perversely, she was born Baptist, being Southern, rural and of requisite financial stringency.

I wince in thinking about my mother's alma mater. I once debated a team in the Brenau College auditorium. Afterward, at the girl's-break dance I was puzzled as to why I was so popular. A constant line of gorgeous girls were cutting in to dance with me. Everyone should enjoy popularity sometimes, but that evening I seemed to be abusing the privilege. Finally, one ravishing red-head offered an explanation, whispering into my ear, "Darling, it pays to advertise." It seems I had debated with my fly open.

I was spoiled early on. In my infancy I was surrounded by hundreds of adoring women—not, alas, from any inherent magnetism of my own, but because I was the only child of the president of a women's college, and we lived on campus. When I was but four years old, Father left Wesleyan to re-enter the active ministry—a singularly ill-timed act from my standpoint, I thought, some twelve years later.

I remember only one of those attentive students when I was four. She was a lovable, upbeat Chinese, who on the campus green would wrap me up in a blanket and have me, legs thus confined, try to walk. In view of my later almost life-long connection with Chinese affairs, it is interesting to speculate why, of all the Wesleyan girls I must have known, that girl from China is the one I adored, and the only one whose countenance I can still picture.

My early years, certainly as compared to the rest of my

life, were uneventful, if kaleidoscopic. As was the custom for ministers of Methodist persuasion, we moved every four years. My accommodating to different schools, making new friends, exploring new cities, settling into different parsonages, made me adaptable and tolerant—some would say to a fault—but the training eased my later life in diplomacy.

I led a standard childhood, reading all the Tom Swift books, going to Saturday morning serial westerns with friends, bicycling with my steady girl friend, exhibiting the usual childish jealousies with regard to a blue-eyed blonde, who years later was chosen Miss Wesleyan. I thrilled over a series of progressively complex chemistry sets, frolicked on father's farms and in their pine forests during vacations, and worked out regularly at the YMCA. Although I persevered doggedly at the Y, except for swimming I dreaded attendance, because most of my friends were better than I was at tumbling and fast-ball sports. That bothered me more than I showed, but I saved my self-worth by usually being first in my class academically, or nearly so, and by being successful in human relations involving all ages.

Surprisingly, the most educational thing I did as a child of ten was to put on plays in the garage with my friends. Through four adult careers I often thought back on the clear lessons I learned as a novice playwright.

Our scripts usually involved royalty; without cavil I was always the king, because it was my garage. The first production got so chaotically out of hand in its latter half that as soon as the final curtain was drawn I rushed almost in tears to Father's study and announced, "I don't want to be an actor any more."

Father stopped typing, took care to register sympathy in his voice and manner, and asked, "Do you want to tell me why?"

I pouted, "My queen didn't act like one. She made up silly lines. My jesters ran all over the stage. When I looked up to heaven to show I was upset, my crown fell off, and everybody laughed. The queen broke wind while I was reading a serious order, and later the background scenery fell down on top of me and a visiting knight, and two guys were hiding behind it to wait their turn. It was awful."

Father turned away from his desk, failing to hide a jiggling of his sparse abdomen, and said, "It sounds to me like your audience was getting more than its money's worth. The laughter coming from the garage seemed uncontrollable. I think you are to be congratulated."

"Honest?"

"Honest. You are probably getting a lesson in how people react to things that can be invaluable to you when you grow up. Next time maybe you should just watch, relax and enjoy. It might be interesting to notice your own reactions, too." He slowly lit his pipe. "Let me know how much money you made. And by the way, I think you should cause the scenery to collapse next time, too."

The take was three dollars and forty-two cents, at seven cents first row, six cents second, and five general admission. Furthermore, the manager had almost sold out the house for our next show, which we hadn't even thought about.

As so often in the adult world, our success was our undoing. We became overconfident, hence lax in both preparation and execution, and our audience dwindled. There is evidence that America today is also to a degree the victim of its success.

Every Sunday I went to Sunday School and to two church services, and almost every Wednesday to prayer meeting. This startling regularity was certainly not from parental pressure, and not very clearly from religious devotion, for even as a child I was unsettled by certain elements of the dogma. The Trinity struck me as a possibly harmless but superfluous construction, and both the virgin birth and the resurrection as of doubtful validity. Whether the conception was "immaculate" or not did not seem to me to be crucial. I probably went to church to listen to the deep, resonant voice of my father, and to delight in his exquisite mastery of words. He was steeped in the grandeur of the King James version of the Bible and in the magic of Shakespeare, both of which he could quote by the yard, and it showed in his often deeply moving sermons. Furthermore, while I was put off by some of the liturgy and the hymns that were self-deprecatory, father's sermons, usually of unexceptionable content, contributed to the fashioning of my character in ways for which I have profited throughout my life. If I had to characterize the ways in a phrase, it would have to be "You really DO reap what you sow."

Despite my early discomfort with dogma, as a small child I was still full of Methodist rites and forms. I accepted the desperate importance of salvation, whatever that meant, so I solemnly baptized the five little kittens our cat had just produced. It was made clear that they were my responsibility in the here and now, and since they couldn't read the Bible, I also felt responsible for their hereafter. I sprinkled their little blind heads with water, reverently intoning "I baptize thee in the name of the Father, the Son and the Holy Ghost, Amen," as I had seen father do scores of times with megavoluble infants. The kittens were no more enthralled than the infants, but I wager they were glad we were Methodists and not Baptists.

My grandparents also were a strong influence in my childhood, especially Grandmother. Manchester was not far from Columbus, Georgia, so I frequently visited them. Grandfather was wise, calm, good, and colorless. Grandmother was homespun-elegant and cultured, for years stylishly outfitted by the finest shops in Atlanta. Later came the depression, when Grandfather's commercial property and peach farms did not keep her in haute couture.

Grandmother used the language almost preciously, yet it was she, almost as much as Father, who started me on a lifelong love affair with words. Once when I was ten she asked me to do something and I replied that I had not been raised to do it that way. Grandmother stifled a gasp and said, firmly but lovingly, "Alfred, *chickens* are *raised; you,* I am reasonably certain, are being *reared.*" A certain degree of articulateness resulting from the tutelage of Grandmother and Father enabled me in school to pass exams with As without saying a great deal, and later in the Foreign Service in reports from the field sometimes to say a great deal cogently and tersely enough to be heeded in Washington.

I learned a lot from my schoolmate peers, too, in summertime vacation visits to father's farms near Baxley, in Southeast Georgia. As an only child, I was surprised to learn how much joy there could be in sharing. We would swim in the creek, romp and tussle in the meadows and explore the woods. We picked a little cotton, shucked a little corn. Tossed a little hay, but mainly tumbled in it, giggling from being extravagantly alive. With uncontrollable mirth we tried vainly to milk a cow. We caught in a tin cup fresh sugarcane juice as it dripped from the mule-powered grinding mill. We exaggeratedly inhaled the aroma of the cooking juice as it turned into thick, golden syrup in the nearby steaming vats.

One evening on the farm Father read to me a letter that my dad had written to me on my first birthday. It made me cry a little and think a lot. It had been written ten years previously, just after Dad learned he had tuberculosis. In simple, non-didactic, caring words it stated Dad's idea of how a life should be lived. He said one should grow perceptibly every year of his life, for when we stop growing we start dying. He spoke of the spark of divinity implanted in every human breast, there either to grow or to fade, as one nurtured or neglected it. He spoke of the need for tolerance of the differing opinions and beliefs of others, and he made it clear that I would have to earn the right to call myself a truly human being.

Mother had a different idea about life and destiny. Evidently she thought I was early cradled in inviolable safety, clutching a ticket to salvation, for she used to remind me that she had "given me to God" when I was two weeks old. I thought that astonishingly presumptuous of her.

Dad's covering note to Father read as follows:
"Savannah, Ga. Sept. 14, 1917
Dear Bro. Charles:

I am sending through J. & C.N. Thomas, Jewelers, a silver cup for Master Alfred in honor of his first birthday. I had expected to write you today, but have been on the go all day and was only able to get a letter written to the boy, which I enclose. It will keep for him till he is a young man. He may open it when you have informed him sufficiently of the more sacred things of life, so that he may properly appreciate its contents.

I am fairly well and working hard for the coming Methodist Conference. Will write more later.
Affectionately,
Elliot
P.S. You may read it and seal it up for him."
Dad was not fairly well. He was soon to learn of the ter-

minal illness that was already taking possession of him.

The following day, as I lay on the wiregrass among the pines, I reviewed in my mind Dad's letter to me, and pondered the difference between the fortunate and the unfortunate. I did not believe in luck. Father had said there was no such thing, and I thought he knew more about the workings of cosmic law than anyone else I knew. If not luck, then what? Much later, I think I came to understand what.

I soon became preoccupied with earning Boy Scout merit badges, swimming at the Y, and discovering the unfathomable, magnetic mystique of girls, so I did not think along these lines again until the summer that I was 16, when for three months I was alone with my tent, horse and dog in the pine woods of the farm. But the lessons of that contemplative summer might not have been so well examined, had it not been for the starkly contrasting, nearly equally valuable summer that preceded it.

Six

The Next
Best Thing
I Ever Did

n my teens life was very good, but largely consisted of surface concerns. We lived in Savannah, and I spent much time at the beach. So, one night after homework I went into Father's study and without prelude hazarded, "May I have a horse and tent?"

Father looked up from pecking on his Oliver typewriter and asked, "Why on earth?"

"I want to camp out in the woods at the farm, take books from your library, fix my own food, ride my horse, and be alone for the three vacation months. I haven't had time to think in years. I want to think about some things I have accepted without really thinking."

"That's a capital idea, son, but I hope you will agree to rifle practice for a year first. Those woods are still pretty wild. A bear was sighted not long ago, there is still an occasional wildcat or wild boar, and there are poisonous snakes. As for this summer, you might want to consider..."

Interpreted, that meant "I'm confident you will decide to..." And I would. Whatever Father had in mind would probably be of unassailable validity or irresistible attraction or both. I thought Father batted close to a thousand in his modest rectitude. At 15 I was not supposed to think he was savvy, but I did, and was even pleased that he was, though I felt a traitor to my kind.

Father continued, "It might be interesting as a prior antidote to your Walden next summer" (so my horse and tent were assured!) "if this summer you went to some large city that offers broad cultural advantages, stayed by your-self at a hotel for a month and 'did' the city."

We agreed on Chicago, and I 'did' it. The first two things I did at age 15 in Chicago were scandalous, because I was not yet an ex-Methodist. I was tall for my age, so I had no trouble getting into the famous, or infamous, Minsky's burlesque. It featured Lily St. Cyr's renowned endowments. The second sin, in the light of my upbring-ing, was to gamble. I lost $7.25 trying to win a camera. To a teenager, in 1932 dollars, that qualified as a disaster.

It was only in the evening of the third day that I felt lonely, and I believe that was because of guilt at having committed the above two 'sins.' The rest of my time in the Windy City was the liberal education that Father must have fondly pictured, and which I hugely enjoyed.

I spent eager days in the Field Museum, the Museum of Science and Industry, the Adler Planetarium, the Shedd Aquarium, the Art Institute, attended Chicago Symphony concerts, Chicago Civic Opera performances, and all the Balaban and Katz movie palaces in the area, where extrav-agant stage shows accompanied the movie, and a full sym-phony orchestra on a great elevator rose from the pit. I swam in then-clean Lake Michigan, ate three hot dogs in quick succession at Wrigley Field while watching great baseball, went to the top of tall buildings (50 stories maximum in 1932), and in a crowded buffet restaurant asked if I could join a fine-looking Afro-American gentleman at a table for two. He was a delight: spoke three languages, had a Ph.D. in psychology, was a member of Phi Beta Kappa, and had a thigh-slapping sense of humor. Today, fortunately, it is hard to remember how remarkable that experience was for a South Georgia boy in 1932.

I ate all the junk food I wanted. I went to church in mock penance for the two evil things I had done, but actually because I had never before seen a church incorporated in a skyscraper. Wide-eyed and shocked, I went through the stockyards and meat-packing plants that were on the outskirts of Chicago at that time. That contributed to my becoming a vegetarian.

Years later I asked Mother how it was that Father let me 'do' Chicago for a month on my own at age 15. She said it was his idea to engender independence in me. She had opposed the trip as unneeded, because I had been "independent from birth, if not from conception, or earlier," she said, in mock resignation.

The next summer I selected a dozen books from Father's library, bought a snake-proof tent and shopped for a horse, carefully looking at his teeth as though I knew what I was doing. I wouldn't have cared if he had false teeth, for a certain roan beauty and I spiritually embraced each other on sight.

I spent three months alone among the pines with Dan, my high-spirited but exactingly obedient horse, with Skipper, my little dog of questionable ancestry but unquestionable devotion, and with books that the beach had too long prevented me from reading.

It was a magical summer. With the exception of my marriage, it was the best thing I ever did. I experienced a unity with nature, knew a consuming love of its creatures and—most valuable of all—gained a burgeoning knowing of my self.

I pitched my tent near a spring with the purest of wonderful tasting water. With saplings I built a simple lot for my horse and fell into an agreeable routine of riding, sunning, rifle practicing, cooking and reading day and night. And thinking. A lot.

I read about the origins of Christianity and of the church—not unexpected fare as gleaned from Father's library, but not recommended fare for the faithful, I soon saw. I read in some consternation about the lengthy and bitter wrangling of the early Christians over doctrinal matters, which often resulted in a sort of five-to-four decision about 'eternal truths' that millions have since accepted as unarguably that.

I read much of the Bible, omitting the begats and most of Revelations, which gave me a headache. I saw why Father exulted in the grandeur of the King James version, but I noted a few *internal* contradictions, such as differing versions of Saul's conversion on the way to Damascus. While that surprised me, it did not disturb me unduly, for I had been taught that while that 66-book collection was certainly inspiring, it was man-written and compiled.

I read how scholars spotted verses in the Bible that were incorporated much later than surrounding verses, as evinced by vocabulary and grammatical constructions that did not exist when the original was written. I questioned the concept of the Trinity even more than I had as a child. I wondered why the Holy Ghost lost interest in women after siring Jesus, and why Jesus was considered the one and only son of God when he himself said God was our Father, too, and we were joint heirs to the kingdom. The Trinity seemed to turn into a Multiplicity, which I decided better fitted reality.

Thus I read myself out of orthodox Methodism, though I still found much of value in Christian ethics. It is difficult to explain what a painful wrenching this was for me, from the religion of my parents and most of my friends. I viewed my father as having downright feral honesty. I think he was incapable of deviousness, duplicity or guile. I never knew him to employ a single falsehood, except the whitest, social kind, such as thanking a hostess for an evening for which he felt no uncontrollable gratitude. He was a scholar, who had read, I believe, virtually all of his very large library. More than once his all-night reading was interrupted by the maid's breakfast call.

Father seemed to love life, the cosmos, and everyone on the planet. He desperately wanted to help people, and I knew he thought he was doing so by espousing the gospel more or less according to Methodism. I also knew that in his own mind he was a bit out front of Methodism and indeed of any Christian dogma. For instance, he thought we couldn't have it both ways about the nature of Jesus: to consider him human enough to be a credible model for us, and also to consider him divine, as one of the select triumvirate. He also thought it peculiar that the alleged one-and-only, unique son of God would say in effect that greater things than these (with respect to the miracles) we should be doing if we had requisite faith.

I was upset for several days, but finally decided that Father was possessed of the same caution that Mark Twain had shown in decreeing that his trenchantly sarcastic book, *Letters from the Earth,* could only be published 50 years after his death. He thought that during his lifetime the world would not be ready for the book's devastating ridicule of very fundamentalist religious tenets.

I recently found a letter from Father on time-yellowed

paper. It was dated Savannah, Georgia, November 6, 1934, three weeks after I first left home to enter Emory University in Atlanta. In it, Father observed, "Doubts have always bothered me, too, son; but less, the more I have studied, thought, worked and prayed. As best I could, I have preached my convictions and kept my doubts to myself. Doubts are good; they make us think. However, doubts involve ignorance, and one ought not to preach his ignorance. Even his knowledge he ought many times to withhold until his audience is ready for it."

For my part, chiefly because of Father's example of scholarship and honesty, I was uncomfortable with some of the crutches that the church offered, while applauding their availability for those who could not walk without them. I became convinced that I was in virtually all things responsible for my course in life, for my experience of reality, in a way for my very being and certainly for my becoming. I decided that was a splendid way for the cosmos to be constructed. At least I could not think of a more satisfactory way. I would not want to be an automaton, or on the other hand something buffeted by chance or luck.

Thus disempowering the dilemma concerning Father's honesty versus his preaching, I turned to getting the most from my privileged solitude and silence.

I dragged my cot out under the stars. I fried bacon and eggs, shifting meditatively around the fire as the gusty breeze shifted the smoke. I encased potatoes in mud and baked them at the fire's edge, later roasting marshmallows in the embers. I then put two nail holes in a large can of condensed milk and lay back on my cot, slowly to suck out the sweet contents, while marveling at the stars, multiplied and made unbelievably close by the rural darkness. I decided to sleep there, rifle at my side, with Skipper on my stomach to warn of any approaching unfriendliness. I felt healthy, blessed and secure. The pine-scented air was intoxicating. Life was good.

I wonder if it has not been difficult for later generations of young people to experience such an unadulterated sense of contentment and security as I did in my youth. The Bomb was a nightmare yet undreamed, the planet was relatively unspoiled, and the comfort, love and security of family life, with rare exception, was still intact. All of that contributed to what I call the background hum of the mind, against which everything else in experience is played out. Consequently, I grew up an optimist as a matter of course. I'm glad, for I am convinced that our background mind-hum sets the wavelengths on which our lives operate, drawing to us people, experiences and circumstances appropriate to the predominant mind-hum.

Just before time for school to start Father came to fetch me. We took a long walk in the woods. I told him some of the thoughts I had entertained in my hermitage, for the most part skirting my problems with dogma. I said, "Here I am entering my last year in high school and I don't know what I want to do in life, or even what to major in when I get to college."

"It doesn't matter, son," Father said with surprising assurance. "The purpose of college is to learn to love to learn. You can specialize later in graduate school if you wish. Just take courses from the most learned, modest and inspiring professors, almost regardless of the subjects they teach, and you'll turn out just fine."

While I did not then find that counsel satisfying, I now think it was some of the best advice I ever received. At Emory I believe I learned more from the nature of the professors, by positive and, more rarely, negative example, than I did from what they taught—which, also, was a great deal.

On the trip back to Savannah we didn't talk much. I found myself studying Father as he drove. He was tall, slender, immensely self-possessed, not quite saturnine, but dignified and often somber. Yet when he smiled he was luminous, for he was a lover of all creation, and that was reflected in his quiet emanations. Only in the last couple of years had he begun to stoop a little. He was 67, an active and totally dedicated minister of a large church. I decided I was fortunate in the seemingly loose, intangible, caring, yet artfully strong tether he had on his son. His round, gold-rimmed spectacles were dusty, but seeing again his clear eyes made me feel secure. He was not handsome (once he had won a cake at Rotary, in jest, for being the ugliest man there) but the qualities etched into that face through the years of study and caring made him almost mesmerizing to look at. The dark red moustache contrasting with his still coal-black, full head of hair and thick, black eyebrows seemed right, for him. I smiled in noting that in honor of his day on the farm with me he wore a soft-collar shirt. It had to be one of mine, for all of his had a starch-stiffened, detachable collar.

I was proud to be the son of this man. I had never heard a word spoken by anyone in his regard that did not show respect and affection. He did not know what it meant to be belligerent or unloving. His jaw neither jutted nor receded. He was totally unassuming, but meek he was not. Father was about the least intimidating human I ever knew, yet I stood in a little awe of him, even while feeling perfectly comfortable in crossing him, on the rare occasions when I had any desire to do so. In writing this more than 60 years later, as a parent I marvel at father's restraint in honoring so completely for a summer's eternity his only child's desire for solitude. I had not seen him for three months, yet we were only an hour and a half apart.

○   ○   ○

In high school I was surprised at being popular, despite not being a football hero. I played in the orchestra, sang in the glee club, was a counselor in summer at camp, was class secretary, class poet, and president of the Hi-Y Club, a collaborative endeavor of the YMCA and the high school. The last was an agreeable association, except at one of the monthly dinner meetings the guys became so rowdy at the table that a couple of biscuits were hurled. (Historical note: in 1933 respectable people, even respectable young people, did not hurl biscuits at each other.) That evening I told Father I could hardly wait to get to college, "where I would find myself dealing with grown people." Father was silent, seemingly looking at a painting on the wall, then finally said, "I hate to tell you this, son, but I'm not sure how often you will find yourself dealing with what you would call grown people."

Just before I left home for college there was an event that succinctly reveals what that remarkable man I call my father was like. One evening I was triple dating in his new Buick, driving down the 'main drag' of Savannah. I was flicking the ignition on and off to make it backfire, soliciting the attention of the passersby. Suddenly there was an especially loud report, after which the car sounded like a ten-ton truck of that era (loud.) I had blown a gaping hole in the muffler. As though that were not enough to slink home with, there came one of Savannah's cloudbursts of semi-tropical generosity, so that I couldn't see. Just then my date, in attempting to shift in her seat, put her foot on mine, and we shot forward, plowing through water that had stacked up in the flat streets of Savannah. We crashed into a telephone pole, knocked out a light, totaled a fender and sent the bumper askew. I promptly deposited my friends at their homes, then about two o'clock in the morning tried to pass my parents' bedroom as quietly as possible. Both father and mother, as always when I was out, were still awake. Father called out, "Hello, son. Did you have a nice evening?"

"Very nice up to a point, Father, but I've wrecked your car."

"Are you hurt?"

"No."

"Is anybody hurt?"

"No."

"That's good. Well, goodnight, son."

I stood there for maybe a full minute in silence. I opened my mouth to say something, but nothing came out. I went to my room and, fully clothed, lay awake for a long time looking at the ceiling—growing.

SEVEN

The
Usages
Of Error

y life at Emory was just about perfect. At that time there were some exceptionally fine men in my fraternity, Chi Phi. The university itself had its priorities uncommonly straight. I don't recall any written campus rules. The unwritten rule, however, was clear: be a scholar and a gentleman, or go home. Some transferred to schools less academically demanding. Others went home.

I followed Father's advice in selecting courses, avoiding the one professor who had a reputation for arrogance, though also of erudition. Arrogance meant that he lacked self-confidence, hence would be a poor model for a young man. I majored in philosophy, because I admired the brilliant and modest head of that department. In those days there was a required course in Bible, taught by the husband of one of Aunt Annie's daughters. He had a puckish humor that managed to stay just this side of iconoclasm. The course served further to validate my drift from fundamentalism. Actually, that became almost irrelevant, because the secular aspects of my life were so satisfactory. The Emory and Atlanta soil that I tilled was fertile.

One month before I was to graduate, Dr. Cox, president of Emory, asked me to take a job immediately, as a favor to the university. A very wealthy man, Mr. Cater Woolford, founder of the Retail Credit Corporation, had asked Emory to furnish a graduate student for the summer who could "carry on a conversation." Part of the job would be to help entertain his guests, either at Sea Island, where he had a suite at the Cloister Hotel, or at his 7,000-acre deer plantation on the mainland that he had bought from the Dupont family. I would be excused from final and comprehensive exams and would graduate in absentia with honors. Mr. Cater had experienced spouse trouble, was morose, and may have needed an interest outside himself. Emory reasoned that if he could be interested in supporting a worthy university, both he and the university would benefit.

It was good duty. I liked Mr. Cater, and was fascinated by his guests, some of whom were quite un-Methodist. I also learned a valuable lesson that Father had earlier pointed out, but of which I had not been totally convinced: wealth does not necessarily bring happiness. Most of the people who I got to know at Sea Island were wealthy and unhappy. I've had Father's contention confirmed elsewhere, at places like Palm Springs, St. Moritz and especially Palm Beach. Of course there are also happy and admirable people in such places, but I am led to believe by the residents themselves that such people are in the minority. Efforts to keep up with the Joneses do not breed the most appealing traits in people.

One day on the beach I gained a certain claim to distinction. I fell ker-plop on the stomach of Mrs. Johnny Walker. Yes, *the* Mrs. Johnny Walker, who was certainly wealthy, and, I learned from her, distinctly unhappy. She was caught up in the luxury of an award-winning nervous breakdown—a catastrophe that turned out to be just around the corner for me, at my young age! I was playing softball and in running backward to catch a fly I stumbled over Mrs. Walker, who I believe was asleep. She was not only forgiving, she was charming and friendly. She advised me never to take a drink. And if I had not met a certain comely young lady in Chicago, who got me to smoking and drinking for closer companionship, I might have successfully heeded her advice. Still, in diplomatic service, where I landed, alcohol, lamentably, is virtually a tool of the trade. It is sparingly used, for one is always on duty, but it is frequently used.

I left Georgia in September for Boston University School of Theology, which was for me a disaster. In part it was I who made it so, for I was spoiled. The dormitory at B.U.S.T., as the institution was familiarly (and to me, not inappropriately) known, was an ancient Beacon Hill mansion that had not been, and was not currently, well kept. There were dust balls in the halls and it was poorly heated. At times the furnace would produce such unabashed belches of carbon monoxide we had to stumble out into the cold for air. There was no bathroom on my floor. In short, it was a far cry from Tom Conally Hall, my fraternity house at Emory, which was a well-kept, beautiful Georgian-style mansion. Nor did the dormitory remind me of the Cloister Hotel at Sea Island. I confess the difference was a problem for me.

That was not the worst of it, however. It seemed to me that piety at the school was paraded, and both faculty and students gave me the impression they had cornered the market on truth. Furthermore, a favorite topic of discussion among the students was what constituted the difference between a $10,000 preacher and a $5,000 one, in 1938 dollars. The professor of Greek opened class with a prayer in a quivering voice, informing the Deity in surely unnecessary detail of the sad state of His world.

To me a religious person had meant someone as unassuming as he was straightforward and able, like my father, who had been my minister all my life until I entered college. The whole scene at B.U.S.T., theological, social and material, confused me and repelled me—especially the theological scene, involving an area of life that I had been taught was of cardinal importance. It literally made me sick.

I became sicker, and was sent to Boston General Hospital, where as a student I was put in a ward with seven others—a circumstance not to my liking. Nor was the arrogant doctor assigned to me to my liking. When I complained to him that my throat hurt, he loudly yelled, "THERE IS NOTHING WRONG WITH YOUR THROAT." I think I had not been yelled at before in my entire life, so to my astonishment, and doubtless to his, I yelled right back, equally loudly, "THEN WHY DOES IT HURT?" Without response he departed with his mouth open. Lab reports could demonstrate no bacterial invasion, so the hurt was doubtless psychosomatic, arising from a desperate need for an excuse not to face the life in which I found myself.

I was sent to a special building of the huge hospital complex, where peculiar cases were corralled. The room was semi-private, the food excellent, attention overly bestowed, and on the staff there were several recent graduates of the Emory Medical School who remembered me from student days.

It turned out that I was not quite peculiar enough to amuse these premier specialists for long. Besides, it occurred to me that I could simply go home and forget theology school, which I suddenly realized was what I desired above all. I was not only sick, but my values had been offended and, I was spoiled. I had not been adequately prepared for the real world, if B.U.S.T. and its dormitory represented the real world. Anyway, it became clear to me that I had a lot of remaking of myself to do.

It took an inordinate length of time to do it. For over a year I felt awful. I was indulging in a nervous breakdown at age 21, and a nervous breakdown is hell. Father had said that hell is when you refuse to take responsibility for your life, thus abdicating your role as creator. Since that is also an unfailing formula for a nervous breakdown, I equate that malady with hell.

The finest physicians in Savannah and Atlanta said there was nothing wrong with me. Well, there *is* something wrong with you when your back aches, you don't sleep well and life becomes insipid or worse. The lab tests, no matter how freely administered, couldn't quantify my malady.

In earlier times, home would have been a splendid place to remake me, but not just then. My parents had retired to the country, where their attitudes and personalities had undergone rapid, fundamental and detrimental changes, largely because of failing health. Father had beginning congestive heart failure and both he and Mother had beginning kidney failure. Both conditions, I would later learn, were chiefly a result of ignorance as to proper diet. Too, Father missed the former professional demands, and to his genuine astonishment, he missed urban life. His attendance at Melton's Chapel near the farm tended to eclipse the traditional leaders of the church, which perturbed him, but he didn't know how to extricate himself without causing misunderstanding.

For my part, in my childhood days on vacation to the farm I found Melton's Chapel fascinating. In those days the men, in black suits and white shirts, sat on one side of the aisle, and the women, in small-flowered gingham, on the other. Both sides seemed to think that God, being quite old, had become hard of hearing, for each side vied all-out with the other in the attempt to overcome the deficiency. The decibels produced by "Amazing Grace," "The Old Rugged Cross" and "In the Garden" were not equaled in my experience until the unforgettable era of my 16 year-old son's stereo. Furthermore, in those days not only country music, but most music produced in the country, tended to be nasal as well as voluble, a peculiarly disagreeable combination. Anyway, it seemed to me odd that one would bellow while walking with God in a garden.

The frequent visiting ministers were for the most part dedicated fear-mongers. One droopy-eyed prelate was especially frightening in his depiction of a jealous and vindictive God. I wondered what my penalty would be for having kissed the little Tippins girl under the back porch, when we were five years old and not even married. The minister warned of God's repeatedly shortening the life span of humankind for having worshiped golden calves. While I did not recall having noted the practice myself, I was still frightened. Methuselah was some 900 years old when he died. Abraham considerably less. Other Biblical figures still less, until currently "three score and ten" was not even the norm, but the Biblically insisted limit. The minister had placed a stretched-out handkerchief on the floor, and, with wails and histrionics that would have been immensely entertaining had the message not been so dire, moved it closer to him with each diminishing of the life span. If that progression were not halted, I had visions of my not reaching maturity.

My welfare and growth had become the central purpose of Father's life. And his only son was a failure, despite the many advantages that had been so carefully provided him. In my silly youthfulness it even bothered me that in his retirement Father drove Chevrolets instead of the accustomed Buicks, yet in part I blamed myself for that necessity. All-in-all, there was a dearth of mirth in the household, and I longed for a visit from Aunt Annie.

I had to get away. I entered a half resort, half sanitarium-hotel near Orlando, run by the Seventh Day Adventists. I was given mineral baths, a massage a day, hot compresses here and there on my stagnating carcass, and was disagreeably stimulated by having something like a fire hose turned on me.

I remained at the Orlando haven for three months, because some idiot inmate told me it took three months to get over a nervous breakdown. Despite all the pampering, or more likely because of it, I made no progress. I now know that it can take three years, or the rest of a life, to get over a nervous breakdown, and also that it can be conquered almost immediately, if one comes to acknowledge what feeds it and does something about it. I suffered from the usual programming that in order to get well you had to have something done *to* you. I now know that to be inverted thinking. I returned home no different, except that I was ten pounds heavier from the sensational, purely vegetarian food.

Home was also the same: sloshing in gloom. To get out of it, to breathe I became an assistant scoutmaster in Baxley, and thus, most unexpectedly, acquired a brother.

I knew what I needed to know about most scouting requirements, but not enough about birds. I learned that the best authority on birds in the county was an eleven year-old boy at the Orphans' Home, so I asked him to spend a couple of weeks in the country to teach me about birds. He seemed to know everything about them except the Audubon names—even that Cardinals are monogamous.

I had to go to Atlanta to be in a friend's wedding, so to his distress I took him back to the Home. I promised him another week with us when I returned, but when I went to get him, he came in crying. His buddies in the Home missed him so when he was away before, they literally threatened him if he left them again. Of course peer pressure won.

Meanwhile, the superintendent of the Home misunderstood my mission. I suppose he thought the folks liked to have a young guest to brighten the place, so before I knew what was happening, he had brought in a substitute. I started to explain that I was only fulfilling an obligation that didn't apply to this boy, but then the boy looked so crestfallen, I said, "Go get into the car. You can have a week in the country."

We never took him back. He is my brother, Phil, to this day. The place was cheerier, all right, but I found his winning personality and good looks inexcusable. I had previously enjoyed all the parental attention; now I felt, erroneously, that I had less than half. I thought in most ways I resented and disliked him—until I decided to watch his tonsils taken out. In Savannah, where Father was chairman of a hospital board, I had witnessed all sorts of gory operations with no reaction other than keen interest, but at the first sight of Phil's blood my knees buckled and I had to stick my head between my knees in order not to pass out. I had grown fond of him and didn't know it. We later had good times together, including arranging simultaneous leaves from Air Corps and Navy to explore Washington and New York.

Probably more than any other factor, it was Phil who cured me of my nervous breakdown. One of the hallmarks of a nervous breakdown is egocentrism; but with the likes of Phil around it was difficult to contrive an egocentric situation for me. Others would not cooperate. Also, Phil would have none of my "dumb slump" as he put it. He would kid me out of my presumed problems, or just clown so outrageously there could be no problems within reach of his vibes.

This most difficult period in my life taught me a valuable lesson: how unfailingly to ruin a life. You just decide not to be happy, for whatever spurious reason happens to be conveniently at hand. Deciding not to be happy can make you sick unto death. It is rare that the decision has much to do with outer circumstance, though outer circumstance usually gets the blame.

Finally, I became sufficiently able to accept life that I welcomed the friendship of a couple of young men from neighboring farms. I went hunting rabbits with one, at first excitedly, because I knew I was a good shot; but I learned that I did not like to kill. I went exploring the Altamaha River banks with the other friend. We would swim in the raw in the warm, muddy water and lie in the sun on an island in the river, far from anyone. I defy anyone not to heal himself in such therapeutic resignation into nature.

Able once again to accept responsibility for the realities I created, I found a position teaching seventh grade history and science at Ten Mile School near the farm. What brought me fully out of the "dumb slump." not surprisingly, was an absorbing interest in the welfare and maturation of others, so that I forgot myself. There is no more wondrous spectacle than watching young minds maturing daily before your eyes, and no more magical therapy than forgetting yourself.

I was a fair-to-middling history teacher, a topnotch science teacher and an unimpressive basketball coach, but I had fun and the students also seemed to, most of the time.

Young as I was, I was surprised that I had no disciplinary problem. I think it was because I respected the students and tried to treat them like young grown-ups, but I was assured by more than one parent that it was mostly because in that era they were well disciplined at home. I was further told that if the need arose the parents would not consider that I was earning my pay if I did not administer reasonable physical punishment, the language most of the children understood in that day and age and locale.

One morning I arrived at the appointed hour to a totally empty classroom. Fifteen minutes later all my students came traipsing in, calling "April fool!" I had not noted the date. If I had thought of that, I like to believe I would have reacted reasonably. Instead, my youthful dignity was affronted and my subconscious reminded me of the parental counseling I had received about discipline. Before my mind regained sensible appraisal, I indicated to the students that penalties were in order.

I suddenly realized that in that case I was supposed to administer "whuppin's." I was terrified. I had never in all my life received one, much less administered one. I panicked in realizing it had not been made clear to me whether girls were to receive the same punishment. It didn't matter. I couldn't "whup" girls. I said either the boys or the girls could pay their penalty, if they wished, by writing 500 times "Discretion is the better part of valor," and handing the work in. The philosophical application of that maxim to the crime committed I recognized as tenuous, but the stateliness of the phrase recommended it as soul-honing for the errant youngsters. I said if writers' cramp did not appeal, the punishment would be swifter. To my enormous relief, all the girls elected to incur writers' cramp, but to my consternation every boy elected to get it over with. I managed to slip my belt from its moorings. Firmly holding the thought that it was honorable to earn the first pay one had ever received, I whacked away, managing to administer a few respectable licks to each of eight presentations.

What surprised me most of all in this unnerving episode was that these boys, whom I had inexpertly but earnestly coached in basketball, blithely continued their cheerful, respectful and friendly relationship with me. If I had received corporal punishment, it would have changed my view of the world and the way it worked.

At Christmas the principal of the school resigned to take over his father's lucrative hardware business, so the board of trustees elected me principal, with three months' teaching experience! I was offered the job for the following year, but meanwhile I had been elected school superintendent in a small town a hundred miles from the farm.

There, at age 25, I was careful at first to wear a hat, and I bought a pair of window pane spectacles, but once I felt accepted, I went roller skating down the street with the students. Teaching the adult Sunday School class of the Methodist Church helped get me accepted. I was a surprising hit in that role. Several remarked how "fresh and applicable to life" my perspectives were. I'm sure none of those dedicated Methodists realized it was because I was teaching Unitarianism. I didn't, myself, until much later, but I was.

My career as a school superintendent ended after a year because the United States entered the World War on December seventh. I made plans to try to get a direct commission in the Navy, as several of my friends were doing.

However, I happened to call on a lawyer friend who had been a general in World War I, a next-door neighbor when we lived in Macon. He advised, "Don't angle for a commission right off; instead, enlist. The most fun I ever had in my life was as a buck private in Uncle Sam's army. You will be given a bevy of tests and you will end up an officer, but meanwhile you will meet a cross-section of humanity that you do not know exists. Won't do you any harm."

I took his advice, for which I subsequently was not moved to render thanks. Clearly, the least fun I ever had in my life was as a buck private in Uncle Sam's army. Still, military life took me to Washington, and to my major life's work in diplomacy—a life that surely was farther from my mind when I was growing up in South Georgia than any other conceivable occupation.

EIGHT

In The
Wisdom
Of The
Army

 encountered the promised cross-section of humanity, all right, especially at the Induction Center in Atlanta. There were three main categories of humanity in the barracks: those who would take me by the lapel and oleaginously inquire, "Do you know Jesus?" or "Are you saved?" On the far other hand, there were those who uttered a stunning stream of expletives profane and scatological, and/or mimed monstrous obscenities. Then there were those whom I could not comprehend at all, much less converse with, because it turned out we did not know the same words.

Gradually there came the numerous tests predicted by my friend the lawyer-general. The resulting sifting process led through a barren blur of other barracks and camps, except that one of these moves housed me in a luxury hotel at Miami Beach, where KP duty was still KP duty. It was there that one of the tests earned me a visit to the commanding officer, who told me with a straight face that my tests showed I was mechanically apt. At that time I hadn't even heard of a Phillips screwdriver. I was put on the train in Miami-weight garb and deposited at Chanute Field, Illinois, in the dead of winter, where I had to wait nearly an hour in a formation outdoors, with snow on the ground, before I was promised the chance to demonstrate my long-hidden mechanical aptitude.

It was worth it. I found myself in the Link Trainer contingent in a swarm of highly intelligent men, every one of them also mechanically apt, by military fiat. I also found myself surrounded by hordes of Yankees for the first time in my life. I think I was surprised to find them reasonably representative of *homo erectus,* but it unnerved me that they went into uncontrollable laughter at my pronunciation of my study companion's name, Pierce. It seems I did not pronounce the 'r' at all.

We studied the flying, dismembering, repairing and assembling of a Link Trainer, a simulated warplane, a fiendishly clever invention that never left the ground. I discovered that I *was* mechanically apt, just as the man said. We all had to master the contraption, in all its unbelievable electronic, mechanical and vacuumatic perplexities. I made the careless mistake of doing too well in the course, so was kept there to teach it. Being a smartypants thus considerably delayed my commission as an officer. I soon became bored, despite three-day passes to Chicago, so, since the Air Corps never taught me to fly except on the ground, I took private flying lessons at nearby Champaign, Illinois. When I obtained my solo license I rented planes and flew about as whim dictated and my thin wallet permitted, getting lost twice, and nearly killed once when the motor failed at 400 feet. The instructor had never told me what to do in such a situation! God Himself must have told me to nose the plane almost straight down, so the rush of air would turn the propeller of the Piper Cub and start the motor. There was no self-starter on the thing. When on the ground someone had to flick the propeller much as one had to crank an early Model-T Ford. The steep dive worked. The motor caught, but those corn stalks were getting mighty big before I soared upward again. As soon as I gained altitude I patterned right down and turned in the jinxed machine. Later I read in the paper that my instructor and the mechanic who worked on that plane were killed, when the motor again failed at a low altitude and they fell into high tension wires.

At Chanute Field I applied for what I thought would be a three-month course in German military terminology. I was comfortable in the language except for specialized vocabularies. I ended up in presumptuously named Paris, Texas. I could rent planes in Paris, but my PFC income soon grounded me. I said as much in not too circuitous fashion in a letter to father. He responded, ending with a P.S.: "Enclosed is a little something to keep you airborne, since you say it is a cathartic in your circumstance. However, you may sometime want to try thanksgiving as a cathartic. You may find it cheaper, quicker and possibly more effective than flying. Even in your circumstance I wot you can come up with a fit subject about which to give thanks. Good luck, and enjoy." I did, and occasionally re-read the letter. I smiled at the "I wot." I had never heard him use the expression before, but it sounded like him. I began occasionally to practice his recommendation, with profit.

After three interminable weeks a new class opened up, as it happened, felicitously, at the University of Chicago. I asked the admissions dean when the class in German would start.

"German? Oh, no. You don't take German. You have your choice among Japanese, Chinese or Russian. Which do you want?"

"I don't care."

"Do you have any experience with or connection with one of those countries, directly or indirectly?"

"No ... Well, in a way. Madame Chiang Kai-shek was in my parents' home a great deal when she was at Wesleyan College. She was good friends with Nona, a girl Father was sending through college.

"It's Chinese for you, young man." I almost laughed at the peremptory way he said that. This academic gentleman with ultrabenevolent, avuncular mein, had—doubtless recently—learned to speak with the crisp finality of a military veteran.

I was delighted at the unexpected change in courses. I much preferred to learn a new language, especially an exotic one. Also, I confess that I did not harbor a consuming yearning to be part of the coming landing on the continent of Europe.

Again, this was good duty. This Georgia boy was puffed up being on the great University of Chicago campus. The food was good, our housing not bad and we could ride horses in the park nearby. I learned later that I once played handball right over (or was it under?) the laboratory where physicists were wrestling with the intricacies of inventing the atomic bomb.

My associates in the China language program were intelligent, well educated gentlemen, possessed of a sophisticated and usually decorous order of barracks humor. In addition, I was in a city of which I had long been fond.

I also became fond of a young lady who lived on the

lake front near the campus and attended the university. She was one of the three or four most beautiful women I have ever seen. Intelligent, graceful and utterly charming, with blond hair, blue eyes, and perfect figure, she was well-reared by her aunt and uncle with whom she lived. They were wealthy, enabling her to dress as I have seldom seen. Not ostentatiously, just in simple, expensive, impeccably good taste. We dated regularly for nearly a year. On Christmas Eve, dancing at the famous Pump Room, she wore a gown that stands out in memory above any other. It was black taffeta with a lacy black gauze oversheath bearing a discreet red rose in the lower left portion. The lines were swirly and elegantly simple. The neckline managed to be both understated and provocative.

Shortly before I was to be transferred to a different post, a young man with a car and a good income took her away from me. We had earlier double dated, so I knew him to be superintelligent. I learned later that, young as he was, he was one of the midwives to the atom bomb birth (the very secret Manhattan project), under or over which I had played. I wanted to think Mary's shifting allegiance was because I was about to be transferred, but I harbored doubts. I do wish I had been a little less Methodist in that relationship, but then that was another era.

Near the end of the twelve-month Chinese course I was suddenly called home. Father was on his death bed. His failing heart and kidneys, in addition to the series of disappointments described earlier, were too much for him. I'm not sure how much my being a corporal preyed on his pride, but he had to be human enough to have preferred that I be an officer by then. He had seen to it that I had the preparation, at least, to make something of a mark in life. Furthermore, my doctrinal doubts, which had begun to show at home, troubled him. Not so much, I believe, on doctrinal grounds as such, as from disappointment that his son could not in greater measure embrace what he had given his whole life to with such devotion. If I had been more mature, I would have held my tongue at home.

Intensifying the blow to Father, I think, was my finding value in Christian Science, though I could not accept its dogma all the way. That interest arose at Chanute Field, because the Christian Science Wartime Minister and his attractive wife had the best cuisine, the largest collection of classical records, and the thickest rugs in the area (barracks are bare), and since they were also wonderful people, I cultivated invitations to their home, where I picked up the literature. Also, when I was stationed for a time at Randolph Field in San Antonio, I dated the mayor's daughter, who was a Christian Scientist. Father did not understand Christian Science, and it disturbed him that I found value in it. That surprised me. In an earlier, stronger day, he would have reacted with more acceptance and understanding.

Father died in the middle of one night. The magnitude of my loss numbed my feelings. I remember simply helping Phil for a while with his homework before we all went to bed.

It was the next day that I felt bereaved to my core. I don't think I showed it, for I had been taught that it was not a class act to show grief, inasmuch as it made others uncomfortable. I was, however, suddenly more cognizant than I had ever been of the magnificent gift I had been given in having 27 years of association with that man. I respected and loved my father. He knew that, but I don't think I ever even once gave overt expression to it, and I wish I had. I very much I wish I had.

The following day, according to local custom of the era, Father's lifeless form was brought back to the house in his casket, after having been prettied up by the undertaker.

His cheeks had been slightly rouged and his lips faintly painted, as though there were blood still in them. Mother leaned over and kissed his forehead. I detected no feeling in the act, though there had to be some. I did not think the seeming lack of feeling was due to training that a show of grief was in bad taste; I felt there *was* no appreciable feeling. While I was pondering that in disbelief, it was suddenly the sight of the distinctive starched, detachable collar of Father's pre-retirement days that sent me to my room to compose myself.

At the memorial service for Father the personal and professional esteem in which he was so widely held was movingly evident. It was so moving I reached over and held Mother's hand, thinking she would need my support at that time. I sensed that she did not. I was puzzled and hurt. I still hurt. I do not know why Mother seemed spiritually to have divorced Father after their retirement, while still ministering faithfully to his creature needs. I think I do not want to understand it, lest I perforce become cynical, and I know that cynicism shrinks the psyche. In later years I have tried to forgive Mother, for there must have been some antecedent cause, to me unknown, for her lack of feeling.

After the memorial service I hurried back to Chicago to make up for lost time, for the Chinese course was both intensive and competitive. There was a test every two weeks, when a few flunked out and presumably went to the fighting front. In fact, of the 165 who started, only 20 of us graduated a year later. Of those, 19 were sent to Fort Riley Cavalry School, and I was sent to the Pentagon in Military Intelligence. I was not chosen because of any uniquely superior performance in the course. Since I was a former superintendent of schools, someone may have concluded that I was more mature than the other nineteen.

Actually, being young, naive and patriotic, I had volunteered for a hush-hush program in which I would be dropped behind Japanese lines in China to perform certain unlikely acts. I was first notified that I had been accepted, but subsequently was told that "another agency" had plans for me, and those plans took precedence. Far better, it turned out to be.

Young and inexperienced as I was, I was thrilled enough just to be in Washington, D.C., with all its monuments, gigantic government buildings, broad avenues, cherry trees and heart-thumping history—plus incomparable contemporary history in the making. Then, and for the ensuing decade plus, our capital city was pretty much the hub of the planet.

For a while yet, it meant another barracks life for me, for I was still an enlisted man. Still, I was content. I had never been, was not then, and am not now, greatly impressed by rank or pomp and circumstance, unless the show is aesthetically appealing or intellectually stimulating. In the Air Corps I was given a free education of considerable value, had a lot of fun after the first two ghastly months, and for some time had associates who were an intellectual delight. That was enough for me. Furthermore, I was pleasantly impressed that my working hours were spent in what was then the world's largest building, far larger than the Cheops pyramid, covering 43 acres of land on a 300-acre plot. This virtual air-conditioned city furnished offices for some 52,000 people in wartime.

After a few weeks at the Pentagon I was commissioned a second lieutenant, perhaps the most distinctive rank in the vast building full of colonels and generals. I fell to mastering the Chinese order of battle in the Chinese Civil War between the Nationalist forces of Chiang Kai-shek and Mao Tze-tung's Communist forces. Having graduated at last from barracks life, I found a room on F Street. I felt reinstated as captain of my soul. I sort of missed the barracks, but not achingly.

In my job in Military Intelligence I managed to please my seniors and settled down to what I supposed would be a comfortable oblivion. This was not to be.

Understandably, after hostilities ended in Europe, the Pentagon was preoccupied with affairs Japanese, while I, almost unnoticed, was plodding away in the Pentagon equivalent of the catacombs, following all things Chinese. With V-J Day, however, the Pentagon seemed to discover that it still had a war going on in China that might turn out to matter to us and to the world.

Virtually overnight, a great segment of the Pentagon almost magically shifted around and reorganized itself, much as a computer screen does when the right key is punched. In view of the resignation of my boss, Major Lau, right after V-J Day, I was about the most knowledgeable person on overall Chinese affairs remaining in the Pentagon. I was about to be put in charge of a bay of personnel, when it was realized that as a first lieutenant I would be overseeing the work of at least one major and various other yet undetermined officers. This would have effected a veritable crumbling of the Pentagon, so I was quickly put into mufti and given the civilian rank equivalent of lieutenant colonel. I was appreciative of the new responsibilities and the promotion, but I soon left the Pentagon, crossing the Potomac to the Department of State. To my astonishment, I had passed the formidable Foreign Service exam.

NINE

The
Best Thing
I Ever Did

ne fine spring Sunday in 1945 when Mother was visiting me, I transferred my church membership to Mount Vernon Place Methodist Church in Washington, for I knew it would please her. There were some dozen of us joining the church or transferring from elsewhere. We were called to the altar at the end of the service to renew our vows. I happened to be standing next to a ravishing blonde. When I returned to my seat and the benediction was pronounced, I asked Mother, "Did you notice that girl in the WAVE uniform standing next to me?"

"Yes, son, and I noticed you noticed, too. But, son, when the minister was having you renew your vows, you really should have been looking at him when you said, 'I do,' not gawking down to your left at some trim blonde with her stocking seams straight."

The next Sunday evening I went into the office of the church secretary who, on seeing me, said to an attractive brunette seated in a corner, "Here's a man who can help you."

I pricked up my ears. "Damsel in distress? My specialty," I announced.

"Not exactly in distress, but I am tired of looking up words," the pert brunette confessed. She wanted me to read a French play to her on which she was to have a test.

When I finished, she said, "By the way, what's your name?"

"Alfred."

"Not Alfred Jenkins!"

"Yes, why?"

"I have orders from three people to introduce you to my sister."

"Who is your sister?

"Martha Lippiatt."

My throat closed tightly. I had already asked the minister the name of the WAVE that had stood beside me. My next question could be predicted.

"What three people have 'ordered' you to introduce me to your sister?"

Impishly, "The minister, his secretary, ... and my sister." I had thought my throat tight before, but at that I nearly strangled.

Soon we were dating. And pretty soon engaged. Within three months, to be exact. *Veni, vidi, vici* too, uncle John! From that day that trim, brown-eyed, beautiful blonde was my pride, my love and my strong support during the next 46 years. In my view and in that of others she was the belle of every ball we attended. She was modest, outgoing, upbeat and quietly energetic, with the most winning smile imaginable. She was loved wherever she went.

When the announcement of the Foreign Service exam came across my desk at the Pentagon, I made an off-hand decision to take it, just to have a look at it. Expecting to go back to the educational field, I was interested in the make-up of exams, and I understood that the Foreign Service exam was uniquely difficult and comprehensive. I was not interested in the Foreign Service, because I didn't know what it was. I was from Georgia. South Georgia, at that. And it was 1945, not the present-day world. For all I knew, the Foreign Service was something like the Foreign Legion, and I wanted no part of that, except in my most Walter Mittyish fantasies. If they had called it the diplomatic service, I would have had a fair idea of its nature. As the time to take the Foreign Service exam came close I gradually learned something about what the Foreign Service was. Still not wholeheartedly, I decided to take the last three days of the renowned Rowdybush cram course designed to prepare one for the Foreign Service exam. Georgetown University gave a four year course with the same objective. I also took books with me on our honeymoon, for the exam was to come right after it. Of course I didn't crack one.

I was astonished that I passed the exam, for some 20,000 people took it that year, simultaneously in a number of cities, and on a sliding scale only 200 were allowed to pass it. Of those, 100 were allowed to pass the oral. My gratitude for the excellence of Emory University training went up another notch.

I took the oral largely because I love a captive audience, which in this case consisted of six high-level people sitting in an arc around a little table at which I sat. At that point those august authorities already knew what you *knew* from the written exam (more comprehensive in those days than it is today). The oral was to tell them who you *are*—

what you are like. The first question was whether I con-
templated committing matrimony. I said I had just committed it, "and that right gloriously, if I may say so." A cir-
culated picture of Martha, which though adulterated by the
presence of the groom, did my cause no harm. The other
questions were substantive, but having been daily inundated in Military Intelligence Service with world-wide
reports of all levels of confidentiality, I may have known
more about many of the subjects covered than most of my
interrogators.

General Bissel, my boss in Military Intelligence, had
given me good advice about taking the oral: "Alfred, I
think there is no danger that you will be cocky, so we
should assure that you appear sufficiently authoritative.
You've been briefing colonels and generals here with confidence, seeming to enjoy it. Go into the oral not with the
idea that those forbidding dignitaries are grilling you, but
that they are asking the questions because they want to
know the answers and will value your knowledge and
opinions." It seemed to work.

I had been warned that there might be tricks, to test
composure and self-confidence. For instance, sometimes a
cigarette would be offered, then questions would be rapidly
fired by the intimidating dignitaries while the victim realized there was no ash tray in evidence. The proper thing to
do, of course, was to interrupt the general, the assistant
secretary or the ambassador and say, "Before I answer that
question, may I have an ash tray?" The receptionist later
told me that some candidates, rather than interrupt the dignitaries, had been known to snuff the cigarette out in the
sweaty palm of their hands or in the cuff of their trousers.
To my mixed disappointment and relief, they pulled no
tricks on me, possibly because, seeing that I knew Chinese,
they wanted me to pass.

On passing the oral and later the physical I suddenly realized I had landed in the Foreign Service. Almost as though I was reading about someone else, I found myself written up in the various home town newspapers of my peripatetic childhood and youth, having my picture taken at Harris and Ewing, buying a homburg (the badge of a diplomat in those days) and in some bewilderment clutching diplomatic passports for me and my bride.

In May 1946 members of the Jenkins clan asked me, despite my preoccupations with entering a new career, to fly down to Macon to present to Wesleyan College a recently commissioned oil portrait of Father. It was a privileged but difficult task for me. The portrait portrayed so well his calm, his wisdom, his goodness and his love. Most of the Jenkins relatives were there, and many friends of Father's, including the retired general who had caused me to undergo enlistment. I was very glad to have that association with Father's memory before leaving the country. I wished father could have known before he died that I was launched on a respectable career. I have tried not to nurse guilt, but I have suffered quite a lot from the belief that my lack of notable accomplishment after graduation from college may have contributed to Father's decline.

The State Department first called me to duty in June 1946, but at my request allowed me to delay, pending completion of my master's degree in education at Duke University. I'm not sure why I wanted to do that. I suppose I still had some doubts about entering the Foreign Service for my life's work, but mainly I think I was heeding Aunt Annie's and Father's advice to get well educated in some line or other, like all good Methodists and maybe even meta-Methodists. So I completed this, my second of four degrees—five if the honorary one be counted. Methodist overkill.

Part of my hesitation about entering diplomatic service arose from the fact that I was a southerner with an intemperate southern accent, and I understood that Foreign Service Officers were all up-East, tall, handsome, wealthy Ivy-Leaguers speaking genuine English, if not English-English, having flawless savoir faire as a birthright and of course clad by Brooks Brothers. That turned out to be something of an exaggeration. Still, I couldn't help recalling an instance when I was at the Pentagon and was called over to the State Department to brief Assistant Secretary Arthur Ringwalt and some of his staff. After the briefing Ringwalt came toward me with hand outstretched, but shaking his head, saying, "Unbelievable. Simply incredible. All that articulate wisdom coming out in a Southern accent!"

Gradually, entertainment in the homes of the FSOs (Foreign Service Officers) on Washington assignment convinced me that I would be accepted by the 'nawthun elite' despite my geographically imposed deficiencies. Atmospherically and psychologically the Foreign Service came to afford me a similar comfort, a similar fraternity, and a similar feeling of personal responsibility and integrity as had the combination of the Chi Phi fraternity and Emory University—that remarkable institution of academic excellence and subtle character-building, blessed, I am convinced, with a faculty and administration of more ability and less ego than most.

We novices were treated like ladies and gentlemen by everyone. The State Department-Foreign Service seemed like a choice club. Indeed, in a way it was that, for the Service was small then. For instance, when you returned from overseas you were cordially welcomed by name by the head of the small administrative office of the Department and solicitously asked about your experiences abroad.

Post-war, the Foreign Service was about to explode in size. It seemed suddenly to dawn on Americans that, at least by any economic or military measurement, our country was the strongest nation on earth, with multifarious global interests and responsibilities. Almost any significant development in any part of the world became of interest to us. Gone, doubtless forever, was the luxury of avoiding the "foreign entanglements" that George Washington had warned us against. We needed a Foreign Service with the capability to report on and influence events throughout the world where possible and, one hoped, where appropriate. The Foreign Service, of necessity, would become less personal in its internal dealings, less, for lack of a better word, genteel, probably a little less self-respecting, and much, much more bureaucratic. Soon communication between the field and Washington would become so instantaneous and cheap that the time-honored 'telegraphese' wording of telegrams sadly gave way to verbosity. Fewer important decisions were made in the field, because it was easy, and expected, to request departmental approval or guidance. There was a compensatory factor: easy communication also facilitated field input into the policy-making process in Washington. Still, the feeling of a personal imprint on history by field officers was diminished. More importantly, the sense of personal responsibility for right action may also have been diminished.

Besides, field input was not always welcome at the department. I recall that some years later Ambassador Parsons and I drafted a lengthy policy suggestion to the department. Back came a very lengthy telegram that said little more than "but your suggestion simply isn't our policy." We were insulted, so I drafted a long telegram that I fear only said "We *know* that. We were recommending altering policy." Fortunately, a bright young political officer, Steve Winship, came up with an incomparably better reply to the department, which I readily substituted for my long, pouting one. His masterful three-word telegram to the august State Department: "Merry Christmas anyway."

Martha thought she had married a staid, small-town school superintendent, but exactly one year from our wedding day, to the discomfort of our anxious families, we were on the high seas bound for the other side of the earth, to begin a life of undreamed-of variety, excitement and hard work, of frustration, glamour, danger and deep fulfillment. I would do it all over again, if I could have Martha by my side.

TEN

An
Optical
Illusion

I t is ironic that Martha was not physically by my side during the battle for Tientsin, for that ordeal and the period following it constituted the most severe test of our mutual support in all of our career. Instead of being with Martha I was with colleagues who, like me, were caught at the office when the fighting started all around us.

During the night spent under rugs we heard small arms fire quite near for a while, then increasingly at a distance. By morning all was quiet, so I went up to my office. The window was broken. The phone was dead. There was still no electricity, so the building was cold.

I started to get up to go to the consul general's office when a People's Liberation Army enlisted man walked in. He eyed me quizzically, but when I greeted him in Chinese he smiled, put his rifle in the corner, sat down and put his feet on my desk. Cocky little fellow, but likable. Bright eyes. Really nice smile. Looked intelligent, rural, and impossibly healthy, even while appearing very tired.

He asked, "Were you afraid during the battle?"

"I suppose so, at times," I confessed, "I think anyone would have been. We were in the very middle of a lot of expenditure of ammunition. But I had much to think about, mainly whether my wife was safe. ... Why did you join the People's Liberation Army?"

"Our country was dying," he replied. "Chairman Mao knows how to save us. ... Why are you in China?"

I tried to explain some of the duties of diplomatic and consular personnel. I attempted then to find out more about him, his family and his hopes for his future, but he didn't seem very interested in himself. He wanted to know about the rest of the world and especially about America.

As I spoke of life in my country he listened intently, but occasionally smiled in polite silence, seeming to convey that he thought I was making up much of what I said.

We spoke for some time, during which I almost forgot the cold. He had a downright regal nonchalance that intrigued me. It seemed incongruous with his lot in life. His supremely contented look, I mused, must come from an *habitual, innocent expectancy of good.* That may sound silly, but to me it explained his ruddy cheeks, his relaxed demeanor during trying times and his health, which was so insistent it was almost intrusive. Given all of the above, I somehow interpreted his boot-shod feet on my desk as a friendly gesture rather than an impertinent one. I can only explain these fleeting thoughts by the fact that I have often learned more from the lowly than from the mighty, and I've certainly known both. I usually pay more attention to the former.

As he had been unable to read the sign out front in Chinese or English, the young soldier suddenly asked,

"What is this place?"

"You are in the American Consulate General."

He frowned. "How far is it to Nanking? That's our next stop." When I told him, he winced. The PLA was largely a foot army at that point.

"How far from Nanking to Shanghai, our next stop? ...From Shanghai to Hong Kong?" I gave him the approximate distances in Chinese li.

"How far from Hong Kong to Taiwan, our next stop?"

"At least 300 li, and it involves water, sometimes as turbulent as found anywhere."

"Mei-yu kuan-hsi. Mao chu-hsi yu fa-tze." (It doesn't matter. Chairman Mao is clever; he has a way.) Then he asked, "How far from Taiwan to the United States? That's our last stop."

"Something over 15,000 li." I didn't tell him other things that might have been of interest, for he wouldn't have believed me.

He laughed. "Nowhere is that far."

"But it is. Would you like a cup of three day-old, cold tea?"

He laughed again. "I have to go. I'm just looking for hiding Chiang Kai-shek soldiers, that's all."

I asked if he wanted to look through our offices, but he said he had done so. He wondered why there were no other Americans in the offices. It seems Tullock had gone up to his apartment. I didn't know where Bob Smyth and Al Wellborn were, but soon learned. A messenger came in, saying I was wanted at the nearby U.S. Economic Cooperation Administration office. The young soldier bid me a cheery goodbye and actually patted me on the shoulder, a rather un-Chinese gesture, saying I had nothing more to fear. Judging from his accent he was from the extreme northeast of China, so he had probably picked up some

Russian customs.

When I walked into the ECA office, there were Bob and Al, two ECA officials, a very good Chinese friend of mine, Lin Pao-ling, who worked for the ECA, and three gentlemen of the People's Liberation Army. Since the PLA habitually wore no insignia I couldn't tell their rank, but they were well dressed and the leader spoke authoritatively. They wore beautiful fur caps, their uniforms were neatly pressed and of good material. Like my earlier visitor, they were ostentatiously healthy. They were dignified and self-confident. The leader looked urban, and his speech indicated a good education. The cherubic youngest of the three appeared to be thirteen or fourteen, but must have been older.

I was introduced to the Chinese and asked to interpret, in order to give Pao-ling a rest. It became evident that the leader and one of the other Chinese understood English, but they spoke only Chinese. The leader said that in the new China foreigners would have to learn to speak Chinese or else have an interpreter. When Chinese went to the States they were expected to speak English, and a cardinal principle of the Government of the People's Republic of China was reciprocity in all things.

There was more talk about the official attitude toward foreigners, i.e., correct but not friendly toward those whose government had not extended diplomatic recognition to the new regime. There was discussion in some detail concerning the activities and objectives of the ECA. The atmosphere was agreeable—more than civil, bordering on friendliness.

While Pao-ling was interpreting, I reflected on the sudden and stark change in the atmosphere of our current experiences. It struck me as unreal. A very few hours ago the Communist enemy of Chiang Kai-shek, our World War

II ally, whom we had strongly supported morally and materially, had been raining hell-fire on Tientsin. When it fell, the day before this meeting, we American officials had no idea what our fate would be at the hands of the Communists. The meeting with this first contingent was reassuring. The cadres that we later encountered, however, were not of this caliber, and tended to be cooler, bordering at times on hostility. I speculated that this first contingent were core personnel, confident in their conduct, whereas later cadre with whom we dealt had to play it safe by being less forthcoming.

We broke up in late afternoon; then Bob, Al and I went to the office and sent a detailed telegram to the Department.

It was long after dark when we finished. Bob Smyth went to the temporary apartment in the bank building. There was no car available, but Al Wellborn and I were so eager to see our wives that we decided to walk the two miles to my house. It was a rash decision, for there was no electricity anywhere in the city. There was not even a car to be seen. It was so dark we could not make out each other as we walked along side by side.

The whole route was composed of commercial buildings, store fronts or walls around private dwellings, so we felt our way by keeping a hand on those surfaces, and steadied each other when feeling with our feet for curb drops. We stumbled over two corpses on the sidewalk not far from the office. They were still there throughout the next day.

About two blocks from the building we were startled beyond description by a sudden, loud, imperious *"CHAN-CHU!"* (HALT!)—so loud that it seemed right in my ear, but I decided it was maybe six paces away. The sentry's command was all the more shattering because the city was utterly, deathly quiet, as well as almost tangibly dark.

Military action was over, and no other activity had yet been allowed. Of course the sentry could no more see us than we could see him. Evidently he didn't even have a flashlight.

"Who are you?" His accent meant he was not a northern Chinese.

"Two foreigners on the way home," I explained.

"You don't sound like a foreigner to me," he said suspiciously.

I started to thank him, but thought better of it. "Nevertheless, we are two Americans on the way home from the office." There was a long, extremely uncomfortable pause.

"Nobody works this late at an office. What are you up to?"

"These are unusual times. We did in fact have to work late."

He yelled, "You are lying!" I became apprehensive. No, I was scared.

"I am telling you the simple truth," I protested. An interminable silence followed. Silence, silence and more silence. Strange how ridiculous thoughts come at unridiculous times. I wished I were a ventriloquist, so I could throw my voice in the hope he would misdirect his fire, if he was entertaining such a notion.

Finally, after what seemed like hours, we started to proceed without permission, when he barked a crisp, *"Tsou-pa!"* (Move along!). We exhaled and gladly complied.

It took us nearly two hours to reach the house. We were weary when we arrived, for the strain of being totally 'blind' was great. At my house the gatekeeper's son opened the gate and surprised me with a hug. "Master, we've been so worried about you!"

Our wives had never looked quite so wonderful.

o   o   o

Public services were reestablished in a remarkably short time, and public law and order were admirable. Potholes in the streets, months old or more, were promptly filled, and the big electric clock in the park near the office began to keep time again.

The mystery was what happened to all the Nationalist soldiers. Not one was to be seen by anyone with whom we talked. Some said they were rounded up, taken to the outskirts of the city and placed behind hastily constructed fences, in the open. That was hard to believe. It was January, and the weather was frigid.

For several days there was dancing in the streets day and night, long lines performing the 'yang-ko': snake-lines of people holding onto the waist of the person in front and taking three steps forward and one backward to the catchy rhythm of drums. One can safely say that for a time there was jubilation in the air, a feeling that China was getting a fresh start. At first many of the foreigners shared this feeling.

The morning after the battle ended Li brought me at breakfast the three local Chinese newspapers. I scanned the headlines of each, read a squib about certain regulations the military intended to enforce, then turned to the editorials. Each of them was scathingly anti-American. I was surprised at the vehemence of the editorials, considering the near-friendliness of the meeting at the ECA office. I reread them, speculating on the import. When Li came in to bring more coffee I asked if he had seen the editorials. He looked down at the floor and I realized I had made a faux pas. I knew that he recognized characters relating to his duties, and thoughtlessly assumed that his reading knowledge extended to comprehending editorials. I hastily said I wanted to refresh his memory of one of them. The three were equally unfriendly, so I chose one at random and read it to him.

I then said, "Li, it looks like Americans may be in difficulty, maybe in danger, under the new regime. From what I know of other Communist regimes, there is often such a thing as guilt by association. If Americans are to be in difficulty it could well mean that Chinese associated with Americans could suffer, too. Mrs. Jenkins has cooked and washed dishes before, and I have mowed lawns. I don't want you and the others to take any risk on our behalf. If you think it best, you are free to leave."

Li closed his eyes a moment, shook his head slowly, and said, "We wouldn't leave you if trouble were certain. But we don't expect any trouble. The Communists have had good intelligence on you for two years." This was, no doubt, from the servants, in both Peiping and Tientsin. If so, it appeared they had done us a favor, from Li's next remark. "They know your beliefs and the policies of the United States are directly opposite to theirs. But they also know that you love China, that you have treated your staffs well, and—maybe the most important, since it's arrogance they hate in foreigners more than anything else—they know that you appreciate Chinese friends at every level of society. They can't be friendly toward you, but I don't think they will cause any trouble to you."

Despite Li's reassurance, we all knew the times were tense. The Wellborns had moved back to their house, and even with devoted servants I was not happy about Martha's being all day at a house far removed from any other Americans, while I had to be at the office.

In asking around I learned that the owner of a house directly across from the three Consulate houses adjoining the airport had wisely left for Hong Kong ahead of the Communists, leaving a business employee as house-sitter.

I convinced the house-sitter that it would be in the interest of the owner if he realized a bit of rent and in addition had an occupant in his house with a diplomatic passport. The passport, in the absence of diplomatic recognition between the governments, technically meant nothing, but in practice was a plus.

I had no idea what a small bit of rent I could get the house for: $85 a month, and it was a marble palace, completely furnished. It had been built originally by and for the Italian contractor who built most of the banks in China. The large, double front door was of intricately carved wood from Florence, Italy. The foyer was grey marble, with steps leading up to a huge reception hall with eight two-story marble columns, marble fireplace and marble winding stairway with a two-story window behind. On the left of the foyer was a well-stocked library with marble fireplace, two large leather sofas and several leather chairs. On the right was a large living room, with fireplace and grey marble columns. Beyond that was the dining room with twenty-four petit-point chairs and a marble fireplace. Bathroom, large butler's pantry and kitchen completed the first floor. Upstairs were three bedrooms, two baths and a large screened porch.

We hated to leave our former servants at the old house, but they were well taken care of by an officer of the Consulate General who took over that house. At the new house we inherited a staff of five servants, who lived on the half-submerged ground floor. They were impressively competent, but too silent and proper for my taste. I never felt comfortable with them because they were humble and submissive, and they didn't smile. The meek may inherit the earth, but spare me from inheriting the meek.

Many incidents underlined the more senior Communists' lack of affection for Americans. One day I was waiting in a small room at the railroad station to go to lunch with a Chinese friend, when several young PLA soldiers came in and started to sing. I happened to be reading a Chinese newspaper, so they struck up a conversation. Their song of the moment I recognized as having anti-imperialist political content. They chided me, saying that's a song I would not sing. I said, "Why not? I don't consider my country to be imperialistic." I didn't then, although I have questioned some of our military and economic moves since. "And I personally am certainly anti-imperialism." They laughed and we all started to sing heartily. We had only sung a few bars, however, when an older soldier strode into the room, said *"Pu hao, pu hao"* (not good, not good) and led the youths out of the room. The average young Communist was open and often friendly, but there was always some earnest cadre around to snuff out any fraternization.

For a while a unit of troops was quartered in our garden, and held their pep meetings under my study window. I wondered if they were trying to convert me. They knew I understood the proceedings, for I had been out in the garden chatting with them more than once. It was fascinating to listen to their pep meetings and study sessions. These rustic youths, who seemed to have difficulty constructing a compound sentence on any other subject, would hold forth with astounding fluency and seeming conviction about dialectical materialism, historical determinism and American Imperialism. Perhaps it was rote learning, but they certainly seemed well indoctrinated.

Even more fascinating was listening, and sometimes watching, their accusation sessions. I recall one when a poor boy was being accused of stealing a garment from another. Actually, I don't know why I say 'poor boy,' for he seemed to be having more fun than anyone else, embroidering on the heinous nature of his crime and engaging in extravagant remorse. His performance could only be explained by his gaining more credit by his penitence than he lost by his crime.

This scene reminded me of the frenzy of the fundamentalist revival meetings which as a youngster I used to attend with our maid in Savannah. I went for amusement, but Lethea's object was to save my soul. The priest-guru was Daddy Grace, who owned a fleet of Pierce Arrows and was surrounded by 'angels' who were said to be somewhat more than attentive. I hated to see Lethea's money go to that con artist, but maybe it was worth it to her.

During my time in Communist-ruled Tientsin I was unhappy being often viewed as not a very nice person, because I was an American. One day I had to go to the Tientsin police station to request that troops leave some U.S. Government property, where their presence was interfering with normal activity. While I was sitting in the waiting room, three female soldiers approached. When I saw them coming I quickly stuffed under my chair the Chinese newspaper I was reading, hoping they would make comments thinking I would not understand. I looked up, smiled briefly, then busied myself going through the contents of my wallet, as though preoccupied. I was rewarded. After eyeing me furtively a few minutes, they spoke softly, but not inaudibly, presumably not expecting me to understand:

"What nationality do you think he is?

"Must be Russian. He is well-dressed and looks content." That seemed to satisfy them for a little, but now they were frankly staring.

The second one had another thought. "Look at his shoes. They aren't Russian shoes ... I saw an American once. I think they are American shoes."

At that the third girl registered facial discomfort of an

order normally reserved for being in the presence of heresy. "Oh, no," she said, "he can't be an American, he has a nice smile." I had trouble not smiling a second time.

o   o   o

In late January a missionary acquaintance told us that my old friend, General Fu Tso-yi had surrendered Peiching to the Communist forces rather than risk massive destruction of the ancient and beautiful city. He is said to have changed his mind a half dozen times before deciding to do so. On February third we read of the victory parade that took most of the day to pass. The troops were equipped mostly with American vehicles, artillery and small arms captured from demoralized Nationalist units in Manchuria and Japanese equipment turned over to the Chinese by the Russians after the Japanese surrender. After the communist regime was established General Fu was given a minor ministry in the government.

China's long isolation caused the Chinese to be ignorant of certain international customs and conventions. That ignorance may have adversely affected the course of history at this time. A couple of months after the Communist entry into Tientsin I had a conversation with a Chinese lawyer friend whom I had known in pre-Communist days, and who, on the basis of things he had said, I had long thought had some connection with the Communists. Presumably he was one of the 'non-Communist patriots' who were supporting the Communists in the interest of a new deal. He explained to me with some pride that since the Communists were not well versed in such matters, as a lawyer he had patiently explained to them that they could not deal with U.S. consular representatives until the establishment of full diplomatic relations. I was appalled. It was he who was not well versed in such matters. There was ample international precedent for full consular relations in the absence of diplomatic relations. However, the damage had already been done. The Communists had indicated that such was their understanding and intent, and they certainly took my friend's advice to the limit. American officials remained in China some 15 months after the Communist takeover, obviously hoping some sort of mutual relations would prove possible and appropriate.

While in China under Communist rule we were in fact regarded as not much more than an optical illusion. We received no mail for over four months, because how could a letter be delivered to a non-existent U.S. Consulate General? The same reasoning caused us not to get licenses for our automobiles. For weeks every day we all rode bicycles the three miles to the office. We had a great time doing it, and were almost disappointed when we were given licenses. Finally we also received our backlog of mail. Some ingenious cadre had the blessed idea of procuring a rubber stamp with the Chinese characters that mean "so-called." That was then stamped before "U.S. Consulate General" on our mail, which we received from then on. Martha's diary states we received three large bundles of Christmas cards on May 20th.

In some ways life went on as usual for a time. The Tientsin Country Club, largely a British creation with a well-kept golf course, swimming pool and excellent cuisine, functioned normally, and movies were still shown there. Smaller parties in homes were held much as usual, with both foreigners and a few Chinese, mostly the employees of the Consulates, in attendance. However, about the time children were prompted by the authorities to denounce publicly their parents for their supposed bourgeois ways, restrictions increased. Only two particularly good friends, Li and Chang, among our Consulate's

Chinese employees continued for a while to come to our house. One evening when we invited them they were atypically late in arriving. I went upstairs onto the back screen porch and saw that a checkpoint had been established about 100 yards from our house. Our friends and the guard were engaged in animated conversation. The guard was holding the bicycle of one of them. Finally our friends were allowed through, but they were shaken.

Only Li ever came to our house again, and that was to take our Alsatian, Rindy, to his house because we were leaving China. Rindy was a huge, handsome dog that we had swapped for our two dachshunds, who fought too much, and who looked silly puttering around eight two-story marble columns. We were distressed when later we read that the Communists were killing off dogs because their barking made eavesdropping difficult.

It seemed that diplomatic recognition was not going to be exchanged soon. Perhaps with the departure of American officialdom in mind, the authorities required the Chinese employees of the Consulate General and the United States Information Service to make collective demands for outrageous lump sums of money, claiming that they had been underpaid in the past. It was an awkward scene in Bob Smyth's crowded office when the demands were made. The fact that every employee was present, from the most senior adviser to the messenger boys, and the fact that several gave indication by their facial expression and bowed heads that they were not eager to be there, emphasized the official backing of the event. Our two best friends among them appeared so embarrassed I felt sorry for them. I did not blame them one moment for technically, at least, taking part in the affair, given the climate of the times. We finally paid the better part of the exorbitant sums demanded.

Over the next eight months both the Chinese radio and the *Voice of America* reported victory after victory of the People's Liberation Army as it swept southward and westward over the vast country. Nationalist opposition was generally reported as weak. Tientsin remained the only major city where the Nationalists made a serious effort to stem the Communist advance, and there were only a couple of major battles fought in the countryside farther south. We had almost no word of what was happening to Americans in other parts of China, except for personnel in the U.S. Consulate General in Mukden. The Communists had entered the city on November 1, 1948. The authorities at first ignored the Consulate General, but later seized its radio equipment and put the staff under house arrest. In February 1950 a Chinese employee resigned his job but refused to leave the premises. Consul General Angus Ward finally escorted him to the gate. The Communist authorities claimed that in doing so he assaulted the employee. Ward and several other members of the staff were arrested and put in solitary confinement in unheated and unsanitary conditions. After a month they were tried and sentenced to varying lengths of imprisonment, but the sentences were commuted to deportation.

The United States had ten or twelve consulates dotted about China at the time of the Communist victory. Many of them were preparing to close down. I feared for my next assignment, because China language officers would by then be in considerable oversupply. I only hoped that I would get some sort of China-related assignment. I did not want an assignment to the Department yet, for it would be too expensive living in Washington on my salary.

In mid-August I received word through Hong Kong that my home leave had been approved. We were not sure that we would be permitted to leave. At least the

Communists had been detaining a number of non-diplomatic Americans against their will. After a cliff-hanging delay we did receive exit permits, and learned that we could take a barge for Taku Bar on August 28, 1949, where a Chinese ship leaving for Hong Kong would pick us up. In Hong Kong we would take the *President Wilson* for San Francisco.

The authorities had to go through our effects, and we became apprehensive that several ancient Chinese objects of art were holding up the proceedings, and that the authorities wouldn't finish in time for us to catch our barge. They finished the day before we were to leave. To our relief they passed everything in our effects except two items: a little daintily embroidered shoe of bound-foot size and a short home movie bit taken in a nudist colony that a college friend had given me for my birthday years earlier as a joke, because I was then President of the Emory Christian Association and he thought it would embarrass me. It didn't. I don't know which supposedly ultrapuritanical Communist cadre found delectation in it.

We departed a few minutes ahead of schedule. Just as we were pulling away from the dock all our servants from the first house ran down to the wharf, calling to us that they had packed us a lunch. They sized up the possibility of throwing it to us, but rightly decided it would land in the water. We were moved to see them waving goodbye. It was courageous of them in the climate of the day openly to show regard for us in seeing us off. Being genuinely fond of them, we were sad to realize that we probably would never see them again. They and many other Chinese friends urged us to keep in touch. Much as we longed to do so, sensing the climate to come, we did not, lest it get them in trouble with the authorities.

Just as we were leaving China in August 1949, so was

Chiang Kai-shek retreating to the island of Taiwan with as much as he could of his military forces, civilian adherents, gold and priceless objects of art.

Needless to say, we were eager to get home, but at the same time sad to be leaving China, for we didn't know whether we would ever be able to return.

As we approached San Francisco on October 8, 1949, sight of the Golden Gate bridge almost made us choke up. Our China assignment was the first time either of us had been out of the country, except for my briefly crossing the border into Canada and Mexico. However, my first exclamation to Martha on landing was not, as I thought it would be, dripping with emotional patriotism. It was, "Look, honey, we're in the land of public drinking fountains!" I don't think there was one in the entire Far East, because unboiled water was not safe.

San Francisco was shimmering in the clear, bright October sun. We almost danced up and down the steep hills of downtown San Francisco, breathing the wonderful, free air of America.

We checked in at the famous old Palace Hotel. When I finished signing in, Bing Crosby tapped me on the arm, smiled and took the pen out of my hand to sign in. I thought it would be thoughtful to appear not to recognize him, so I just smiled in return. In our suite we saw television for the first time.

o   o   o

In Washington I was occupied with consultation at the Department. Walton Butterworth, the assistant secretary for the Far East, called me to his office to discuss a few matters. His main concern was whether I thought we should extend diplomatic recognition to the new regime in China. I said I thought the Communists were there to stay

for some time, and that some day we would find it necessary to recognize them. However, I saw no need for haste
in extending formal diplomatic recognition, if only because
I did not believe that in their present frame of mind they
would return the compliment! As it turned out, for reasons
I shall discuss later, we were unwilling, indeed one may
say, unable, to recognize the regime for almost a quarter of
a century.

In Georgia I had trying business to attend to. Mother
had died while we were in China. Since Father had passed
on previously, there was the will to probate. Furthermore,
the home at my parents' country place where they had
retired had burned to the ground just before we left China,
destroying Father's large library, much of it irreplaceable,
and all Mother's dishes and vases that she had hand-
painted at Brenau and Wesleyan. Aunt Lizzie said that in
Mother's declining last days, when she was semi-deliri-
ous from kidney failure, she repeatedly said things like,
"Put that aside in preparation for our going to China to see
Alfred." Poor dear, she was in no condition to go to Baxley,
six miles away.

I went to the charred homestead site and for a while
lay down on the grass under the mimosa trees in the garden,
where I was inundated by memories of my childhood and
youth. The mimosa trees grew with limbs strategically
placed for small boys' climbing. The cement bird bath,
now toppled and fragmented, had been a center of fascination whenever we sat in the garden in pre-pesticide days.
The high-hedge quadrangle, now scraggly, was where, in
my ignorance as to the deleterious effects, I used to sun-
bake nude by the hour. The pump house still stood, where
first gasoline then electric power brought incomparable
tasting well water to the house. The house site itself offered
a surprisingly small pile of rubble. Had all my parents' tan-

gible effects, the various accoutrements of a former more social life, gone up in smoke? Or had there been valuables left still intact that had been carted away? No matter. The site remained for me a symbol of the privilege I had been given in the associations there. How sorely I wished I had expressed that appreciation more openly! The previously described gloom nine years earlier did not even need to be shrugged away. It was no longer in my reckoning.

The battery radio by my side announced that on October first the Chinese Communists had established the "People's Republic of China," with Peking as its capital and Mao Tse-tung as its Chairman. Under the mimosa tree, all that seemed very far away.

My thoughts then tried to embrace something of the new Southland which, as the old one, had once shaped me. Evidently it had changed astoundingly in a very few years. I could see that, even in driving through the countryside from Macon. Houses that had been of unpainted wood, sometimes with cracks in the walls through which one could see outdoors, had been replaced with red brick "ranch style" houses. Farm machinery instead of mules was in evidence, usually in the open, partly to advertise that it existed and partly because housing had not yet been provided for it. A new Ford or Chevrolet would be parked out front, and sometimes a Dodge or better.

I drove by little rural, "consolidated" Ten Mile School where I had been principal. In the vicinity I passed a new Buick. A finely gloved hand stuck out and waved at me. The voice inflection of the "Hi, Mr. Jenkins!" helped me recognize that it was formerly little Sally Mae Brewer in the sixth grade, who had at that time worn one of her two dresses the entire year, and had been obliged to drop out of school for two weeks at harvest time to join her two brothers on their then unmechanized farm.

Meanwhile, the nearby town's timber and turpentine moguls, some wealthy lawyers, bankers and insurance salesmen, even the revered family physician, began to chafe under Roosevelt's new graduated income tax. Still, it gave new hope to many by reducing somewhat the enormous difference between the very rich and the rest of the populace. Untold numbers of jobs were created through the use of federal funds derived from the graduated tax structure.

The fate of some of the urban rich was even more drastic. Some outstandingly worthy institutions, such as Duke University, were endowed by the immensely wealthy before the graduated income tax came into effect. After that tax, however, many an urban mansion or estate became a community college because hiring several servants for the upkeep was no longer practical.

Also contributing to the South's new prosperity was the U.S. Government's recognition that the absence from farm fields of menfolks at war meant reduced income at home. Payments designed to cover much of that loss came along with the monthly checks for military service. Also, many an impecunious plowhand became a major or lieutenant colonel in the Air Corps and sent home substantial checks.

With these thoughts and memories I fell asleep on the grass, only to be bestirred by the sun in my eyes. I glanced once more at the rubble that was the country home of my parents, then stretched luxuriously in the thought that I was to drive into Baxley to spend a couple of days with the living: my brother and his family, where Martha was soon to join me after prolonging her visit with her large and close-knit Lippiatt family in Pennsylvania.

Even the delights of being back home and of being with our families did not block out of my mind thoughts about my next assignment. I reasoned that it would be an important determinant of the nature of the rest of my career.

ELEVEN

From
"Fragrant Harbor"
To
"Beautiful Island"

inally the word came. To my delight I was to be chief of the Political Section of the U.S. Consulate General in—Hong Kong! Not only was Hong Kong a fascinating and delightful place to live, it was the choicest assignment in the world for a China language officer, certainly at my level of seniority, because it was destined to become the uniquely important, chief 'listening post' with respect to mainland China for years to come.

In December 1949 Martha and I arrived via Pan American Clipper in the Fragrant Harbor, which is the translation of Hong Kong. Fabulous Hong Kong, pearl of the Orient, crossroads of the East, one of the few remaining bulwarks of a dying imperialism, daily recipient of hordes of frightened, disillusioned and dispossessed mainland

Chinese. Bustling Hong Kong, haven of free-thinkers and assorted plotters; bulging little island of nefarious intrigue and British law and order; land of titles and tinsel, squatters' camps and mansions, exciting restaurants, unexcelled scenery. Cadillacs and Rolls Royces weaving around a few remaining rickshaws; double-decked streetcars; seas of pedestrians: Fukien farmers and Shanghai sophisticates, students, merchants and mechanics from all over, in flight from the 'workers' paradise,' graceful Indian ladies in colorful saris with diamonds planted on their noses, little urchins in their innocence incongruously singing songs of praise to Mao while breathing the freest air in a radius of many miles. The captivating combination of the ineffable calm of the East and the know-how, energy and reliability of the rugged British. And abundant evidence of the almost pathological energy of the Chinese, too, *when motivated.*

When I arrived there were only four officers in the Political Section of the Consulate General. When I left, eight months later, I had a staff of 18 officers, secretaries and locals. It had become our chief listening post in the attempt to gather, interpret and report on developments in the mainland of China, and would remain so during the 23 years when we had no official representation there. We who did the reporting on events in China came to be known as the 'China Watchers.'

The Political Section spent a great deal of time debriefing people who left the mainland, whether legally or illegally. When the land border became difficult to penetrate, many Chinese swam through shark infested waters to the freedom of Hong Kong. Some estimates had no more than fifty percent making the crossing alive. One day the British chief of police took me on a tour of the land border between Hong Kong and China. He told poignant stories of the lengths to which Chinese on the mainland would go in order to enter Hong Kong. Some Chinese successfully slipped across the land border, the Hong Kong Government endeavored to return virtually all illegal immigrants. In 1979, for instance, 89,241 were sent back, but most of them would try again, some as many as eight or nine times.

Hong Kong offered opportunity for a life of more dignity and freedom than was possible on the mainland at this time, including an economy of free enterprise, which certainly did not exist in China in the 50s. I said it seemed to me the Chinese in Hong Kong would be so grateful for such a life that they would not insist on political franchise, or be restive under largely benevolent British control.

The police chief thought a moment, and said, "Do you remember when we were driving along Nathan Road in Kowloon and saw that carefully groomed, stylishly clipped poodle on a leash? Compare him to that unkempt mongrel gamboling in that field over there, romping about freely with another dog. Who is happier? Get the point? Human nature, too."

I talked with a Chinese who had made it through the shark-infested waters to Hong Kong. To my surprise, he was thinking of returning to the mainland. The British would have gladly facilitated his return, for the magnitude of the refugee problem was troubling.

I asked, "Why on earth do you want to return?"

He smiled. "Well, it is true that my country is a prison. I did not like that at all when I was there. Still, most of the time it offered a measure of security. Although there is almost unbelievable underemployment— people 'goof off'—there is almost no unemployment. Life is drab and uninteresting, even a little fearful. But one eats, and is clothed. Hong Kong, even as a colony, is certainly no prison. It is amazingly free. But it is a jungle. I find that I am afraid in a jungle, and unsure of my future."

Among those who fled the mainland were wealthy former Nationalist generals who, cognizant of the great outcry in Washington, "Who lost China?" were eager to gain U.S. backing for a 'third force' to retake the mainland. Third force because at that time we were not backing the Chiang Kai-shek forces that had retreated to Taiwan before the Communists' onslaught, and certainly we were not backing the Communists on the mainland of China. We were "waiting for the dust to settle" before making up our minds about a policy toward China.

An annoying chore I had at the time was returning gifts foisted upon me by third force aspirants who thought I could be instrumental in gaining U.S. support for them. The gifts were not usually offered in person, for most knew they would be rejected. They thought, however, if the gifts were left on my doorstep in the night or delivered by messenger, I might receive them. I could not and did not, except for one gift of no great value, the donor of which I was never able to locate.

During our time in Hong Kong I was extremely busy in writing reports, vetting others' drafts, interviewing escapees from the mainland, fending off the third-force aspirants and entertaining professionally useful people. I had so much on my mind that, although tired at the end of a workday, I did not sleep through the night, but would often half awaken several times, prompted by an idea I wanted to remember. I formed the habit of keeping three by five slips of paper by my bed. I would scribble an idea on one in a sleepy stupor, fling it on the floor and fall almost immediately back asleep. I think my restlessness was due in good part to the heavy food involved in entertaining and being entertained.

We were often entertained by incredibly wealthy Hong

Kong Chinese. I was not all that excited by pheasant under glass, though I did own to a liking for caviar, thin toast and vodka so chilled it was syrupy. The old, established Chinese families tended to be delightful. In contrast, there were numbers of *nouveau riches* who were ostentatious, shallow and sometimes boorish.

I had an especially vivid dream one night, evidence that my life-long interest in metaphysical matters was not entirely eclipsed by professional pressures. In my dream it seems I had been studying with an elderly guru for some time. Moments under his spiritual tutelage seemed to mock time and defy evaluation, so deep was the understanding that he imparted. He understood the riddle of Being and Becoming. One morning, after the great philosopher had partaken of his breakfast of a few almonds and two sections of orange with a bit of the peel, he turned his radiant face toward me and said, "My son, you have made the requisite progress to receive the formula for the All—the Absolute. Follow me to a more holy place in which to receive the Ultimate." Consumed by gratitude, I followed him up, up above the clouds to the pinnacle of majestic Mount Omai. He stood for a moment as in prayer, the wind blowing through his flowing white hair. Then he turned to me and said, "Keep this in your heart, and see that you impart it to no one: *ch'uan po an shih, wei lao ti-pan, ch'ing wu ch'i tso.*" His form simply evaporated, and I sat bolt upright in bed, yet still in the usual stupor. I grabbed pencil and slip, and quickly scribbled in Chinese the priceless, immortal formula.

The next morning, as I lay stretching in bed, I suddenly realized that there on the floor I had the formula for the ultimate Cosmic Truth. I grabbed the one slip in Chinese from the several on the floor and with trembling fingers read *"ch'uan po an shih, wei lau ti-pan, ch'ing wu ch'i tso."* which, translated, reads, "Please do not leave your seat until the boat is docked and the gangplank lowered." It was the admonition I had seen on the ferry when we lived in a hotel in Kowloon and I had to cross the harbor to go to the Consulate General on Hong Kong Island. I suppose it is good advice after all: wait patiently for the right moment before stirring.

The stark contrast with China was welcome indeed. We enjoyed the beach at Repulse Bay, the free port shopping, the current movies we hadn't experienced for several years, and, in a way, I suppose, the 'big name' people constantly going through Hong Kong. I recall meeting Orson Welles at Repulse Bay, and the actress, Linda Christian, wife of Tyrone Power, at Consul General Rankin's house. She was visiting Hong Kong while her famous husband was making a movie in Manila. I remember her because of her beauty, her overly precise speech, and the quite unbelievable length of her cigarette holder. By coincidence Martha and I had advance tickets to see Tyrone Power in "The Razor's Edge" that very evening.

When we told Ms. Christian of our plans, she vigorously drew on her cigarette, wafted a long cloud of smoke that seemed to come from her shapely ankles, and said, "Ahhhhh, yes. I think that is Ty-rone's best pick-ture. It is so...somehow deep, somehow." Having read the book, we did not dispute the trenchant appraisal.

At that time in Hong Kong about the only Chinese who spoke Mandarin were the white-sleeved policemen from Shantung province in north China. I was told they were lonesome, not being able to speak with the local Chinese, a fact that was confirmed in an acutely embarrassing incident. One morning I was driving down the steep, winding road from our house on the Peak to the office. The road was being resurfaced one half at a time, and there were large, empty oil drums separating the two halves. As I rounded a curve on the wet pavement I skidded, knocking over a couple of drums, which on the steep incline knocked over I shudder to think how many more. They rolled in every direction down the steep hill, with unearthly din, banging into each other, into light poles, scarring lawns and gardens, and menacing pedestrians and vehicles. A policeman, dodging an oil can, ran up to me, and my heart sank. I had visions of losing my driver's license on top of a fine. The policeman was menacing, but he was speaking Mandarin! I phrased profuse apologies in Mandarin. The policeman registered in quick succession anger, incredulity, astonishment, recognition and effusive fraternity. He grasped my hand, said the mishap could have happened to anybody on a steep, wet road, and invited me to supper! I fully intended to accept, but the incident was just before my transfer to another post, and I never made it.

o   o   o

The Consul General, Karl Rankin, was sending out invitations to 800 persons for our Independence Day celebration at the Hong Kong Hotel, when the radio announced that war had broken out in Korea. I had no idea that a disturbing telegram which I found on my desk a few days later was related to that war. The telegram suddenly assigned me to Taiwan!

I thought I must have enemies in Washington, for the island had been expected to fall to the Communists at any time. A United Press story under a Washington dateline had appeared in the Hong Kong press in late November 1949, quoting "well-informed sources" as saying the United States had "virtually written off any chance of saving the strategic island of Formosa (Taiwan) from the Chinese Communists." The staff there for a year had been awaiting orders to evacuate on short notice. Such an assignment appeared to be a banishment, compared to the Hong Kong assignment.

Karl was in Tokyo conferring with General McArthur at the time, doubtless about the likelihood of the Chinese entering the Korean war if United Nations forces fought in Korea. As soon as he returned I rushed to his office to ask anxiously, "Karl, have you any inkling why I am being transferred to Taipei?"

"More than an inkling. I asked for you. I'm being transferred there myself, to head the U.S. mission as minister. At least for a time, you are to be my number two." That was no banishment. It was evident that United States China policy had changed. We were, to some significant degree, it appeared, going to support the forces on Taiwan.

"Thank God," I exclaimed. Karl Rankin was one of the ablest officers I came to know in my entire career. It was a joy—and a choice education for a junior officer—to work under this man, who later was made Ambassador to Free (Nationalist) China.

Martha and I were distressed when we learned that she could not at first accompany me. I was fortunate in inheriting a pleasant Japanese-style house from a good friend who was being transferred out of Taiwan, and I did have Kuan with me, the top-notch Peking cook, which made life easier than it would otherwise have been. It was hard enough for a time without Martha, but three months later she had fought her way through the Department and was by my side in Taipei. The outbreak of the Korean war and the consequent resumption of military and economic aid to the Chiang Kai-shek Nationalist Government, the epidemic of schistosomiasis among the Communist troops marshalling for an aborted attack on Taiwan, all meant the island was almost certainly safe for the foreseeable future.

During our two years in Taipei the Embassy staff was materially augmented, and the military and economic development of Taiwan got underway, with very substantial U.S. military and economic aid. A good percentage of the ablest and most experienced businessmen and industrialists from the urban centers of the mainland had accompanied Generalissimo Chiang Kai-shek and his forces to the island. Taiwan soon was benefitting from their expertise and American aid. In a very few years the per capita income in Taiwan was ten times that on the Communist mainland.

Martha and I became friends with Bill and Mary Sun, senior members of the Presidential staff and close friends of the Chiangs. As mentioned earlier, Madame Chiang, nee Soong Mei-ling, attended Wesleyan College while Father was there, but a bit before my time. In Taiwan we were with her on a number of occasions, and she was always very kind to us. I believe all three Soong sisters thought a lot of my father. I have in my study the wedding photograph of Soong Ching-ling and her husband, Sun Yat-sen, the first President of China, that Madame Sun had autographed and sent to my father. Twenty-one years later, when I was in China with Kissinger, I had the pleasure of calling on Madame Sun Yat-sen. She reminisced nostalgically of her happy college days in Macon and spoke warmly of my father.

One evening we were invited to an intimate family dinner with the President and Madame Chiang. There were only six at table, the Chiangs, Bill and Mary Sun, Martha and me. It was a friendly, not an official occasion, of course (I was only a Second Secretary of Embassy and Consul), so nothing of great import was discussed, but it was a pleasant, homey evening. I recall that the president persistently complained to Madame Chiang that plain white rice was served, whereas he thought foreigners liked fried rice. Madame Chiang first answered him in his native Chekiang dialect. When he persisted, she answered him in Mandarin, so we would understand. When he again returned to his fried rice theme, with unmistakable conclusiveness, but pleasantly, she answered him in English, "I *know,* dear."

President Chiang was of average Chinese height, slender but well proportioned, surprisingly youthful in appearance, He had a ready smile.

No one can fully appreciate Madame Chiang without meeting her personally. She has been one of the world's most fascinating, talented and beautiful women, always exquisitely dressed and erect in carriage.

The president congratulated me on my Chinese. I responded with a common literary phrase that means the president is "overly laudatory." I knew the phrase contained a character with the same phonetic pronunciation as the president's surname, but that did not seem to matter, until I saw Bill Sun blanche. I still don't know why it was a *faux pas,* but evidently it was.

The Korean War and the "Who lost China?" theme caused U.S. politicians to want to underline their anti-Communist convictions, particularly as Senator McCarthy began to exploit and heighten the tense political atmosphere with false allegations of Communists in the State Department, academia and the military. A stream of senators and congressmen visited Taiwan, and of course the Government of Free China, as it was often called, was eager to have them come. There were many other dignitaries who came through in those two years, from General Claire Chennault to Joe Louis. General Chennault had gone to China in 1937 on a survey mission, and remained to help Generlissimo Chiang build an air force. He had built the volunteer *Flying Tigers* before U.S. entry into the war in Asia in 1941. Joe Louis, of course, was a former heavyweight champion. He gave an exhibition match in Taiwan. A number of us at the Embassy entertained him in our homes. I think he probably had been sharper mentally before his head had been pounded to a pulp, but he was modest, friendly and comfortably likable.

I looked forward to my first assignment to the Department, as Officer-in-Charge of Chinese Political Affairs. That was possibly the most vulnerable position in all of Washington during the McCarthy hearings, which were in full swing. I was busy with office demands and in making speeches all over the country explaining our China policy, or the seeming lack of one because of the conflicting American interests inherent in the "China tangle." Therefore, I did not focus on the shameful McCarthy hearings until a few able and innocent acquaintances and friends of mine fell under the Senator's axe.

It is a disgrace that neither Secretary Dulles nor President Eisenhower for so long lifted a finger to protect these people. Finally, it was the ever-lethal weapon of sarcastic humor that began the decline of McCarthy. A screamingly funny recording came out spoofing the McCarthy Senate Unamerican Activities Committee Hearings. It was entitled "Point of Order"—a phrase often used by McCarthy in the Hearings. About that time the press turned against McCarthy, but by then I fear it was simply a barometer of his incipient decline. The *coup de grace* was not administered, as I recall it, until Eisenhower finally invited all the senators to a White House function except McCarthy. The Senator's demise, politically and physically, soon followed. By then it was a politically safe move on Eisenhower's part, for McCarthy had become discredited in almost all quarters.

In the summer of 1954 I went for six weeks to Geneva,

ostensibly as a member of the United States Delegation to the international conference on Korea and Indochina. Actually, since mercifully my responsibilities did not encompass the Vietnam problem at that time, I was there because the Chinese Communists were also there. My task was to negotiate with them for the release of some 80 Americans being held on the mainland of China against their will. They were in fact hostages—held for what leverage was not entirely clear at the time, but with hindsight it may be seen as an attempt to gain an offer from us of diplomatic recognition. Many of those held were students, missionaries and businessmen. The Chinese claimed that 13 were spies. So far as I know, there was no truth in that.

My opposite number in the negotiations was one of the Chinese officials who, in the Panmunjom talks in Korea, had maintained, from the Communist viewpoint, an unsullied record of vituperation and bombast against the United States. Yet here at Geneva he dealt with me with unfailing civility. That puzzled me, until I began to wonder whether the alleged fraternal collusion established between the Soviet Union and China soon after the Communists came to power was wearing thin.

I think it was that, and more. I believe the Russians had been acting arrogantly; that is, taking at face value the polite Chinese fiction that they regarded the Soviets as big brothers. Such, although acceptable for a time, was the height of pretense for the ethnocentric, xenophobic, inherently self-confident Chinese. The Chinese have always been well practiced at make-believe, even antedating Communist times.

Arrogance as the cause of growing disenchantment with Soviet advisers in the Chinese midst is of course an oversimplification of what was a complex and increasingly difficult relationship, but in later days it was the one problem most referred to by Chinese with whom I talked.

Up until April 22, 1960, the Sino-Soviet dispute was kept secret. On that 90th anniversary of Lenin's birth, however, the Chinese challenged the Soviet leadership of the world Communist movement in an article entitled "Long Live Leninism," in effect saying the Soviets were heretics so far as Communist orthodoxy was concerned, hence not worthy of leading the world Communist movement. That made the rift public. When the Soviet Union refused to support China in her border war with India in the fall of 1962, the USSR indicated a preference for a non-Communist friend over a Communist maverick. That was the last straw, indicating no hope of reconciliation. An article in the Chinese periodical *Red Flag* on March third, 1963 appealed to all "genuine" Marxist-Leninists worldwide to denounce the "revisionist" Soviets. The definitive fragmentation of the world Communist movement had started. It would be virtually complete thirty years later.

When I had been in Geneva for some six weeks, it was time for me to return to my responsibilities in the Department. When the Chinese at the Geneva Conference learned that I was returning to Washington, at our next meeting they asked what would happen to the talks. I sensed they were fearful they would not then continue, so I purposely said I did not know. While that was technically true, I was reasonably certain they would continue. The Chinese promptly announced the release of 16 Americans, evidently in the attempt to insure that the talks would continue, under some auspices. They got their wish: the level of the talks was raised, because Ambassador Alex Johnson took over. Later the talks were moved to Warsaw, where they continued for some 134 meetings over 17 years.

As early as the winter of 1958-59 I had my suspicion confirmed—in my mind, at least—about problems in Sino-

Soviet relations, though I don't recall any sinologues who agreed with me. My conviction was more due to a fluke than to perspicacity. I was at a reception on the top floor of the State Department where I spotted a senior Soviet official whom I had known earlier. He looked awful. Bleary-eyed, spirit sagging.

I said, "You look terrible. What's the matter—been staying up too late plotting against us?"

He smiled and said, "No. It's not you. It's those goddam Chinese. You'd better be glad we've got them and you haven't." He meant in the Communist, as distinct from the Free World, camp. I silently agreed that the Chinese, as adversaries, can be as nettlesome as anyone on earth. I thought of the Panmunjom talks in the Korean settlement, and the Warsaw talks that settled virtually nothing.

China was a hot subject at this time, and I did a great deal of public speaking all over the country under State Department auspices. I had the temerity to suggest in a couple of speeches that I thought the Chinese and Soviets were having difficulty, which was no brilliant deduction on my part, in view of my Geneva experience and the conversation at the State Department reception. I met with incredulity in the universities, where half my speaking was done, as I had for the most part within Washington officialdom. Yet the following year the Soviets left China. They took with them the blueprints of numerous projects in which they had been assisting the Chinese. We learned after the fact that Khrushchev as early as 1956-57 realized that in helping the maverick Chinese Communists he was creating a Frankenstein. He began to withdraw aid, notably in the sensitive field of scientific development.

Sharing the stage in Akron, Ohio with Sir Rob Scott, deputy chief of mission at the British Embassy in Washington was a special event. The British policy toward

Author as a student of Chinese at University of Chicago in 1943.

The Mercury Mamie Eisenhower rode in Ike's second Inaugural Parade became Jenkin's personal auto.

Departing Taipei, Taiwan for Washington; Alfred and wife, Martha.

The Jenkins family, Alfred, Martha, Stephen and Sara, departing New York for Sweden.

U.S. Ambassador to Poland Jack Cabot with Jenkins at Warsaw talks.

King Gustav of Sweden (on the left) with Jenkins in seat of honor on His Majesty's private railroad car.

The author at his desk at American Embassy, Stockholm.

Famous photo of Kissinger and Jenkins at El Toro, California, fueling stop on China trip to arrange Nixon visit. (AP Wirephoto)

Jenkins enroute to China on the clone of Air Force One.

Jenkins and Kissinger on conducted tour of industrial plant near Beijing.

Jenkins with wife, Martha, receives State Department's Honor Award.

Chinese dignitaries welcome Henry Kissinger and party.
Jenkins is on the right.

Chou En-lai and dignitaries assemble in Great Hall of the People to greet
Kissinger's party. Jenkins is on left.

Kissinger, a secretary, Winston Lord and Jenkins at the Whispering Wall at the Temple of Heaven in Beijing.

Jenkins flanked by Kissinger's secretaries on roadway to the Ming Tombs.

Author speaks at Emory University on Alfred Jenkins Day, proclaimed by then Governor Jimmy Carter.

American University press conference in Washington airs Jenkins' China views.

Famed astrologist Jean Dixon greets Jenkins at Washington party.

China was very different from ours, since they had recognized the Mao regime soon after its inception. Accordingly, our semi-debate attracted a good bit of attention. The British traditionally recognized a new regime as soon as it was in control of the country, while we often refrained, out of political, moral or frankly economic concerns.

During my Washington assignment in the Office of Chinese Affairs Martha and I received our first invitation to a White House function. That evening I returned home from the office just before eight. I struggled into white tie and tails and Martha into an extraordinarily beautiful Chinese gown. We left our house barely in time to get to the designated southwest gate of the White House at the appointed hour. Halfway into town Martha screamed, "I forgot my gloves!" (the above-the-elbow white kid gloves that were *de rigueur* for a white tie affair.) If we went home for them we would be late. If Martha went without them we would be subject to private censure and maybe ridicule. We decided not to be late, and Martha, bless her, decided to enjoy the evening to the fullest, irrespective of the unintended *faux pas*. Sure enough, when we greeted the Chief of Protocol, the distinguished Honorable John Simmons, his whole body gave a quick jerk as he looked at Martha, but, being John Simmons, he said nothing. Of course, Ike and Mamie were imperturbably cordial, gloves or no gloves, as were our foreign ambassador and senator friends and seemingly everyone else. We were told later by a mutual friend that Perle Mesta, the renowned Washington "hostess with the mostess" was put out by Martha's wearing the gown most talked about and because Martha, in addition, was "the prettiest woman in attendance."

There was one other extremely embarrassing event of the evening. In going up the stairs from the southwest entrance level to the East Room we joined a crowd that was ascending the stairs closely together. It being difficult to look down, I inadvertently stepped on the small train of the gown worn by the wife of an ambassador of a Western European country that I prefer not to name. The ripping sound stabbed me in the chest, but I couldn't undo the damage. Who would have expected a train at a time like that, taking up two steps in the stairs? If looks could kill, I wouldn't be writing this.

The very next morning after the White House reception my office phone rang. I heard the voice of some senior official in the administrative side of the Department say, "We have a DCM-ship for you."

"What's a DCM?" I wanted to know.

"A deputy chief of mission. You would be the number two man in the Embassy, directly under the ambassador." DCM was a recently coined term. The classical name for the job was Counselor of Embassy.

"Where would it be?"

"Jidda, Saudi Arabia."

"I like my present job," I hastened to assure the voice.

"Yes, but this would be quite an honor. You would be the youngest and most junior DCM in the entire U.S. Foreign Service. May I stop by your office and talk with you?

"I suppose so."

Twelve

Saudi
Arabia

 was talked into taking the job on a dare. It was not such a terrific honor, after all. It became apparent that they hadn't found anyone else willing to be number two under the incumbent ambassador in Jidda, for no one could get along with him, except at exorbitant cost. He had the reputation of being pathologically, if not psychotically, egocentric and psychologically sadistic. I thought I could get along with anyone, so I agreed to take the job. I later found no cause to question his reputation.

It was the policy of the State Department to fashion one's career so that approximately one-third of it would be spent in Washington, one-third in the officer's area of specialization, if any, and one-third out of that area abroad—supposedly in order to prevent a specialist from "going native" in the country he knew best. However, Saudi Arabia was the only assignment in my career that was not China related, save for two years as a senior inspector and one year as deputy director for Southeast Asia. I was assigned to Saudi Arabia not so much to satisfy the requirements of the third category above, but, as I have indicated, because I was both gullible and overconfident. Even when assigned to Sweden, an important part of my job was to meet periodically with Chinese officials in Warsaw when we had no diplomatic representation to the Mao Tse-tung regime. All my Washington assignments were related to China or East Asia as a whole.

I arrived in Saudi Arabia with a strike against me, being a Far East specialist instead of a Near East one. I suppose all Near East candidates were hiding under rocks, knowing Ambassador Wadsworth, or at least knowing his reputation.

Very soon after I arrived in Jidda the Ambassador said, "I'm glad you are here now, Mr. Counselor. You're in charge. I'm going to Istanbul for the opening of the new Hilton Hotel."

The next day I attended the ceremony that dedicated the King's former palace in Jidda as a university. In walking from building to building a young Saudi with an elfish smile fell in step with me and chatted amiably in what one might call fluent 'drugstore cowboy' English. After much relaxed banter I finally asked,

"By the way, what's your name?

"Mohammed."

"Mohammed what?"

"My dad's the king."

"Oh...."

Had I suspected such, I would have phrased my last query more carefully. Meeting him, however, was serendipitous, as I shall explain.

My first audience with the king will be vivid in my

memory forever. It was an all-new experience, since it was soon after my arrival, and I had not yet accompanied the ambassador on such visits. When the door was opened for me to enter the audience chamber I was flabbergasted. His Majesty seemed to be a half-mile away. In the huge room there were something like 14 or 16 enormous crystal chandeliers, Czech I believe, and many thick, overlapping oriental rugs between us. I was so overcome I forgot I still had my homburg in my hand. Some minister ran up and snatched it from me. The length of the room was lined on either side by cabinet ministers and princes.

I was nervous. Not that I am intimidated by kings, but I had visions of my first audience being a certain failure. I had been instructed to request agreement by His Majesty to something involving Israel, to which it was entirely unlikely he could agree. Evidently the subject is still classified, for two days recently spent in the National Archives building in Washington failed to produce the report of that audience, although there were scores of other documents I had signed while I was in Saudi Arabia.

I presented my case with sepulchral solemnity. His Majesty responded in kind, but without a definitive answer. I set forth my second line of offense, certain I had lost my case. During the interpretation of my second try, in sadness I looked around the audience chamber. The young prince with whom I had enjoyed such a pleasant conversation at the university dedication caught my eye and gave me a ludicrously exaggerated wink that contorted his face grotesquely and made it next to impossible for me to keep mine in suitable shape. After that I lightened up and engaged in a bit of levity with His Majesty, joking about both the delight and the envy that "we Jiddawis" experienced on hearing of the discovery of plentiful underground water at His Majesty's capital of Riyadh, "even if it was the

French who finally found it, after we Americans had failed." I was told later that one doesn't indulge in that sort of thing with a king, but my ignorance evidently paid off. His Majesty suddenly was in a better mood, and to my surprise my request was granted! I think I owed my success to that blessed, contorted wink, though a kind word from Sheikh Yussuf Yasin, His Majesty's senior advisor, may have been involved.

When Wadsworth returned from Istanbul I learned of a habit of his that I found eminently satisfactory. He almost never came to the office. He would select a couple of projects that struck his fancy, dealing with them from his residence, and leaving all other matters to me. I not only ran Chancery, I had to be 'mayor' of the American Embassy compound, which housed almost all of the staff. I had to go to the residence frequently to inform His Excellency what I and the rest of the staff had done, other than what was obvious from the outgoing and incoming telegrams and dispatches that my secretary delivered to the ambassador at least once a day.

The ambassador was addicted to bridge. No matter how many guests were at table, on the conclusion of the meal he would say, "I'll take you, and you, and you for bridge in the Louis Seize room." It is hard to believe, but I was expected to amuse the other guests in the sun room. One evening when, as Dean, he entertained all the ambassadors accredited to Saudi Arabia, after he had disappeared into the Louis Seize Room with three anointed ones, the others decided they had enough of that sort of foolishness. After conversing politely with me for a decent interval and indicating that I was not to blame for any ambassadorial discourtesies, they lined up to thank me for the evening and headed for their limousines without a nod to the Dean. I made a studiedly tongue-in-cheek gesture toward the

Louis Seize room, but they observed that the Dean was much too busy to be disturbed. I made no protest, considering their action to spring from genius. When the Dean heard automobiles starting up outside, he realized what was happening and ran out of the house, slapping his forehead and apologizing. It was too late. Some had already driven off, and the rest were appropriately cool. The ambassador's health declined from that point until his retirement.

Wadsworth refused to be in residence when a naval vessel called, if the captain would not agree to making a formal port call. According to the ambassador's boast, as the presidentially appointed Ambassador Extraordinary and Plenipotentiary, in a formal port call he would be accorded 19 guns.

I admit that in view of the ambassador's sadistic treatment of his staff (working them to the bone, often needlessly, then belittling them) I could not resist enjoying an occasional instance of his discomfort. A choice one of these was one afternoon when he was pompously briefing a couple of Washington dignitaries at the residence, with charts and all. The ambassador was between stocky and portly, was studiedly dignified, ample-jowled, of precise, fastidious speech in English or French, and, being wealthy, of Episcopalian persuasion, though so far as I could see he never granted the Deity an audience. His self-image, when intact, was that of *"l'ambassadeur parfait,"* the title of a book I noted in his library.

Just as His Excellency was getting into the joy of revealing to the visiting dignitaries his mind-boggling grasp of Middle Eastern intricacies, he began to hiccup. Now it is self-evident that ambassadors, bishops and royalty must avoid the hiccups at all cost. Few things in life are as leveling as the hiccups, and of what earthly use is a leveled ambassador, high prelate or monarch? The visiting dignitaries struggled valiantly to maintain their composure. Not I. I crept to an adjoining room to quake, from where I could appreciate His Amplitude's masterful rendition of the ambassadorial hiccup extraordinary and plenipotentiary. After a couple of massive eructations, His Excellency's epiglottis had begun punctuating his presentation with sudden and uncontrollable closures that seemed to levitate his amorphous frame. They shook not only his ample abdomen, but also tinkled the crystal sconces above the credenza against which he was leaning and heaving. Finally, with punctuated apologies, he excused himself for a time, to return a bit later full of yet untapped wisdom, renewed confidence and bicarbonate of soda.

The ambassador had the decency to be out of the country a great deal of the time, thus leaving me in charge. While I was charge d'affaires the Imam of Yemen and Nasser of Egypt paid their first visits to Saudi Arabia, as did the Shah of Iran. State dinners in the palace for visiting dignitaries were an extraordinary experience. Seven or eight courses of French cuisine served on Dresden china for well over 400 guests in the huge state dining hall under (I think I counted) 32 huge crystal chandeliers. Instead of five kinds of wine, five kinds of milk: cow's milk, buttermilk, goat's milk, camel's milk and, I was told, mare's milk. At smaller banquets, instead of having finger bowls at the table, after dinner when we were seated in the garden, servants came by and poured over our hands *Evening In Paris* perfume from large flasks.

Saudi Arabia was not a favorite posting for women. For instance, the telephone system in the mid-50s left much to be desired. Often a messenger was the better answer. At one point, there was an article in the local paper stating that a modern dial system was to be installed. Nothing happened for months, so I asked the Embassy's chief Arab consultant what had happened to the plan.

"It was scrapped long ago."

"Why? It sounded like a wonderful idea."

"The authorities realized that without a central operator to go through, unauthorized persons would be able to use the phone."

"Unauthorized persons?"

"Yes. Women," he explained, matter-of-factly.

Saudi Arabia was nominally dry in more than climate, but when we went to the homes of diplomats of other countries represented in Jidda we were served drinks of all sorts. Their liquor was brought in under cover of the diplomatic pouch. In U.S. usage, this was prohibited. Martha and I were embarrassed having to serve Coca Cola when our friends dined at our house. Finally, Martha called over the Marine sergeant, head of the guards at the Embassy, and said, "I understand that Marines can do anything. Will you kindly ask your men to build me a still?" They did. We would give an all-night bridge party in order to tend the still, the produce of which must have come off something like 180 proof. We would perform this rite on the servant's evening off, but they knew of it. They called the potent product 'sadiki juice' (brotherhood juice). Actually, the king knew about it, too. The Embassy compound, in universal diplomatic usage, was regarded as American territory for all practical purposes, but I thought it best for His Majesty to be aware of what we were doing. His response was something to the effect that his hearing was not what it used to be. We received the impression there would be no difficulty, so long as it did not come to the attention of a very conservative Moslem religious group known as The Society for the Suppression of Vice and the Propagation of Virtue. We called them The Virtue-Urgers.

Even though I found elements of our life in Saudi Arabia most satisfying, after two years I found myself eager to return home. I found it uncomfortable to be in a society that was so convinced, like much of Christendom, that its religion had a monopoly on truth. In the view of the local people we were infidels—a sentiment warmly reciprocated toward Moslems, I fear, by most of the limited number of Christians in Saudi Arabia who took their Christianity seriously.

One fine morning in April 1957 I received welcome word of my next assignment: a year at The National War College at Fort McNair, District of Columbia. "War College" was something of a misnomer. It was more of a foreign affairs college, designed primarily to broaden the vision of military officers of colonel level whose record made it likely that they would advance to flag ranks. A few officers from Departments other than Defense were accepted each year—six from the State Department and the Foreign Service, presumably on the basis of professional promise, but perhaps I was simply being rewarded for having weathered a stint as deputy to Wadsworth. In any event, the year broadened my vision more than I could have imagined.

When we landed in New York I headed for a large drug emporium, for I was beginning to develop a discomfiting cold. Antihistamines had appeared on the market while we were overseas, and I was bewildered by the variety on display. A gum-chewing, very short-frocked clerk approached. I smiled at her and said, "I have an incipient cold. Can you suggest something?"

She stopped chewing, looked at me quizzically, then disapprovingly, and said, "Yeah. I suggest you speak English." At that I felt a warmth of recognition similar to seeing the Golden Gate Bridge on our first return from overseas. I knew I was home again—and unquestionably in New York.

Thirteen

A
Controversial,
Abortive
Book

 began a year at the National War College in Washington in September 1957. It was a unique and valuable experience—unique because of the restricted entry, and valuable because of the prodigious amount of information provided through lectures, study materials and discussion groups.

The College was designed to bring about greater understanding between the civilian and military components of government, as well as greater understanding among the military services themselves as regards their respective areas of effort—their capabilities and limitations. As stated at its inception in 1946, "The College is concerned with grand strategy and the utilization of the national resources necessary to implement that strategy...Its graduates will exercise a great influence on the formulation of national and foreign policy in both peace and war...."

Usually the day started with a lecture by the best authority that could be obtained on the topic of the day, flown in from anywhere. It was at the College that I first saw Henry Kissinger then a Harvard professor, and raptly listened to his lecture. I was impressed. I said to my seat mate that I'd like to get to know that man. His response was, "Fat chance!"

The highlight of the year was the field trip. The world was divided into four or five areas, and the class divided accordingly, each group being provided a four-motor plane. I chose to go to Africa, where we visited thirteen countries. We were briefed in each country by the president or equivalent, the prime minister or the foreign minister, and by specialists in various fields. My deepest impression was the stark diversity depicted in Africa—politically, economically, socially, and in education, hygiene, climate, topography and degree of modernity.

We witnessed the dying days of colonialism in that part of the world. I shook my head when the authorities of the Belgian Congo said they expected to retain political control of the colony for years, because they had the foresight to provide a better material life for the natives than the colonies of other European countries. Liberation of that colony came on the heels of the others.

One day in Brazzaville I was lunching with Jim Greene, the medical doctor assigned to our plane, when he remarked that since he did not have to attend the briefings he hoped to arrange a side trip to see Dr. Albert Schweitzer at his hospital in Lambarene. I immediately said I was going with him, if I could get permission from the commanding general of our group.

In remarkable coincidence, a lady in an adjoining booth overheard our conversation and came to our table to offer advice. She was returning home after spending some time at the Schweitzer hospital, writing a book about the doctor. She said there was a regularly scheduled plane that would get us to Lambarene fairly early in the morning, but she knew of none that would return us to Brazzaville late that day, a timing necessitated by the departure of our group early the following morning for Luanda. She said if we decided to take the morning plane we would find on arrival one Pierre at the airstrip, with a lorry to pick up supplies for the hospital. She gave us a note to Pierre asking him to take us to the dock immediately. There, if we were lucky, we would find a dugout. We should flash a fistful of francs at the owner, say ooga, ooga, which means quickly, quickly, point up the river and say "Schweitzer."

I came out of the next briefing to meet a dejected Dr. Greene. No way to get back in time. I said I was prepared to charter a plane if necessary, in order to visit with Schweitzer.

Jim was as determined as I to find a way to spend a little time with the remarkable philosopher, theologian, musician, physician, Nobel laureate—Jim out of medical interest, I out of philosophical. I had read almost everything Schweitzer had ever written.

When I emerged again from briefings that I scarcely heard, Jim was smiling. An unscheduled Air France plane was to put down in the late afternoon at the Lambarene air strip, to drop off medical supplies for the Schweitzer hospital! We were in luck.

When Pierre deposited us on the dock the next morning, we found not only two dugouts, but a one-lung, putt-putt motorboat of unappealing vintage that we quickly hired. That made much faster the two-mile trip up the Ugawa River to the hospital dock. On the dock was one of the nurses, who invited us to go on up to the doctor's office.

There was no receptionist to stop us, so after hesitating we simply walked in. The good doctor was binding up a boy's foot. Schweitzer received us politely, but with reserve. It turned out he thought we were newsmen, because we had cameras hanging around our necks. When I gave him my card, however, the doctor warmly welcomed us, suggesting that we go on to the dining room, where he would join us momentarily. That extraordinary, craggy face with the busy eyebrows and unruly hair, seen as he carefully tended to the little native boy, swam before my eyes as we walked uphill toward the dining room. Only a deep reverence for all life and a spiritual union with all nature could have built such a face as this octogenarian youth possessed.

Just as Schweitzer entered the dining room, one of his doctors asked me which of Schweitzer's books was my favorite among those I had read. Since I had read my favorite in German, I answered, *Aus Meinem Leben und Denken* (Out of My Life and Thought.) Schweitzer said, *"Sie sprechen Deutsch!"* and we launched a happy dialogue on many subjects that lasted until Jim and I boarded the plane.

When he heard we would have to leave before long to catch our plane, he suddenly left the room.

"Why ... Did I offend Dr. Schweitzer?" I asked one of the doctors.

"Oh, no, he's gone for his hat. He's going with you down the river to the airstrip."

"That's very kind, but I must dissuade him. It's too much..." The doctor was getting along in years, and the equatorial sun is nothing to take lightly.

"It will do no good. No one can manage him. We've all quit trying."

We had asked the putt-putt to return mid-afternoon, and there it was. Dr. Schweitzer and his head nurse boarded the boat with us, and off we went. I saw nothing short of adoration in the eyes of the boat owner as he looked at Dr. Schweitzer.

We talked of a number of things, but the doctor had two main themes. I knew him to be a religious man, or rather a very spiritual one, but he spoke with deep feeling about the divisiveness of religions in a world that had to learn to be one. He thought that especially in the era of The Bomb we could no longer afford the luxury of various, often mutually inimical, would-be monopolies on truth. Everyone had to learn that truth came in different garb. That led to his other main theme: The Bomb. He said we were living in the most dangerous period in all of history. Whereas human folly had previously been held in check by the inexorable laws of nature, we now had control over the most elemental powers of nature before we had gained control over ourselves. He tried to get me to say that I would beg my government simply to scrap The Bomb unilaterally (as though I would have any appreciable influence in that regard) because it was insanity. I agreed as to its insanity, but said that as long as there was so much misunderstanding and mistrust and even animosity between us and our friends on the one hand and the Soviet Union and its allies on the other, the insanity of that confrontation meant we would have to retain the insanity of The Bomb. He still didn't buy that reasoning, but we continued to talk animatedly, as though we were old friends. As a result I'm afraid Jim got the short end of the visit, but he assured me he had learned what he wanted to know from Schweitzer's head nurse who had accompanied us.

The road from the dock up to the air strip was very steep. The good doctor locked arms with me and was practically pulling me up the long hill. I became out of breath, being just able to come out every now and then with a

"Jawohl, Herr Doktor," while Schweitzer talked excitedly about his plans for the next 20 years. He was 84; I was 42.

While we were waiting for the plane and Jim had a chance to talk with Schweitzer, it occurred to me that my son and daughter would value a picture that I had taken of the great man. I asked his nurse assistant if Schweitzer would object to my taking one.

She promptly replied, "Oh, no. He's the most accommodating man in the world."

Her inflection in saying that, however, caused me to respond, "But he'd rather I didn't, wouldn't he?"

"It is true he is tired of being 'Niagara Falls.' You and he have enjoyed each other so much, if you 'forget' to take his picture, he will remember and love you forever."

The plane landed, we were handed a bag of edibles the hospital kitchen had prepared for us, and we said good-bye.

I then did something which at the time I thought to myself, "Father would not approve of this." I engaged in a little would-be innocent subterfuge, although I had been carefully taught that subterfuge was never innocent. Father had maintained that while it may not harm the 'victim' at all, it always damaged oneself a little. That should not be taken lightly, for the self is about all we have, ultimately. I'm afraid I hazarded the damage this time. I snapped one quick picture of Schweitzer from inside the plane where he could not see me. Schweitzer therefore was not disturbed, but Father disturbed me.

("But, Father, I was thinking of my children.")
("Hmmm.")

The plane was overloaded with goats, Singer sewing machines and people. It had been practically squatting when I saw it on the ground. It was a C-47, and I knew when C-47's were squatting, for the U.S. Air Force had flown me around in them in Saudi Arabia. We did get successfully airborne, en route to our next stop, Lastourville. We were there some twenty minutes for some obscure reason, then took off, or rather attempted to do so.

We were bumping along the dried mud and grass airstrip when a tire blew. A C-47 has only one tire on either side, so the prospect was not pleasant. The pilot had the choice, I quickly reasoned, of cutting the motor, so when we flipped over the plane might not explode, or gunning the motor on the bad wheel side, so that we would stay on the so-called runway until we came to a stop. He evidently attempted the latter, but to no avail. We went off the runway into the sand at a good clip. With the sudden halting by the sand of forward propulsion we up-ended so that we almost stood on the nose of the plane, but we did not flip over. We plopped back down, splintering the struts. I'm sure my fingerprints are still on the armrests. We all piled out, convinced we were in Lastourville for a time.

We spent the night at the home of the only white man for nobody knew how many miles around. We were treated as royally as treatment goes in the middle of Congoland. Beds with mosquito-netting were set up, we were given a satisfying dinner considering that no one was expected, were offered native female companionship for the night if desired, and after excellent French cognac went to bed not too much out of sorts with the world, even without the proffered native companionship. Our host had a two-way radio, and had informed the U.S. Consul General in Leopoldville that we were safe but delayed. Our tour group was in turn informed.

One wondered how often this sort of thing happened, for 'Air Chance' to have someone so well primed for guests. That sobriquet for a usually splendid airline would be unfair elsewhere, but in the Africa of those days it seemed appropriate.

The next morning new underpinnings were flown in, and by noon the plane was declared airworthy. I asked the pilot if we could take off right away. He said, *"Mais, monsieur, le déjourné."* (But, sir, the lunch.)

And what a lunch! Fine Scotch whiskey before the meal. The pilot and co-pilot made alarming inroads on a fifth. At table among other delicacies, a whole cooked sheep standing on all-fours was brought in, dripping with pili-pili, a hot African sauce. At *each plate* was a full bottle of superb Bordeau, which the pilot and co-pilot finished off with alacrity. The luncheon group of some five passengers and two crew by then had become effusively convivial. When the pilot finally observed that perhaps we should soon get underway, remembering the squatting C-47, I asked if he was not going to make a little trial flight before we all took off. He stood up and with uncertain equilibrium bowed low, and said, *"Mais, monsieur, c'est vous qui êtes pressé!"* (But, sir, it's you who are in a hurry!")

This prompted the assemblage to rise, raise their glasses and cry, *"Vivent les diplomats pressés"* (Long live hurried diplomats!") It was wild—and by then late afternoon. I asked the young English salesman, a fellow passenger inured to African travel, if we were really going to take off with the pilot in his condition. He replied he would not want to fly with him if he were *not* soused. I was not comforted.

We loaded, gained speed, and thank God, I supposed, became airborne. Right away the wings began dipping back and forth. Heart in my mouth, I asked the Englishman what was going on.

"Relax. He's just waving to the nice people down there who were so good to us." I accepted his explanation without relaxing, tensed by visions of the well patronized fifth of Johnny Walker and the drained Bordeau.

We landed at Brazzaville after dark, and to our delight were told that the neat little launch nearby was to speed us across the Congo to Leopoldville. We crossed in style, disembarked, and were received by the U.S. Consul General, who was very solicitous of our welfare. We assured him all was well, and he assured us that we were indeed fortunate that such was the case. He explained,"One does not cross the Congo at night, but I understood you were in a great hurry, so I arranged the passage. There are heavy mahogany logs floating in the Congo River, which is very swift at this point. Those logs are impossible to see at night, and they could splinter a launch and make fish bait of its occupants. See that man over there on that bench, slumped over as in prayer? He's the relieved owner of the launch."

We were too late to join our group, but arrangements had been made for a commercial flight to Luanda the following morning, and for accommodations in Leopoldville that night. We spent a few moments feeling guilty for having caused so much concern, but soon decided to reward ourselves for being alive with a splendid dinner at our hotel that included caviar, escargots, tournedos and parfaits.

o   o   o

Back at Ft. McNair, I was faced with the necessity to produce a term paper. The papers were to be no more than 7,000 words. Being in the military milieu, I soon learned that was exactly what was meant. My 'paper' ended up being book length, so I was advised to hand in only the Introduction and Chapter Six of twenty chapters. Length was partly the reason, but I suspect a more important reason was that the paper was considered too controversial for the War College library, where it was destined to rest. It examined the religious elements at play in the fashioning of our early history. I doubt that today it would be so controversial. I had chosen for my subject "A Philosophy for United States Foreign Policy", thus attempting to combine my two favorite subjects (I had gotten over my earlier peeve with philosophy as being mere epistemological busy-work). Since I had majored in philosophy and had experience in foreign affairs, I pictured putting my feet up on the desk and dictating my paper in a couple of afternoons, leaving plenty of time for golf. That did not happen.

It was at the time of the Soviet sputnik, the first man-made earth satellite. It is difficult today to remember the extent of the impact on U.S. officialdom, as well as on the American public, of that Soviet 'first.' Practiced as we Americans had long been in strutting, we now went though a flagellating soul-searching of our supposed lethargy and other deficiencies—especially with regard to educational standards, and most especially with regard to the sciences. Suddenly the Communist threat appeared to be an *avant garde* threat. We were behind. Why? What happened?

What concerned me—a concern that prompted my term paper—was the belief that the Communists had a recognizable, well-articulated philosophy for their foreign policy, wrong-headed as it was, while we did not. It seemed to me that Communist philosophy was at least clearly understood as being based on the dogmas of dialectical materialism and alleged historical determinism. A Communist world was said to be in the making, and the outcome inevitable. Communism proposed a theory of humankind and of existence purporting to encompass all the natural and social sciences. The Communist philosophy for foreign policy, therefore, followed dogmatically from its entire system of thought. Uprisings from the masses of the non-communist world, long used and abused by greedy industrialists would spell the doom of imperialism. This trend would accelerate as the masses freed themselves from the opiate of religious superstition.

On the other hand, a philosophy for United States foreign policy cannot rest on dogma, if only because we as a people do not subscribe to any one dogma. In our culture, dogma usually means religious dogma, and certainly we are not unified on that ground. Everything else is supposedly science, or derived from scientific thought. Like the American experiment in democracy and free enterprise itself, it must be a function of unpredetermined, open-ended growth. Ultimately it rests upon the beliefs, the understanding, the insights, the will and the determination of the public at large—at a given period. The fact that those things are so varied in our culture would seem to make it difficult if not impossible to present to the world the philosophy underlying and sustaining our foreign policy in terms as terse and understandable—and as globally marketable—as the Communist doctrine. Invalid as the latter doctrine and the underlying philosophy was and is, and has more recently been *proven* to be, that did not dispense with my problem of adequate international marketability of our philosophy and its practical implications. It is important to remember that in 1958 the Communist 'menace' was viewed as very real indeed.

One does not delve very deeply into the possible underpinnings for a philosophy for foreign policy before recognizing the need for examining underlying concepts of the fundamental nature of the cosmos and of humankind, for it is such basic scientific, philosophical and religious beliefs that cohere and prod a civilization, giving to a people a recognizable character. That character in turn determines their beliefs and assumptions, hence their actions.

When our nation was founded, there was considerably more agreement as to the beliefs that supported Western civilization than there is today. As Louis Halle pointed out in his lucid study of *Civilization and Foreign Policy,* speaking of a much earlier period in our history:

"The vision that has supported Western civilization is that of the world as a battleground in the struggle between good and evil. God and Satan represent, with an actual or symbolic reality, the two opposed principles. Man was created in the image of God but succumbed to the Temptation of Satan in the Garden of Eden. This, in terms of legend, is the Original Sin that accounts for the evil in human nature. Christ's sacrifice, however, betokens man's hope of redemption ... The purpose of life is the salvation of the soul. This is the essential theme not only of our religion but of our classic literature and art. It is also—and here we come to what is relevant to our problem—the theme of our statecraft. It explains those conceptions of individual freedom and responsibility that have animated and indeed determined our political evolution. Our own national constitution is the expression of a philosophy that cannot conceive of a man's moral enlargement except in terms of freedom. The organization of society, according to that philosophy, must be designed to provide the opportunity for nourishing the spark of divinity in our breasts, and human freedom is not to be justified on any other basis."

Such assumptions in fundamentalist religious terms are not widely accepted today. For about a century Western civilization has been passing through a revolutionary period in its beliefs as to what is valid concerning the scientific nature of the cosmos, and of humankind. This revolution has been going on with respect to religious beliefs as well.

I dealt in detail with these themes in my book length paper. Suffice it here to observe that the diversities in religious belief in our society arising from doctrinal sectarianism within Christianity and Judaism have been compounded by increasing representation of other Eastern religions in our midst, and above all by the insistent demands for reorientation of thought by scientific disciplines such as physics, archeology and the science of the mind. I think we all understand well enough what Walter Lippmann meant by erosions of doctrines wrought by "the acids of modernity" to leave it at that. Whether the resulting trends in basic beliefs in science and religion are good or bad for their impact on foreign policy is less pertinent to the inquiry that I was embarked on than the fact that they existed, and that they existed in such diversity and multiplicity. Since we have no unified societal view, we cannot as a people state any one version of our philosophical underpinnings without offending some significant segment of the populace, while satisfying another.

This dilemma was underlined on the one day in the War College course devoted to a consideration of religion as related to national strength. On that day there had to be at least three speakers: a Protestant, a Catholic and a Jew. Even then we omitted perhaps a score more religions represented in America, Islam, Hinduism, and Buddhism, for instance, being only a start. Furthermore, not one of the three persons invited to speak could speak in any detail, at least, for all of Protestantism or all of Catholicism or all of Judaism.

In the question period my hand went up first. I didn't mean to be naughty in asking the question. I really wanted to know how these gentlemen would answer it. I said, "As I understand it, the Bible, among other things, is primarily an account of the growth of humankind's understanding of the nature of God and of man and of their relationship over a period of about twelve hundred years. It seems to me it records considerable growth in that understanding, from the Old Testament through the New. Are we to believe that such growth came to a screeching halt somewhat less than two millennia ago with the canonization of those 66 books, and that further growth in understanding is not to happen, or at least not to be authoritatively chronicled?"

All three gentlemen took a shot at an answer, though they may have preferred to take a shot at me. I would not dare put words in their mouths at this point, but the general outcome, in my opinion, was that the Protestant made an embarrassing botch of his attempted answer; the Catholic jumped into the breach, temporizing eruditely. It seemed about to be left in that unsatisfactory state, when the Jew, who had already endeared himself to the audience with his intelligence, humor and honesty, raised his hand and asked, "May I come to the defense of Christianity?" He then launched into a sprightly account of how Christianity had, because of its very diversity through the centuries, evidently met the needs of widely diverse peoples. He received more than polite applause, largely because he had already established rapport with the audience. I was reasonably satisfied with the Rabbi's answer, but it still seemed to me that canonization closed the way to growth in understanding beyond the 1200 or so years chronicled in the Bible.

Actually, thousands of books have been written which record further growth, but for the most part they are supposed to be consonant with reason, whereas the Bible must be taken on faith wherever it is "unreasonable".

I continued to be unhappy with some of the problems I had in Methodist dogma, for I was still nominally a Methodist. It was at the War College that I made the overt transition from Methodism to Unitarianism. The chief reason was doctrinal, but there were others. The minister at the largest Unitarian church in Washington was learned, expressed himself beautifully, and the music was superb—sprightly, invariably up-beat, and as disciplined as the Cleveland Symphony.

At the time that I wrote my paper, it was clear that the United States had the responsibility to lead the Free World in its efforts to preserve and extend the areas of freedom in the world. American foreign policy, with its moral and material supports then reasonably intact, was the single most important element in freedom's insurance. For that reason it was important not only to us, but also to others what sort of philosophical underpinnings bore us up.

I came to see that we have no choice but to base our foreign policy on democratic precepts rather than on a philosophy more basic than precepts. Any agreed dogma, although it may lend itself to being cogently articulated for public consumption and global salesmanship, would become set in concrete, as is the wont of dogmas. It would spawn a list of dos and don'ts logically following from that dogma that might or might not be valid for that time and circumstance and society, and could well be ruinous guidance for another time and circumstance and society. History has often shown that a dogma in concrete is dangerous and often lethal when there are other, contrary dogmas juxtaposed and fixed in just as firm concrete. Witness the Middle East, where contending exclusive claims to truth have contributed to such tragic carnage.

Democracy, in its essence, must be undogmatic, hence fuzzier than either secular or religious dogma. It is cumbersome, its machinery creaky, subject to special interest influences from labor, management, the military-industrial complex and a hundred other forces. Yet it appears to be the safest, surest provision for society's needs, that has yet been devised.

I am indebted to T.V. Smith and Edward C. Linderman for their masterful description of the democratic process, which I have very slightly revised:

When diversity, made possible in the first place by a free climate, results through the democratic process in compromise, and the relative success of the tested compromise results in popular consent, with its by-products not only contentment, but also a bit of education to add to the fund of socially inheritable knowledge, this constitutes progress. We may then go on to the resolution of other diversities, which may be newly arisen from the changes wrought by the first resolution of diversities. This is the great *democratic* dialectic, and it is neither materialistic nor deterministic. It may indeed involve material goods, but this is different from philosophical materialism. It is the demonstration *par excellence* of the interplay of free wills—the 'divine spark' in enlightened and enlightening action.

Democracy, therefore, implies that we live in a world of moral consequence: that we are free (insofar as our political, social and material environment permits) to make our countless daily choices of this rather than that, and that we will profit from the right choices and suffer from the wrong ones. We are handed responsibility right along with freedom. Democracy, therefore, is mature business.

Participatory democracy, however, is the only democracy that will work over the long haul. The degree to which we spurn the opportunity to participate in our democracy today is the true concern, not our diversity of beliefs, which, if in an atmosphere of tolerance, is strength, indeed fits the very requirements for the raw material of the democratic process!

It seems to me that a democracy, if its sayings and doings are to ring true at home and abroad, must make every effort to act in character with the preponderant tenor of its basic beliefs, even though they may not be able to be stated in agreed, dogmatic form. That is not easy to do. I do not think we did it very well in Vietnam, lamentably the area of my main concern for the year following the War College, although as Deputy Director for Southeast Asian Affairs I also had responsibilities relating to Laos, Thailand, Burma. Cambodia, Malaysia and Singapore.

FOURTEEN

Dear
Old
FE

n 1958 I was in favor of our Vietnam policy of supporting South Vietnam militarily and economically in its struggle against Communist North Vietnam. Like most Americans, in and out of government, I then thought our policy right, because I did not believe that the people in the south wanted to assume the Communist yoke that had been imposed on the north. Also, some feared that the Chinese Communists, heady with their rapid takeover of China, might press southward to the "breadbaskets" (a term more apt in that day than in this) of Southeast Asia in order to help feed the huge Chinese population.

Even during the first year that I was charged with responsibilities in that part of the world, I began to have doubts as to the wisdom of our course of action in Vietnam. On an orientation trip to the area I became convinced that the government of South Vietnam was neither effective nor popular, hence was a weak reed for us to lean on. I also gained a better understanding of the highly nationalistic dedication of the Viet Cong military forces in the north. My increasingly lukewarm support of our policies in Vietnam, moving toward opposition, began to show in meetings within government. Of course, in public speaking I followed the established line. The government cannot, or at least should not, speak with oppositive voices. Gradually I spoke out less and less even within government, for doing so seemed to accomplish nothing except to estrange me from most of my colleagues.

Fortunately, after I spent one year in the Office of Southeast Asian Affairs, Jeff Parsons, assistant secretary for the Far East, rescued me from Vietnamese affairs by naming me Planning Adviser for the Bureau of Far Eastern Affairs, familiarly known as FE.

I was uncomfortable with the words "Far East" in my title and in the Bureau itself. "Far East" was a term originated by the British, who approached the area by traveling east. It seemed to me that the region was our "near West", since it constituted the nearest significant land masses on that side of our continent beyond Hawaii. Furthermore, to the people living in the region, the legitimate question was, "Far from what? Here we are." It seemed to me the implication smacked too much of colonial times. I waged a battle—a noisy one, I fear—to change the name of the Bureau of Far Eastern Affairs. There was strong opposition on the part of some, who had invested their careers in "dear old FE"—dear in large measure because of the ever memorable tenure of that grand Virginia gentleman, Walter Robertson, as Assistant Secretary for Far Eastern Affairs. Also memorable was his hard-nosed United Nations adviser, Ruth Bacon, who for years appeared almost single-handedly to keep the Chinese Communists out of the

United Nations.

I wrote a number of memoranda on the undesirability of calling our near West the Far East, perhaps with more passion than the subject warranted, but I thought the nomenclature denigrated the area, and I didn't think that was smart. East Asia was clearly destined to loom larger and larger in our future and in the future of virtually everyone on the planet. Finally, the deed was done. We became the Bureau of East Asian and Pacific Affairs," with the acronym EA/P.

Much of my attention in that assignment inevitably centered on Vietnam. I added an additional worry to that of the weakness of the South Vietnamese Government and the fanatical dedication of the Viet Cong in the north: the Vietnamese terrain was not congenial to our kind of warfare.

I tried to get across in meetings that in Indo-China we were fighting nationalism even more than we were fighting Communism, and there is no more formidable, implacable 'enemy' than the force of nationalism when arrayed against one, unless it be that of a dedicated religion, and Communism filled that bill also, except for its non-theistic aspects. The simplicity of the anti-communist theme in the United States blinded us to the primacy of the nationalistic concerns of the Vietnamese, both north and south. Some six years later, when I was on the senior staff of the National Security Council, Averell Harriman, then Assistant Secretary for East Asian Affairs, called me to his office to discuss possible new courses of action in Vietnam. Things were not going at all well for us, and would soon be going worse. I was appalled at the widespread use of defoliating poison and dumbfounded at the idea he mentioned of building a fence across Vietnam. I thought the fence idea was crazy and said as much, but I did not have the

expertise to discuss some of the other issues. I can't believe
that building the fence was seriously considered, but it was
not just mentioned in passing. For the most part I remained
in sad silence, my unhelpful conviction having become
self-evident. My opinion was not again sought on Vietnam.
In any event, my responsibilities at that time were China
and Korea

When I was planning adviser for EA/P we were still
under the spell of Kennedy Camelot. Red tape was to be
cut, and anti-communist miracles were to be performed by
decisive, immediate action and plenty of it, with minimal
time squandered in consultation with the specialists around
town.

As evidence of this youthfully invigorating but
supremely naive climate, one morning I received a phone
call from Walt Rostow, an old and admired friend who was
at that time deputy national security adviser at the White
House. Walt asked what I thought about doing something
or other. I said, "I think it would be in our interest." Walt
said, "Good. I think you're right. We'll do it," and hung up.
I don't remember the subject, but I do remember that it
was one on which an interdepartmental meeting normally
would have been held, drawing on the expertise of quite a
number of people before a policy would be agreed upon.
Again, that was not evidence of haste or bad judgment on
Walt's part. Most of the town, and especially White House
officials, were seized of the Camelot complex—for a short
while. They had to be, if their services were to be retained.

Camelot fever was not confined to the White House. In
that same period I once phoned the Secretariat, the administrative office for the secretary of state, to get approval for
a certain course of action. I was prepared to express the
idea at that level and to receive an answer in a few hours or
perhaps on the following day. I phoned instead of writing a

memo because there was moderate urgency to receive authorization. Instead, my call was immediately put through to the Secretary of State himself, Dean Rusk. I gained approval for what I wanted in five seconds instead of in perhaps 24 hours, but the secretary should not have been presented with that request cold—or at all. One of his deputies could have appropriately made the decision, and normally the secretariat would in the first instance have relayed the proposition to him so that he could at least briefly deliberate over it before giving an answer. Rusk was playing the part required of him by the president, that "young man in a hurry."

Upon taking up the assignment for EA/P I was given an orientation trip through all countries within the purview of the Bureau of Far Eastern Affairs. The highlight from a personal standpoint was the stop in Taiwan, when my old friend, General Chiang Ching-kuo, then Minister of Defense, gave me a dinner party and a beautiful silver gift that by regulation had to go to the State Department's warehouse instead of reposing on my dining room credenza. It was "old home week" with the Americans and Chinese in the Embassy.

One interesting duty of mine was to coordinate the annual Chiefs of Mission Conference in Baguio, the Philippines. It was a gathering of all the U.S. ambassadors in East Asian and Pacific countries, when current problems and future prospects were gone over by those who knew what they were talking about. It was a fascinating and informative few days, invaluable to a planning adviser, and nakedly revelatory of the caliber of the several ambassadors.

Following one of these conferences, I accompanied the assistant secretary, Jeff Parsons, on a trip through East Asia. We had consultation visits in Manila, Saigon,

Singapore, Bangkok, Rangoon and New Delhi. Since it was just the two of us on tour, we generally had small, intimate dinners with the top leader(s) of the region, often accompanied only by our ambassador to the country, so that discussion could be as nearly candid as possible. I particularly recall an evening with Lee Kuan-yu, prime minister of Singapore. He was impressive. Highly intelligent, quick-witted, well-informed, enthusiastic and personable. After giving an account of recent developments in booming Singapore and of his plans for the future, he spoke at considerable length praising the successes and the growing strength of Communist China. It sounded very much as though he was radically pro-Mao Tse-tung. Nevertheless, I finally said, for Lee's benefit, "Jeff, I think the prime minister is not so much indicating his admiration for the Mao regime as he is trying to insure that we remain strong enough in East Asia to counter that regime, if events require it." Lee smiled and made no rejoinder.

Our evening in the home of Ne Win, virtual dictator of Burma, was not so reassuring. He had a certain charisma, but it was evident that Burma was saddled with a highly authoritarian political and economic structure that did not bode well. Not that Lee Kuan-yu was by comparison a Jeffersonian democrat. Lee was, however, brilliant and perceptive, and his citizenry had the energy and inventiveness of the Chinese when motivated. He knew how to motivate them.

I have searched for an excuse to mention the consultation we had in New Delhi with our Indian Ambassador Elsworth Bunker, but I was so fascinated by the caliber of the man that I did not retain the substance of our discussion. I only saw Bunker again at one small dinner in Georgetown and at a couple of larger parties. I can only say that he impressed me as being a gentleman through and through, an honest one, and with a modesty strongly augmenting his great capability. An interesting sidelight is that he is the only American ambassador to have married an American ambassador—Carol Laise, a lovely lady who at the time was ambassador to Nepal. I first knew her when she was ambassador to Norway and came to dinner at our house in Stockholm.

I have consistently maintained that the State Department, and especially the Foreign Service, is composed of generally able people, many outstandingly so. To any who may question that, I offer a couple of things to bear in mind. The first is that the business of the State Department, for the most part, is trouble. It is obvious that not many complex international problems are solved quickly and entirely satisfactorily. After all, the world is composed of sovereign states, not easily subject to the benefits of the democratic method of problem-solving. We Americans are an impatient breed, and the State Department often gets blamed for lethargy or inefficiency when it is actually exercising prudence and the best timing of exceedingly complex actions. The second thing to remember is that the State Department is not only a Department within the Executive Branch, answerable to the White House, but in our system of checks and balances in government, the executive branch itself shares responsibility with the legislative and judicial branches, despite the myopic, self-serving assumptions of an occasional president.

When will we get better government? When we get a better citizenry that the government must reflect in all its composite complexities. It succeeds right now in that reflection more than most people with their own special interests and limited visions can believe, or stop to think about. We will get better government and a better world when the conscience and the consciousness of the citizens of our country and of the world are substantially raised, and almost certainly not before. At least, not in a democracy. It looks like better government is ultimately up to you and me and our neighbor. If we think about it, would we wish to have it any other way?

I must mention one factor on the other side of the ledger. With all of State's true strengths, there are of course weaknesses. A major one, it seems to me, is the accusation that too often it waits for problems to arise, rather than foreseeing them and attempting to avert them. I used to wonder why this was so. I think in significant measure it is because so many of the senior people in the State Department have had legal training. I do not mean to denigrate the legal profession. With the exception of attention to a few standard precautions such as preparing a will, lawyers are *trained* primarily to address problems after they have arisen. What one is trained to do, one tends to do, because one does that well. Legal training is undeniably useful in many aspects of problems that State faces, so the presence in the Department of those of legal training is desirable. There is simply a downside: lack of the habit of looking far enough ahead to avoid, where possible, problems arising.

During my tour of duty as planning adviser I had to move my residence twice. On returning to Washington from Jidda we had rented Admiral Tex Settle's house on 32nd Place. He retired when we had been in it only a year, so we moved across the street into Admiral Pine's house. After one year in it, the admiral was retired unexpectedly and needed his house. We decided we'd had enough of that, so we bought a house in Georgetown, on "O" Street, from where I could walk to work.

Historic Georgetown was delightful. As an article in

American Motorist put it, "Georgetown is a way of life, an attitude, a symbol, a completely separate entity from the rest of the District of Columbia, as defined as if it were walled." It is an 18th Century village named for King George II. Although now surrounded by Washington, it antedates the capital by half a century. Within its few square blocks live high administrative officials, judges, legislators, writers, artists and other notables and strugglers. In a way it is a homey place, with small shops such as a book store, a drug store and a 7-11 sprinkled through the residential area, and all manner of smart, avant-garde or frankly tacky shops on Wisconsin Avenue, a main thoroughfare that runs through Georgetown. We retained the house until several years after my retirement from the Foreign Service, living in it on Washington assignments and renting it whenever we were abroad, to Ambassador Jake Beam, to Anne Chamberlain, a most attractive divorcee who was a successful writer, and to Abigail McCarthy, ex-wife of Eugene, the senator and presidential candidate.

When it came time for my next assignment, the Bureau of East Asian and Pacific Affairs wanted to send me to Seoul, Korea, as Deputy Chief of Mission. I heard through a friend, however, that Jeff Parsons, who had been made ambassador to Sweden, wanted me as his deputy. The Bureau carried a lot of weight in the assignment of its own people, but Jeff Parsons was pretty weighty in his own right in the Service, so there was a flattering bit of a tug-o-war. The Seoul assignment carried ministerial rank, but the chance to work with Jeff again, and in Europe for a change, was appealing. I just kept quiet. Finally, Jeff got his way, and I was glad. I went as deputy to Ambassador Parsons in Stockholm. It turned out there was more method than just humoring either Jeff or me, in sending a China specialist to Sweden. In addition to being Deputy Chief of Mission, I was given the role of adviser in the Warsaw talks with the Chinese. Warsaw was our point of contact with the Chinese when we had no diplomatic representation in China. I went from Stockholm to Warsaw nineteen times in my not quite four years in Sweden. For Martha and me, in most respects, our time in Sweden was a great joy.

FIFTEEN

Scandinavian Pomp, Chinese Circumstance

 was surprised how much I felt at home in Scandinavia. I had long taken satisfaction in the belief that through the years I had become simply an Earthling, transcending such limiting categorizations as white, Anglo-saxon and French, meta-Protestant, southern, clean-shaven, cautiously liberal and transnational in thinking. I discovered that I was in truth a Westerner—global-thinking in most ways, but still a Westerner who had learned to love the East. I almost felt guilty. Philosophically, I was so wedded to the idea of oneness in general and one-worldness in particular, believing that oneness, viewed in almost any way, was consonant with basic cosmic law, that I did not want to feel more at home in the West that I did in the East. I often toyed with the idea that if there is such a thing as reincarnation I must have been Chinese at some previous

time. Actually, Christianity in its first few centuries did not reject the idea of reincarnation, but the priests evidently decided they would have a better hold on us if we had only one chance for salvation.

Yet it was a relief to be out of the tensions of the East that were characteristic of the time. There were problems in Sweden, too, but at first I scarcely saw them. The combination of free enterprise in production and socialism in caring for the citizenry seemed like a sensible formula. As a matter of fact, while capitalism was a dirty word in Sweden and socialism a dirty word in America, the two systems were remarkably similar. The United States had a bit more capitalism than Sweden, and not quite as much socialism, but there were generous amounts of each in both countries. Later I came to believe that Sweden's almost confiscatory tax rate to fuel the welfare state drove some of its wealthiest, and perhaps some of its most talented, citizens to take up residence abroad. Furthermore, many Swedes complained that the 'cradle-to-grave security' caused too many youths to be lethargic and inordinately interested in sex and drugs.

Given the degree of democracy and free enterprise in Sweden, at first I thought it incongruous that there was a monarchy atop socialist Sweden. It is not surprising that there has been serious talk of doing away with the monarchy, and equally unsurprising that it has not happened. The monarchy is a symbol of national unity and loyalty that is real, and, I suggest, satisfies the love of pageantry and pomp that religion has largely lost in Sweden. At the same time royalty in Sweden is so down-to-earth it threatens no one. At dinner one evening at Ambassador Parson's residence, King Gustav charmed us all by his relaxed friendliness. I was told that he refused to be crowned by the archbishop in the cathedral at Uppsala, preferring to let God and the people crown him in their own time. Both evidently did a good job of it. He was known and loved for a regal rejection of self-importance.

One evening at dinner his disarming queen, of English origin (sister of Lord Mountbatten), captivated Martha with her complimentary comments on Martha's Chinese gown, and with an almost neighborly account of something or other. Perhaps it was His Majesty's gall bladder operation. King Gustav VI died in 1973 at age 90. He had both unassuming majesty and a keen sense of égalité. He was choice. You could see it in his eye, in his smile, in his bearing and hear it in his speech. No wonder the Swedes loved him.

Sweden's films, plays and opera productions are unsurpassed, and of course Sweden was the home of the legendary Ingrid Bergman. I regret that I once contributed to her untimely death: at one party I lit her cigarette for her. She was charming.

Ingmar Bergman's production of *The Rake's Progress* I rank with Lawrence Olivier's *Richard II* and Helen Hayes in *Victoria Regina*. Swedish productions in political satire restaurants have offerings as sophisticated and funny as anywhere in the world. The Swedes take vacations of respectable length, the archipelago being a favorite destination.

The Swedes have a relaxed view of nudity, which I can relate to up to a point or two. I see self-damage in the degree of shame the many brands of Christianity have put on the issue. There is validity, it seems to me, in considering the God-given human form to be a matter of personal responsibility, of requirement for careful nurturing as being the temple of the soul—as a vehicle for self-mastery, but not a matter for inherent shame. I like to swim nude, but only in circumstances that offend no one. Long before we had an indoor swimming pool in our Virginia house that permitted that privilege, I spent two summer vacations on the Island of Sylt, German territory south of the Danish border in the North Sea. I was by myself on the first visit, since Martha had taken the children to Pennsylvania prior to my home leave to put them in school for a full semester before we would return to Sweden. The second time, the four of us were together. Sylt seemed to be a choice playground for the German elite, and lots of Danes and Swedes—the rich, the beautiful, the talented and a minimal sprinkling of slobs to lend a touch of reality to paradise. There were virtually no Americans. I was told the Germans "hadn't told *American Express* about it," lest the place be overrun. There were two stretches of the more than 20 miles of white sandy beach that were generally accepted as areas for those who preferred to swim nude. No fence, no sign even, certainly no police. When in my walks I came upon the nude areas, I doffed my trunks and experienced the balm of innocent freedom—until a British friend advised against it. At that time, because of my participation in the Warsaw talks with the Chinese, my picture with story was occasionally in newspapers and magazines. My friend pointed to the cliffs above, saying there were news photographers there with telephoto lenses who delighted in unauthorized exposures of those who were publicly recognized. I was not a buff buff to the extent of wanting to appear *au naturel* in *Stern*.

Since philosophy and religion have been undercurrent themes throughout my life, largely because of the life-long dedication to both on the part of my father, perhaps I should observe that it seemed to me that most Swedes took their government-sanctioned Lutheranism *cum grano salis,* to say the least. Surely that is unfair in the view of some Swedes, but the idea was confirmed by Swedish friends of ours who had visited relatives in Minnesota and were startled to find that the transplanted Swedes there still took their Lutheranism seriously! Indeed who is likely to be serious about a tax-supported religion, as was the case in Sweden? One's most basic beliefs, it seems to me, must stand on their own merit or collapse. In Sweden it appeared to me that the religious genre of basic beliefs tottered, if it hadn't well nigh collapsed.

Once we made the mistake of taking the children to the Anglican Church, where at least the service was in English. The liturgy, I'm afraid, had the worshippers groveling in worm-of-the-dust unworthiness. That night on climbing in bed Stephen said, frowning, "Daddy, were those people in church bad people?"

"Of course not, son."

"Well, I didn't think so. I know some of them and they are real nice. Why did they say 'there is no good in me' in such a moany way?"

"Good question, son." To myself I supposed it was hoary, obstinate tradition, stemming from times of less understanding of the damage that self-damning thoughts can bring.

A rare treat during our time in Sweden was accompanying Adlai Stevenson to Uppsala for his graduation address at the university, and his tour of the 'nations' on the campus, roughly the equivalent of fraternities. A number of amusing, lengthy poems flattering to Stevenson or poking fond fun at him were offered at the various nations on the campus. They evinced a great deal of effort in preparation, for they were clever as could be. Stevenson responded *ad lib* to each in prose, of course, but with humor and apt references easily of comparable excellence to the students' carefully prepared offerings. The students howled. He won the campus hands down in an impressive tour de force.

Stevenson stayed at the ambassador's residence, and Jeff was thoughtful enough to arrange a dinner and evening for just the three of us. I saw why some people said Stevenson was too intellectual, and maybe too gentlemanly, to be president. I don't think he could have stomached the expected—and allegedly necessary—wheeling and dealing.

Stevenson invited me to call on him in the Waldorf Astoria Towers whenever I passed through New York. I was able to do so on three occasions. He was our Ambassador to the United Nations at the time. He indicated he did not really want the job. I said I could not think of anyone else who could handle the responsibility with nearly so much effectiveness. He said, "But they have made me just a debater, not a policy maker."

We each confessed our disenchantment with our Vietnam policy though he was much further along in his opposition than I at the time. We commiserated with each other because of our requirement to support it in public.

In the first visit, after a half-hour or so, I said that I knew something of the impossible schedule that Stevenson followed, and made a move to leave. He said he was not pressed at the moment. Soon we found ourselves, no matter what the ostensible subject, talking about the status of the "human experiment" at this stage in its evolution. We both thought that alongside all the horrendous things going on in the world there were evidences of slow but fairly steady growth in human consciousness. Stevenson thought a careful reading of history would give cause for cautious optimism. Still, considering the fact that for the first time in history we had the scientific and technological skills to banish hunger, poverty and misery for all people, it was difficult not to be impatient with the pace of our maturation.

Stevenson was pessimistic about the Washington

scene, saying that there was too much malice abroad there, too much damaging gossip and ruthless power-seeking. He was nostalgic for the Washington of World War II and for some fifteen years following it, when there were numbers of "mental and moral giants" in government. I thought and almost said aloud, then thought better of it, "Yes, and it was your prominence, your personal integrity and your respect for the sacredness of responsible government service that helped attract people of that caliber to Washington."

On Stevenson's face in repose there was a *Weltschmerz* in the lines around his eyes and mouth. Often, however, his incomparably sophisticated humor would light his eyes and turn those lines upward. I remember thinking during that visit what a joy it would be to live next door to him. It was mutual interest in the somewhat pompous "human experiment" theme that largely accounted for the rapport I was privileged to enjoy with that truly great man. There are few pleasures to equal spending relaxed time with an erudite, witty, articulate, honest and caring man or woman. I have had but two full-fledged heroes in my life, other than Lindberg when I was a child: Adlai Stevenson for his high intellect, his sophisticated wit and his moral character, and George Marshall for his long range vision, his wisdom and his unshakable integrity.

Dean Acheson, former secretary of state, also visited Stockholm, and Jeff kindly again arranged a dinner in his home for the three of us. I admired Acheson for his intelligence and his way with words, and I thought he had been a very good secretary of state. He also looked like a secretary of state, which I believe was a somewhat negotiable asset in foreign affairs. He was, however, aloof, having little time for the ordinary run of humanity. I never saw him speaking to anyone at the Metropolitan Club in

Washington except to those of more or less his equal in
stature, which meant he was inordinately silent. He must
have been lonely up there. I was disappointed that he did
not converse freely that evening with Jeff and me. He was
either too tired or I was too junior, maybe both. If he had
opened up, I like to think I could have held up my end of
the conversation. Who knows, we might both have profited.

Speaking of high intelligence and a way with words,
three or four of the most memorable evenings I have spent
anywhere in the world were spent in the apartment of
Gunnar Myrdal, in the Old Town section of Stockholm.
He liked to give stag dinners for six only, so there could be
meaningful discussion. After dinner we would sip excellent red wine and discuss the world's affairs until all hours.
The world-famous economist wrote several classics about
the poor in America and in developing countries. He wrote
An American Dilemma, one of the first books to investigate
racial problems in America. It was controversial in 1944,
baldly and boldly pointing up the contrast between the
vaunted American ideal and the reality of segregation and
other forms of discrimination. For lengthy periods he lived
in the United States, of which he was clearly fond, despite
his criticism of our faults. When in Sweden he became
chairman of a committee on Vietnam and took part in
demonstrations against the Vietnam war, of which there
were many. He emphasized that he was protesting the war,
not implying anti-Americanism. In 1974 he was given the
Nobel Prize in economics. Alva Myrdal, his wife of 61
years, won her own Nobel Peace Prize for her tireless
advocacy of nuclear disarmament. Both Myrdals played
important roles in designing the Swedish welfare state.

I could not object to Myrdal's finding fault with the
United States, for his criticisms came out of a genuinely

high regard for the "American experiment." I have often contrasted his service in criticizing us with Krishna Menon's disservice in criticizing us so vitriolically and self-righteously. Menon was sometime defense minister of India, but at the time I had lunch with him in New York he was Indian Ambassador to the United Nations, where he did not exert himself to spare us from embarrassment. Detecting the remaining traces of my Georgia accent, he proceeded for some 15 minutes to give me unadulterated hell for our tolerating a second-class citizenship (this was in 1957). Finally, I put my hand on his arm and said, "Excellency, despite my accent, I was taught at the dinner table as a child that the congenital circumstance of skin pigmentation or the lack of it was about the poorest criterion for judging human worth that could be devised. However, we have a problem in the South. We are gradually making progress, but it cannot be solved overnight. For unfortunate—no, for shameful—historical reasons there is just too much difference yet in the average white and the average Negro" (that was the accepted term then for Afro-Americans) "in education, in speech, in cleanliness, in social conduct, even in health and morals, so that both races would be uncomfortable if fully thrown together right away. Progress will continue, and I trust will accelerate. Meanwhile, Excellency, I wonder whether in your desegregation problems in India you have had any experience by which we might profit."

To the credit of the inveterate sourpuss, he actually smiled, saying, "I do not wish to criticize you unjustly." That is probably as close as he ever came to saying "Touché!"

The attitude of Swedes toward the United States was a mixture of many ingredients. Sweden was, of course, technically neutral in the East-West, that is, free world-communist bloc confrontation of the era. Neutrality arose partly from ideology, inasmuch as Sweden considered herself to be a socialist country, and partly because of the discomfort of geographical proximity to the Soviet Union. Many Swedes have relatives who have settled in the United States. Swedish hearts were for the most part with the West. Every now and then there was evidence of strong affection for America, except with reference to the Vietnam war. There was scarcely concealed jubilation when Soviet missiles had to be withdrawn from Cuba, and the outpouring of sympathy at the assassination of President Kennedy was far beyond anyone's expectation. A silent candlelight procession to the Embassy was participated in by a very large number of students. As soon as definite word was received that President Kennedy had been assassinated, all scheduled radio and TV programs were canceled and somber music was played the rest of the evening. The king phoned Jeff that evening and called on him the following morning. Several religious groups held memorial services. We were told that the only other time the palace flag had been flown at half mast other than for a member of the royal family was for Dag Hammarskjold, Swedish Secretary-General of the United Nations.

Nevertheless, the Swedes never wanted to be taken for granted in their silent allegiances. Count Wachtmeister, later ambassador to the United States, one night at dinner at our house, perhaps because of some presumptuous statement I had made, politely reminded me that Sweden was neutral. I said, "Yes, but you are neutral on our side, aren't you?" He smiled and let it pass.

o   o   o

A dinner in the spectacular City Hall was given for Lyndon Johnson on his visit to Sweden when he was vice president. I'll never forget it, for earlier I had emphasized to his advance team that the Swedes have the habit of punctuality almost to a fault. It is (or was—I don't know how much customs have slipped) not much exaggeration to say that if you invited 20 people to dinner, they virtually all would congregate outside your door moments before eight o'clock in the evening, and the senior guest would punch the doorbell on the hour. Or so it seemed from inside the door, when they all streamed in.

I showed up in the Johnson suite at the Grand Hotel a half hour before time to go to the City Hall. I was scheduled to transport Vice President and Mrs. Johnson from the hotel to the City Hall in my car. I don't think Lady Bird was thrilled by the prospect of the mere Deputy Chief of Mission's escorting them, but she was too gracious to show it openly. Well, not very openly. Jeff planned to receive them at the City Hall. The hour that the vice president was to show up at City Hall came and went, and he was still telling jokes—masterfully—in his hotel suite. LBJ was a raconteur par excellence. Even his off-color stories, by far the majority, were so well told, and usually so amusing, they tended not to offend. I looked ostentatiously at my watch a number of times, but I confess that I did not break in to remind him of the Swedish reverence for punctuality. There is no denying that LBJ had a 'presence' that made it difficult to interrupt his laid-back performances.

He was sporadically a charmer. I would come to like him when later I was on loan to the White House as Johnson's "China Watcher." I admired his domestic objectives and achievements, while decrying his stubbornness regarding Vietnam. As for Mrs. Johnson, when I first met her she impressed me as being tough as nails. I thought she shared and abetted her husband's vaulting ambition. In her later days in the White House, however, I came to regard her as one of the most gracious, socially savvy and attractive denizens of the Washington jungle.

Back to the scene in the Johnson suite. I was told by the Embassy's political officer, who was present before I arrived, that the most famous artist in Sweden had been prevailed upon by the Embassy to bring a number of his representative works for Johnson's approval. It seems that the vice president liked to purchase one painting from each country that he visited. The officer said that after no discernible deliberation amid stories, the vice president had settled upon the smallest of the paintings, valued at $400. He said Johnson said to the famous artist, "I'll give you $100." We all wanted to sink through the floor. The artist, after he regained his composure, was reported to have said, "Mr. Vice President, it will be my pleasure to give you the painting." The vice president reportedly then said, "Thank you."

The vice president borrowed my car, a white Buick convertible, to ride in for his street parade in Helsinki, Finland. The only other convertible that we could locate in Stockholm was gold colored, and that did not seem to convey the right message. A picture of the Johnsons riding in my open car appeared on the front page of the *New York Times Magazine*. The Counselor of Embassy in Helsinki sent me a copy of the picture "as a little balm by offering visual evidence that your car was used." He was referring to the fact that my car was in an accident while with the Johnson party in Helsinki and required moderate repair. Fortunately, the Johnsons were not in it at the time. Later, when I was assigned to the White House, President Johnson autographed the picture for me.

In view of the distaste I had developed for the more archaic tenets of religion, I'm afraid I occasionally took pleasure in poking fun at them. One day when we were skiing at Storlien, considerably north of Stockholm, I noticed on the wall of the lodge a map that showed a little town over the border some 60 miles into Norway by the name of Hell, so I boarded the train and went to Hell. The town consisted of two small stores, four houses within view, and a railroad station. To my delight there were post-cards in the station depicting said station, with HELL in large letters. I bought a card and sent it to my minister in Washington. On it I said, "Contrary to popular opinion, this place is a) not overpopulated; b) already frozen over; and c) the road to it is not paved with a damn thing." I was told later that, being Unitarian, he read it from the pulpit.

The Swedish military once invited me to Uppsala for a celebration. At the luncheon the commander of the base offered to give me a supersonic ride in a two-seated trainer. I eagerly accepted, but when we got up from the table our Embassy air attache took me aside and said I shouldn't accept. He said in my position I was public property, espe-cially as charge d'affaires (Jeff was in Washington serving on the Promotion Boards) and I should not take unneces-sary risks. He admitted I would probably be safer in the trainer than I would being driven back to Stockholm from Uppsala, but if anything happened to me in the plane, such as a burst blood vessel in the eye in a supersonic turn, he would find his ...then he used an indelicate expression indicting that he would be in difficulty for not having stopped me. I had to 'remember' an engagement in Stockholm that would not allow time for the flight. I was determined to fly supersonically at the first opportunity, however, so some time later in returning from Paris I took the Concorde. We traveled a little over Mach 2, and I saw the sun set twice that day, since we were traveling west faster than the earth turns.

Throughout my tour in Stockholm every four to eight weeks I went to Warsaw as adviser in the talks held there with the Chinese on matters of mutual interest, since we had no diplomatic representation in mainland China. At the Geneva Conference on Indochina in 1954 it was agreed that Chinese and American representatives would meet periodically. The Warsaw talks were an outgrowth of the negotiations, mentioned elsewhere, that first Ed Martin and then I held in Geneva, attempting to get the Chinese to release a number of Americans being held in China against their will.

Alex Johnson was the first U.S. representative at the ambassadorial level in the talks growing out of the ones Ed Martin and I had held. Johnson met with the Chinese ambassador in Geneva and then in Prague. Ambassador Jake Beam headed the talks in Warsaw for the first two times I went there, but he had already received an assignment to the Department and had contracted to rent our house in Georgetown. I understand from mutual friends that Ambassador Beam elected to retire from the Service because he was inappropriately left by Kissinger uninformed concerning an important issue involving the ambassador's area of responsibility. After all, an ambassador is a presidentially appointed envoy "extraordinary and plenipotentiary" to care for American interests in his country of assignment. The advisability of Kissinger's stepping in to conduct affairs in the country would be questioned by many; to leave the ambassador uninformed of what went on is very hard to justify. Those who knew Jake well seem to think his leaving the Service was a distressing loss to the country. After Jake Beam left Warsaw, Ambassador Jack Cabot took over. It was a joy working with that personable Boston Brahmin in my trips to

Warsaw, and getting to know his delightful wife, Elizabeth. I have three oil paintings in my hall now that she kindly spotted for me at a bargain in Warsaw, when I did not have time to shop.

In the talks there were four on each side of the green felt table, across which we hurled in a most gentlemanly fashion quite ungentlemanly accusations. I had to get off a lengthy telegram to the Department right after each meeting. The scribe's verbatim account followed a few days later. I finally taught myself shorthand in an attempt to avoid writer's cramp in taking notes. A record of the proposals put forth by each side can be found in Kenneth Young's book, *Negotiating with the Chinese Communists*. He spent a couple of long evenings with me in 1967 while writing the book, taking copious notes from a speech of mine that covered the talks and the negotiating methods of the Chinese.

About the only thing ever agreed upon at the Warsaw meetings was the date for the next meeting. Frankly, the tenor of the talks seemed to me at times to be almost childish, often petulant and endlessly accusative. Each side seemed to be not so much debating across the table as talking for the benefit of their exigent constituencies back home—the Chinese making anti-imperialist brownie points in Beijing and we making anti-communist brownie points in Washington.

Actually, I almost came to like the first of the two Chinese ambassadors who participated in the talks, Wang P'ing-nan. When I encountered him outside the talks he was more than civil. This caused me to do him a disservice, I fear, but I certainly had no intention of doing so. Jack Cabot asked me one evening in his office what I thought of Wang. I said I thought he was a likeable man who had to say the disagreeable things he said, but I sometimes wondered if he had his heart in it. Almost immediately after that, he was replaced by Ambassador Wang Kuo-ch'uan, who was a great deal tougher in word and atmospherics. The transfer of the first Wang was doubtless explained a bit later, when we learned that the Embassy was "bugged" with numerous microphones implanted in the construction. I feel sure my remark to Jack Cabot was relayed to Beijing by the Poles.

One weary afternoon after my recently less than mastered shorthand gave me difficulty, I decided I needed a drink. Though I should have known better, I went to the bar of the Communist government-owned hotel and ordered a martini. Before I had quite finished it I realized I had been given a drug-laced mickey. In moments it made me terrifyingly lascivious. I retained sense enough to head straight for my room, lest I tackle the first waitress who passed, a misdeed that I supposed the authorities hoped would happen.

I know next to nothing about drugs, except the prescription kind from a course in pharmacology taken years later at chiropractic college (accurately labeled toxicology there), so I do not know from what "recreational" drug I obtained such an all-consuming, disabling, innocent high. I confess that it was disturbingly pleasurable physically, but I do not care to seek a repeat less innocently, because I find that degree of abdication of the self to be distasteful.

o   o   o

At a meeting in October 1964 we were handed for forwarding to President Johnson a message from Premier Chou En-lai stating that "China exploded an atom bomb at 15:00 hours on October 16, 1964, and thereby conducted successfully its first nuclear test." It further declared, "The Chinese Government hereby solemnly declares that China will never at any time and under any circumstances be the first to use nuclear weapons."

At least talking was better than fighting, but it was frustrating that the talks virtually got nowhere. In April 1965 I was called back to Washington for consultation at the Department concerning the Warsaw talks and in New York with Adlai Stephenson on Chinese U.N. representation. At the Department we discussed several possibilities designed to produce some movement in the talks, but the Chinese were still reeling from the disastrous economic results of Mao's so-called *Great Leap Forward.* The "backyard furnaces" not surprisingly produced steel of unusable quality and the new and venturesome agricultural techniques were a fiasco. Three years of bad crops followed, causing widespread malnutrition and, reportedly, pockets of starvation. The Chinese did not want to negotiate from weakness. Besides, Mao's Great Proletarian Cultural Revolution was being planned, and it soon became evident the Chinese were in no mood to deal with the hated imperialists.

Nevertheless, President Johnson in a speech at Lancaster, Ohio, in September 1966 said:

"In Europe our partnership has been the foundation for building bridges to the East. We and our friends in Western Europe are ready to move just as fast, and just as far, as the East is prepared to go in building these bridges.

"In Asia, we have a similar hope, though today it is clouded by war and by bitterness. But still we look to the day when those on the mainland of China are ready to meet us halfway — ready to devote their enormous talents and energy to improving the life of their peoples — ready to take their place peacefully as one of the major powers of Asia and the world."

In other public statements it was reiterated that when that day comes, the Chinese will not find us unresponsive.

Meanwhile, we were determined to work as best we knew how to increase the likelihood of that day's coming.

SIXTEEN

Hate,
Fear
And
Love

n leaving Sweden I was offered an assign-
ment as a senior inspector for the State
Department-Foreign Service. The job carried rank equivalent of ambassador. I
would have to travel about the world
inspecting the effectiveness of the job that
American embassies and consulates were doing, and writing efficiency reports on all personnel charged with so-
called "substantive" duties, for example having to do with
political or economic reporting. An administrative inspector traveling with me would report on the performance of
the administrative and consular personnel. It meant six
weeks inspecting abroad, followed by three weeks in
Washington inspecting the Departmental support and guidance offices related to the Foreign Service offices abroad
that had just been inspected. I readily accepted, for it was a

highly responsible job professionally, and it was time for the children to have stateside schooling.

My reintroduction to Washington included an episode that on reflection strikes me as characteristic of the era. About one thirty in the morning in the second night in our Georgetown house on returning from Sweden, I was doing an acrostic puzzle sitting on the floor in the upstairs sitting room (our effects were held up by a strike) when I heard simultaneously the door bell, door knocker and kicking against the front door. I ran down, flung the door open and there stood Bobby Kennedy. He looked a little sheepish, and said, "I'm Bobby Kennedy." I said, "I know. I'm Alfred Jenkins." We shook hands and, after inquiring about the whereabouts of the previous occupant, he left. I should have asked him in. From what I learned of his nature later, I imagine he would not have minded sitting on the floor in the study and having a nightcap with me. I got to know him slightly at the Metropolitan Club, but soon after we met there and smiled about the nocturnal encounter he resigned from the Club because of its anachronistic racial policy. I came to admire him on that and a number of other issues, while finding him personally overly intense. I debated leaving the Club myself, but decided to stay and work from within it toward the same principle that Kennedy was honoring by leaving it. It was not long before the racial barrier was broken, followed considerably later by the gender barrier.

In my two years I inspected overseas missions in perhaps 30 countries on three continents. Fascinating as I found the travel, the local sights, the local dignitaries, the U.S. Foreign Service personnel, the varying character of each post under varying leadership on the part of ambassadors, consuls general and consuls, the most gratifying thing was discovering how very professionally the work of representing our country's interests was generally being done. There were only a couple of cases where I had to turn in distinctly adverse reports, and these were on very senior personnel. Power often corrupts.

I shall mention Embassy Beirut, not in the context of adverse reporting, but because my six weeks in Beirut had a profound effect upon my view of the human condition. I was first charmed, then alarmed.

Charmed, because Beirut was justly known then as the Paris of the Orient. It had at least two fine hotels, the Phoenicia, which was new and spiffy with a Frenchy atmosphere of not-quite-innocent sauciness. The stools at the bar, for instance, faced a series of large glass panels showing the underwater scene of the swimming pool, which was at the ground level above. The swimmers were in respectable swim garb, at least by Gallicly tolerant local standards, but they were often unaware that they were on display from the neck down. The hotel personnel were well trained, young and vibrant. The other fine hotel was the insistently staid George V. Old, confident, seaside, with superb cuisine, wondrous service and the most velvet vintage of *Chateau Neuf du Pape* that I have ever tasted. A dinner club, the Lido, offered stage extravaganzas of Parisian scale and charm.

The 'pillars of the community' whom we met were cultured, often witty, and spoke French with captivating style. Perfect strangers were often friendly. One young fellow with whom I conversed on the strand conducted me through a museum and art gallery and then insisted on my going home with him to meet his sister and mother.

I was alarmed by Beirut, because of the electrically charged 1965 atmosphere of potentially devastating societal explosion. The formula for death and destruction was precise: multiple major religions well represented in one small country, each with a tenaciously held monopoly on 'truth' that was incompatible with the others' monopolies on 'truth.' Still another major religion was in a juxtaposed country that was paranoically insecure (Israel). And of course there were economic considerations (translate 'greed') adding to the varied drives toward oppositively envisioned solutions to the multiple confrontations. I was brought to see this mess first by Ambassador Porter, but even more tellingly by the able younger officers in the embassy who had less establishment connections among the populace, and in many conversations with Lebanese of varied walks of life.

It dawned on me, not for the first time, but for the first time starkly, that one's religion was usually a matter of geographical location at birth. And of course in America, where there is such a smorgasbord of religious offerings, geography, ethnicity and family finances all combine to load the dice in favor of a given faith, or no faith—or rather a secular faith: I doubt that anyone has faith in nothing. If I had been born in Mecca or Medina, I would have been—at least in childhood and probably for life—a devout Moslem, and I would have known I had the one and only 'truth,' or at least the only complete 'truth.' All other peoples would be infidels. Indeed, even within Christianity, if I had been born to my Jenkins clan a generation or two earlier, I would have been born a relatively wealthy Episcopalian, comfortable with somewhat convoluted ritual and a touch of pomp, instead of being born a relatively poor Methodist, with an erstwhile tendency to be smug in my 'more spiritual' simplicity.

What a riotous theological tangle attended the time when the Middle East was aflame with the reaction to Saddam Hussein's rape of Kuwait! Hussein had declared the war a jihad—a holy war, meaning God was on his side.

The highest religious authority in Saudi Arabia, however, had just as insistently declared that God was on the opposite side, as had President Bush in proclaiming it a moral war. Presumably God would not be on the side of immorality. I felt like asking if the real God would please stand up—provided He, She or It was not hopelessly confused along with the rest of us. If there have been UFOs and in the superior perception of the occupants they have comprehended our self-wrought catastrophes and atrocities and have in revulsion darted away into space, I don't blame them. The human experiment obviously has a great many problems to resolve. To solve them will take assumption of personal responsibility, not supine reliance on incantations of salvation.

The tragic spectacles of the Lebanon of 1965, the whole Middle East of many years and the Ireland of the past decade are enough to tempt a person to become a Buddhist. Buddhists are pacifists *and,* non-proselyters, hence at least not knee-jerk confrontationists. Not that I extol any one religion. On the contrary, I recommend answering the increasing call to eclecticism, tolerance and ecumenicism—all else having failed us for centuries on end.

Thinking along that line reminded me of a wondrous visit I had with a savant in Inner Mongolia. Once in Kalgan in the province of Chahar, on a leisurely summer evening in 1948 I was greeted by a pleasant, outgoing Nationalist soldier. At first I thought his intent in striking up a conversation was to practice his English, but in view of his education and my belief that he was an officer in enlisted men's clothing, I came to believe he may have been assigned by General Fu Tso-yi to keep a friendly eye on me. He said I should call him Chang. We talked of the Nationalist-Communist civil war for a while, but as we became better acquainted, surprisingly our interest turned to religion.

"My mother is Buddhist, maybe a little Taoist, and my father is a Christian," he said. "I see some good in all three, but my father is unhappy with what he thinks are my mother's 'stubborn ways.' I think my father is the stubborn one, though of course I never say that. When he scolds my mother for her 'unChristian beliefs' she doesn't fight back, she just smiles. I think in that way she wins and my father loses."

I laughed appreciatively, and agreed. "Are you a Buddhist or a Christian?" I wanted to know.

He laughed in turn. "I'm neither one, and maybe both. Probably more Taoist than anything else. Anyway, I think you should meet a master that I know, who is perhaps mostly Buddhist, but he refuses to label himself. I will take you to see him tomorrow if you wish." Of course I wished it. "He will love you," he assured. "He loves everyone."

The next day Chang came for me in a jeep and we drove to a small outlying village. Chang only accompanied me to the gate of the residence of his friend. He told the coolie who answered the bell who I was, then left. The coolie called to the household manager to come. They conducted me to a small, comfortably appointed sitting room and explained that their master was "handling a problem." This was stated as a fact, without any apology for keeping me waiting. As they brought tea and cakes, they said they hoped I would be content to rest a while. I was happy to do so, for they were choice company. In fact, they provided a clue as to the remarkable nature of the master of the house whom I was to meet. They seemed to enjoy serving me and making me comfortable, yet they were not in the least servile. In quite atypical Chinese fashion, they seemed to regard each other as equals. Their faces combined serenity with such child-like openness it would have been comical, had it not been magnetic. They reminded me of a combination of Albert Einstein and the big-eared, wide open Alfred Newman of MAD magazine. I gestured that they should sit. They smiled, but continued to stand. They asked many questions about my life, some of them quite personal, but in such a matter-of-fact manner, there was no embarrassment.

After some fifteen minutes the door to the master's study opened and the 'problem' visitor passed by. I was ushered into the master's study. As I approached him I wondered how I should address him. I used a Chinese title that is roughly the equivalent of 'honorable sir,' but at that my host tossed his head back with a little chuckle, so afterwards I simply addressed him as 'you,' as he addressed me. I realized Chang had never called him by name.

When I walked in, he did not at first rise to greet me, but instead intently looked me over for a few moments, after which he flicked his head to one side and seemed to eye me in the periphery of his vision. He then rose to welcome me.

I had been eyeing him, too. He had an enormous head on a large-framed, not obese, body. I first thought he was bald, but later realized his head was shaven. He wore no glasses. His dark eyes, despite his presumably advanced age, were as clear, wide open and waterless as a child's. His nose was more aquiline than the usual Chinese nose. He was not pure Han Chinese. His teeth were regular and white. In repose his face was all but unlined, but wrinkles appeared around his eyes when he smiled, which was much of the time. His skin seemed almost translucent.

My host neither shook hands nor placed his hands together in the usual Buddhist greeting. He approached close (almost seeming to sniff me!), lightly touched my left rib cage with the tips of his fingers—a very un-

Buddhist gesture in my experience. I was reminded of
Chang's expression "perhaps Buddhist," as though the tag
didn't matter. I thought I received a slight electrical shock
when he touched me, but rather than its being some esoteric phenomenon I thought it might be static electricity
from the rug.

The master said in cultured mandarin, "Yes ... yes, you
are welcome. Chang has told me about you. I see that you
have been served tea, so let us go up to the temple grounds
to talk. I discuss supposed (an unvocalized 'hunh' through
his nose) troubles in this room, and you have not brought
me a trouble." He laughed infectiously and called for his
rickshaw. He had a basket of fruit prepared to take along.

Since he was perhaps twice my age, maybe more, it
was natural that he ride and I walk the less than a quarter
mile to the temple. As we started out he asked, "Why do
you come to me today?"

I hadn't really thought about that. I had merely trusted
Chang's recommendation, for what purpose I was not sure.
"To learn from you, I suppose." I immediately thought the
"I suppose" would have been better omitted, but it was
said.

He laughed. "No. We shall commune." He laughed
again, quietly. He took out some beads and began to finger
them. I sensed he would as soon be silent for a while.
Always smiling, he frankly stared at me, silently, most of
the way up the hill. Surprisingly, I found that entirely comfortable, perhaps because I was moved to stare right back,
and that, too, was comfortable. I wondered why that was
the case, and why I was strongly drawn to this man. I think
it was because he seemed to be totally, but totally, without
pretense. Then it dawned on me: that freed us both!

We stopped beside the temple. "Let us sit out here in the
shade. You may go into the temple to have a look—and a

sniff, if you wish." He cackled. "But you will find the incense is too much to bear for long. The trees out here smell better." He laughed extra long. "The temple building is nothing special, but here is special."

He was right about the temple. It contained an overwhelming statue of the Buddha, several mirrored columns, and scores of burning joss sticks and incense. It all smelled of well-intentioned, trusting, relatively benign ignorance.

When I returned he had cut open, cored and peeled apples for us. "Do you like your work in diplomacy?"

"I am still in the State Department's China Language School in Peiping. I like that very much, and I believe I shall also like it when I am in a more normal assignment in diplomatic service. My friends who are, say that it is very fulfilling. They also say that if you have a responsible position it can be extremely demanding. The work is varied, and there are long hours. Even entertaining is with serious purpose, and in a sense you are always on duty. You never know when there will be an emergency, day or night."

My friend seemed to ponder that. After quite a while he said, rather to himself, "Being is what is seminal, not doing"... (then, looking at me) ... "But you know that."

"I know it intellectually, but ..." He laughed and put his hand on my arm so quickly it startled me. He did so, as if to prevent my finishing the sentence. I think he did not want me to state out loud the somewhat negative thought that would have followed.

We were silent in complete comfort for some time. I think I had never before experienced time as being so irrelevant. I do not know how long we were silently content, but suddenly I realized that it was not long before the appointed hour for Chang to pick me up, and I had not "bled" this savant of what I felt was a storehouse of refreshingly unadorned wisdom.

I tried to enter that storehouse by saying, "I don't want to seem dramatic, but I really want to make my life count. I think I have a beginning knowledge of what to do in order to make that more likely, but I think I know much less about what to avoid doing—and I have an idea that the non-doing matters a lot."

Again, his quiet laugh. "That is a typical Western concern, dear friend. It is because in your culture you are taught fear."

I blanched a little. I did not understand the connection then, and I was offended. "I do not think of myself as being fear-ridden."

"I know. With you it is on the subconscious level, but it is endemic in your culture. It is one of the few things that, if one feels it necessary to look for such things, one may not admire about your culture."

"I have not been taught fear. 'Fire and brimstone' teaching was never taken seriously in my upbringing."

"No, but the remaining subconscious effects of that and related earlier teachings are in your culture nonetheless, even if not in terms of a bygone belief in a geographic hell and a personal devil—it just isn't on the conscious level, in conscious people." A fairly long silence. "It crops out in the fear of being "bad" or simply "not proper" in ways that harm no one, including the self. Americans often don't even have the security of family and clan solidarity. That lack constitutes a form of fear." More silence.

I couldn't think of anything to say at the moment. Finally he continued, "Fear is unattractive. That is why …" (with emphasis) "… Americans who have been in my country tend to 'fall in love' with it. It is because they find so appealing friendships with Chinese who have not been schooled in fear. Hate is not the opposite of love. Fear is. The very smell of fear is repellent. Animals know it.

Humans don't sense it consciously as a rule, but they do subconsciously, and react to it instinctively. The lack of fear is enormously attractive, even magnetic in the literal sense, and the *total* lack of fear comes across as pervasive love. ... You are probably thinking there are unattractive Chinese, too—" (I *was* thinking that) "—even despicable ones, if your consciousness is constructed to receive such impressions. But if you are here long, you will surely come to love China. The chief reason will be because the overwhelming percentage of Chinese have not been taught fear."

I did stay in China long enough to love it, and I think his reasoning, though by no means the whole story, has rock-solid validity.

My host continued, "But here we are picking apart and analyzing ... Let us enjoy." He took out his beads again. Chang was waiting when we returned. I greeted him, then turned to the master. I did not know what a proper leave-taking would consist of, so I just smiled appreciation. The master returned a magnificent, lingering smile, lightly touched my temple with the tip of his middle finger, muttered, "Good," then turned and walked into his house.

I thanked Chang profusely when he dropped me at the hotel, but I realized I was not very polite on the drive into town because of my silence. I was thinking, why didn't I even inquire as to my host's name? Why did I not ask whether he was monk or layman? Why didn't I ask dozens of questions to claim his wisdom, when I might have?

In the next day or two I saw why. If I had come away with dozens of 'nuggets,' each might have adulterated the other. As it was, I had come away with two stark, lasting and resplendent 'nuggets:'

1) Being defines, undergirds and is more elemental than doing; and

2) there is nothing—but nothing—to fear.

It is love that expunges fear, and the lack of love that produces it. I remembered what Chang had said about the 'master' I was to meet. He would not only love me because he loves everybody, he also loves every*thing*. I did not quite understand then how that could be possible. I think I do today.

SEVENTEEN

Terminal Illness Of A Dynasty

ne Sunday afternoon in the spring of 1966 I was lying on the beach at Lima, Peru when a telegram from Walt Rostow was brought to me. Walt was asking me to join the Senior Staff of the National Security Council at the White House. He was National Security Adviser to President Johnson. I was happy at the prospect of working with Walt, an old friend whom I respected.

My first act on the National Security Council staff was to write a memo to Rostow suggesting that we should get out of Vietnam. What I suggested may have been perceptive, but making the suggestion to Walt at that time clearly was not. I thought I could presume to speak my mind concerning a policy that I thought was destined for failure, but that memo simply served to drop a curtain between Walt and me on the subject of Vietnam. We never discussed it again, in all the time I was at the White House. At that point I did not realize that Walt was just as hawkish as President Johnson, who could never with any grace admit defeat—or anything less than success—on any issue. Fortunately, my responsibilities on the National Security Council staff involved only China and Korea.

I was sad. I think if we had gotten out of Vietnam about then it would have saved the Johnson administration and permitted him a second term. True, I had read articles reflecting on the shakiness of President Johnson's integrity when it stood in the way of his ambition, but I had great respect for his domestic program, for his seeming personal devotion to and belief in it, and for his ability either to charm or to bludgeon others into accepting it.

For a time Walt did not want me to accept public speaking engagements. I assume he thought I might not follow the official line on Vietnam. I certainly did not follow the line in some private government circles, but I carefully did so in public, elaborating it as convincingly as I knew how, as established policy, without overtly subscribing to it. He must have soon realized I was at least a reliable government servant, for he authorized (arranged, I assume) a *Time* reporter and photographer to interview me in my office. The picture of me before a map of China in the resulting *Time* article of January 27, 1967 was captioned "The watcher of the China Watchers," implying that I oversaw the other "China Watchers" in the State Department and elsewhere. That was an inadmissible exaggeration, though I was a primary funnel to the White House of opinion on China through Rostow, who probably had the attentive ear of the president on foreign affairs more than anyone else in Washington at that time, and through him I probably had the last word on China with the president.

We of my ilk were called "China Watchers" because in the absence of any diplomatic representation on the mainland of China we "watched" all the bits and pieces of overt and covert news, rumor and innuendo emanating from or about China, and tried to arrange them into some recognizable and meaningful composite. It was not easy during the roller-coaster era of the Cultural Revolution, the very time that I was on loan to the White House.

The day that issue of *Time* came to our house I saw our son, Stephen, reading it in the library downstairs. He did a double-take when he came upon my picture in it. He read the article, went back and focused on the "watcher of the China Watchers" caption under the picture, snorted, tossed the magazine aside, and said, "If they wanted to sell their magazine they should have run a picture of the watcher of the watcher of the China Watchers" (his photogenic mother.) So much for the likelihood of complimentary recognition for Dad from a fifteen year-old son in the 1960s.

I seemed then to have the green light to speak in public again, so I did so, far and wide. Unfortunately, it came just after I had rejected the invitation from an old college chum and fraternity brother, then president of a North Carolina College, to speak at his institution. I explained that in my position on the National Security Council staff I had to avoid a public profile. He saw the *Time* article two days after my rejection, and wrote me a teasing "what the hell" letter.

I was not only free to speak around the country as duties permitted, but was encouraged to give background briefings to the more reliable newsmen and columnists on my interpretation of the Cultural Revolution, the frenzy of which was threatening to tear China apart. I met with most of the leading news-folk in the Capital of that era, but perhaps most of all with Joseph Alsop, the columnist who at that time was immensely influential in government and throughout the country. At that time I was impressed by the high caliber of the Washington press corps in general, and came to have a healthy respect for the contribution of the press to the democratic process. I confess that I favored Alsop because he was generally regarded as almost uniquely influential in forming public opinion, he was a conveniently close neighbor in Georgetown, was a captivating conversationalist (if you were able to discount his egocentrism), and his French cook offered one of the best cuisines in Georgetown. If we wanted to meet on her day off, we met at the Metropolitan Club. It was the habit at the Club to be seated in the dining room by the maitre d', but Joe, totally in character, I fear, would invariably sweep by him and select his own table, unlike any other member I ever observed. I managed to be more amused than embarrassed.

Joe developed an excessive confidence in my appraisals of the goings-on in China, but my reputation on that score was in good measure due to the excellent briefings I received in turn from some sharp officials in the Central Intelligence Agency. In Alsop's column the day after one of our many luncheons he would usually over-agree with me by about thirty percent. He was no stranger to poetic license, if it helped to dramatize a basically valid point or to turn a phrase with style, at which he was a master. With all Alsop's considerable, but somehow not very offensive, arrogance, he was a warm, thoughtful and devoted friend. He passed on a few years ago, and I miss the visits I used to have with him.

Despite being on the National Security Council staff, on only about a half dozen occasions was I actually with President Lyndon Johnson, not counting his three-day visit in Stockholm as vice president. I believe I only met with him once in the Oval Office and once in the Cabinet Room, once for an evening on the presidential yacht and once for a White House luncheon. Nevertheless, I came to know him well indeed through colleagues and by pretty close observation. He was one of the most complex prominent figures I have ever known. He loved power and had over-leaping ambition. Yet he was the common man's friend. His domestic achievements were almost in a class by themselves. He could be the most persuasive man in town, yet he was brought down by a war he could not sell. He was a man of great feeling, of no small vision, often a charmer against whom there was simply no ready defense. He was characteristically thoughtful of his staff, sending us huge, frameable Christmas cards with personal messages, and gifts like gold tie clasps or cuff links with, not surprisingly, "LBJ" on them all.

It pained me that the President of the United States could sometimes be boorish. One day when we were meeting in the Cabinet Room of the White House with some dozen of the leading China scholars from universities all over the country, the president punched one of three buzzers under the table, the one that brought him a Fresca. When he had half consumed it, he asked, "Would you gentlemen like something?" No one would.

While I was on the National Security Council senior staff, President Johnson invited me to go on a dinner cruise on the Potomac aboard the *Sequoia,* the presidential yacht, The occasion was his entertaining the Asian ambassadors in Washington. The dinner went beautifully, but I probably made a misstep. At one point during cocktails the president headed for an empty seat next to me. I had always been schooled that foreign dignitaries should be given the place of honor, and what more honorable place than next to the president? Accordingly I gave up my seat to some Eastern ambassador—the Burmese, I believe. Johnson was silent and seemed miffed. He soon arose and went elsewhere. I was told later that he had intended to offer me an ambassadorship to a certain country where I think I would not have been particularly well suited. Only China interested me for assignment, so I'm glad I tried to be polite in surrendering my seat, thus saving me the embarrassment of being unenthusiastic about the president's offer. A bit later I was offered the ambassadorship to another country, but Walt immediately scotched that idea, saying it would be a waste to send his China specialist to a country so far removed from Asian affairs. I was appreciative. I would not have minded serving in that particular country, but I preferred to wait for a China assignment.

After dinner on the yacht we were invited topside, where we were shown two films produced by the United States Information Agency about—LBJ. On conclusion there was no applause. Secretary Rusk caught my eye and smiled helplessly and Averell Harriman lifted his eyes to the sky.

Johnson was at times demanding of services beyond belief, or at least beyond normal practice. After his visit to Stockholm as vice president, I congratulated the head of the Secret Service contingent traveling with him on a difficult job well done, indeed on their helpfulness to me with regard to a couple of unusual Johnson demands on the Swedish authorities. He replied, "Thank you, Mr. Jenkins, for noting and appreciating our efforts. We don't always experience that satisfaction. But I can tell you, if this had been the president (Kennedy) instead of the vice president, it would have been less than half the trouble." Lyndon Johnson was a big man, and did some big things, yet at times he could be socially inept. Still, I liked him, and hated to see the Vietnam war defeat him.

As implied earlier, I had long been convinced that it probably would. I had strong doubts about the validity of the 'body count' figures of Viet Cong killed that came in from the field, based on all I learned from both Vietnamese and Americans on my three visits to Vietnam and from my assignment in Southeast Asian affairs during the early days of our aid to the South. I had to bite my tongue when I had reason to talk with General Maxwell Taylor, a couple of doors down the hall from my office. I thought we would not win the Vietnam war because of the terrain that was unfriendly to our type of warfare, because the South Vietnamese government was unpopular and inept, but mostly because we were opposing nationalism even more than communism. Of course we could have technically "won" that war, if we had virtually annihilated North Vietnam. That would not only have brought on our heads the opprobrium of much of the world, which we began to earn in adequate measure anyway, but would doubtless have brought China fully into the fray, and the Korean experience did not make that possibility attractive. Furthermore, I did not view the Vietnam war as one that absolutely had to be won. I could not buy the idea of a Communist juggernaut rolling over Southeast Asia, and certainly I could not buy the concept of the domino theory that posited the fall seriatim of other countries of the area if Vietnam fell. Aside from China itself, Vietnam was the only country in the whole area where Communism had early aligned itself with nationalism. That was the really difficult-to-beat combination. Since that was not the case in other Southeast Asian countries, I did not believe that relatively puny Chinese efforts to subvert those other countries would be availing. Still, not only was Vietnam not my business, I probably did not have the full take of intelligence from the field on that subject. My platter was full enough with a China in horrifying turmoil during Mao's so-called Great Proletarian Cultural Revolution.

It has been an awesome thing to watch in the past four decades what is probably the world's oldest continuous civilization determinedly taking itself apart—at times, as during the height of the Great Cultural Revolution, seemingly blasting itself apart, with both method and madness—and then just as determinedly attempting to put itself back together again in vastly different form. During these years the Communist leaders set their country upon a new and different path, destroying the vestiges of its historical social order based on Confucianism, and attempting to build a new social order on Mao's brand of Communism, based on nothing less than a reconstituted human nature. Not surprisingly, that tall order is proving to be impossible to carry out.

Mao's most desperate attempt to achieve it was the decade-long so-called Great Cultural Revolution, beginning in earnest in 1966. Most scholars accept the date August 18 as the official start of the revolution, when the hundred-acre Tienanmen Square, filled with one million young Red Guards, thunderously wishing the Chairman long life. That same Square was the scene, more than 20 years later, of the most pro-democratic, hence anti-Mao demonstrations yet seen in China—and the scene of horrendous government slaughter of its youth.

Mao's principal aim in launching the Cultural Revolution was to reinvigorate the spirit of the Chinese people, to recover the spirit of self-sacrifice, egalitarianism, hard work, and confidence in the future that spurred the early years of his military revolutionary period (especially in his Yenan base), and which indeed characterized the very early years of his regime. Mao's age added urgency to this objective, if his dream was to be furthered after his passing. A secondary aim, allied with and viewed as necessary for the success of the first, was getting rid of a number of senior Communist leaders that Mao viewed as standing in the way of achieving his first aim. Once the press was again under Maoist control, this was done in an atmosphere of a virtual deification of the chairman by the press and in mass rallies with every fist holding high the "Little Red Book" of Mao's thoughts. This mass hysteria of Mao-worship was in large part whipped up by the urgings of Lin Piao, Mao's designated successor, who may have encouraged the Mao-worship as a cover under which he allegedly plotted to kill the chairman. In any event, the extravagant praise of Mao at this time went to such unbelievable lengths it led many to believe he was being more ridiculed than honestly praised. In the East, words do not necessarily mean what they seem to say. Extravagant praise may mean precisely the opposite. It could mean that the one praised had so lost prestige that he needed spuriously pumping up.

A sample from the Chinese press:

"Chairman Mao, Chairman Mao! You are the ... wonder of our era. Your glorious works contain the most penetrating thinking, the richest contents, the most brilliant theories, the most simple words, the highest prestige, and the greatest strength. Every sentence in them is a truth. One sentence equals 10,000 sentences. Your theory on political power growing out of the barrel of a gun, and your great call for combating self-interest and repudiating revisionism have most concentratedly, scientifically, and correctly expressed the universal law for the proletariat in China and throughout the world to seize political power, win victories in revolutions, consolidate political power, and carry the revolution through to the end.

" The whole world is shaking and the people of the five continents are shouting together with joy that Marxism-Leninism has developed to a new phase of Mao Tse-tung's thought, and the world has entered a great new era of Mao Tse-tung's thought." Could anyone believe that was NOT tongue in cheek? Just as the British take the prize for understatement, surely the Chinese then took the prize for overstatement, even besting the Soviets at the game. The sycophantic drooling about "the red, red sun in our hearts" went on and on. Yet a bit later it was widely reported that when Chinese spoke disparagingly of the infamous "Gang of Four" of Shanghai origin, who for a time were largely running the Cultural Revolution, they would often spread *five* fingers apart, representing the fifth member of the "Gang," Mao himself.

Through the Cultural Revolution Mao attempted to consolidate his authority over the country, to reverse what he considered to be a trend toward "revisionism" (a rightist drift toward an incentive economy and bourgeois mores), and to temper the younger generation through struggle for carrying on the Chinese revolution with something like its pristine fervor. Much of the party cadre had become complacent and lethargic, and the bureaucracy self-serving. The less extreme, non-Maoist policies, reinstituted after Mao's disastrous *Great Leap Forward,* had gradually gotten the economy moving again, only to be disrupted by the Cultural Revolution. Mao attempted to use the youth in the "Red Guard" phenomenon as chief agents for purging the bureaucracy.

To license teenagers to bring down their seniors was heady business for them. Hundreds of thousands of youths milled about the country, most converging on Beijing, and in effect disrupting much of the nation. The Red Guards' peregrinations en masse seriously compromised the transportation system, already a weak link in the Chinese economy, and that resulted in shortages of food, fuel and raw materials.

A large number of prominent figures were dismissed from their posts, or even jailed, accused of having followed an "anti-party, anti-socialist black line." In late 1966 even party Secretary General Teng Hsiao-p'ing and Chairman of the Republic Liu Shao-ch'i were denounced, and soon ousted. Not long thereafter Ch'en Po-ta, then presiding over the Cultural Revolution, claimed that Liu and Teng, together with P'eng Chen, ex-mayor of Beijing, had engaged in a plot to kill Chairman Mao. Evidently opposition to Mao was startlingly widespread among the most senior members of the Party, for a very few years later an article in the theoretical journal, Red Flag, claimed that Lin Piao, defense minister and supposedly Mao's closest comrade-in-arms, had kept a "sinister notebook" detailing plans for a plot to overthrow Mao. The article said this showed that Lin's never being seen without his book of Mao quotations and constantly shouting long life to Mao was a cynical sham.

The Red Guards not only were instrumental in bringing down numbers of officials who opposed Mao, they destroyed untold quantities of priceless antique art objects as being unrepresentative of the new China, and visited public torture and at times death upon individuals deemed to represent ancient ways. Not surprisingly, there was also a rash of suicides during the Cultural Revolution.

In the supercharged atmosphere of the time the Red Guards made absurd demands. They wanted to revamp the traffic light system, for it was inconceivable for red to be the stop indicator in a Communist society. They wanted to change the name of the capital from Beijing (Northern Capital) to Tung Fang Hung (The East is Red).

Still, the Red Guards were by no means unified in their allegiance. They fought among themselves, as did the workers in the cities, and even the farmers. Stemming from a quiet paranoia typically characteristic of totalitarian states, the vast majority of the citizenry were not so much committed ideologically to one side or the other as they were simply striving to end up on the winning side. In the tense emotionalism produced by the Cultural Revolution, however, it was difficult not to be pressured into commitments. Those who made a serious commitment knew that they would not likely be forgiven by the opposition if it won out. They usually concluded, therefore, that they must fight on with whatever means they had. Since the Party had traditionally won out, the tendency was to side with the bureaucracy, but by the spring months of 1967 most were betting on the Maoist revolutionaries.

To some extent the factional fighting was a power struggle between the entrenched and the aspiring. In part it was prompted by a clear and wide generation gap. Most of the positions of responsibility were held by men of advanced age who participated in the famous Long March of the 1930s, and until the Cultural Revolution there was little upward mobility—indeed, not very much even at that time.

Mao met a degree of opposition that must have surprised him, as he turned to various segments of Chinese society for support in his Cultural Revolution. His final reliance had to be on the military, which eventually brought a measure of order out of the alarming chaos, but even its allegiance was not monolithic.

Most activities requiring harsh and onerous party control collapsed during the Cultural Revolution. For example, the corvee peasant laborers on rural construction projects returned to their villages with impunity and gratitude. Huge numbers of urban students forcibly settled in rural areas to "bring knowledge" and at the same time to learn from the peasants, to get their hands dirty, to see suffering, to hear of the past, and—not incidentally—to free the cities of troublemakers, took the opportunity gleefully to flee back to the cities. Usually the peasants were as happy to see them go as the youths were to go.

It is obvious that there was extensive disruption to the economy during this chaos, but possibly the greatest cost of all to the nation was the fact that the educational system was a shambles for a decade.

In a very real sense Mao's basic opponent would seem to be human nature itself. He was trying in a romantic way to remake humankind in a hurry. One of his most misguided, ineffectual devices for doing this was the usages of hate: class hatred at home and a generalized hatred against foreigners—chiefly against the United States and the Soviet Union. However, at least 36 other countries were roundly denounced in this period, some of them supposedly good friends. The sharp deterioration in Sino-Soviet relations was largely occasioned by what the Chinese saw as the progressive *embourgeoisement* of Soviet life and the decreasing international militancy of the Soviet Communist Party.

In January 1967 I wrote to Ambassador Parsons in Stockholm with respect to the Cultural Revolution:

"This Wagnerian enactment of the failure of a dynasty, for all the world to see, will certainly damage the image of Communism itself as a way of life and of governing, and this may be the most far-reaching implication of this whole incredible show (the Cultural Revolution). Not incredible in that it was unexpected; I think you and I have long thought the last days of Mao and the post-Mao era would be ushered in with considerable convulsion. While musing on the beach in Lima last spring I began to wonder if the convulsion were not in the offing, but it came a bit sooner and with more madness than I had expected. The madness, it seems to me, comes largely from the phoniness of Mao's revolution. It is inverted——a revolution instigated from the top, with little felt need in the mass base (at least in the context Mao had it), until a carefully pre-deified Mao stirred up the base. No wonder it's going awry, since it is fundamentally anachronistic. The Yenan syndrome is not reproducible in today's China. Meanwhile, so far as senior personalities are concerned, it seems to be open season on almost everyone by almost everyone, and especially by that inflated virago, Chiang Ch'ing (Madame Mao Tse-tung), who is suddenly a big shot and enjoying every minute of it.

"I said last August that I thought Mao was on the skids physically and perhaps mentally, and that Maoism was definitely on the skids politically. I see no reason to believe otherwise now, except that mentally Mao may still be intact in a way, though unbelievably misguided."

Madame Mao evidently helped bring about the Cultural Revolution and was a prime leader in it. She was the Number One deputy in the Central Cultural Revolution Team established in the summer of 1966. It was ostensibly headed by Ch'en Po-ta. Later that year Madame Mao became adviser on cultural matters to the Liberation Army. She was thus probably mostly responsible for a production of "The Red Detachment of Women," to which, for my sins, I was subjected at least three times during the Kissinger trips, the Nixon trip, and later when I was stationed at our Mission in Beijing. It was impressive ballet calisthenics, but hardly "cultural," and unfortunately the

Chinese characters shown on a screen to upper right during the songs made the dreary, heavy political content linguistically, and, in confusing measure, philosophically semi-comprehensible.

Chiang Ch'ing's sudden and spectacular emergence to prominence must have been especially satisfying to her, inasmuch as she had long been unpopular with the Party, being regarded as an upstart, arriving in Yenan as an unknown B-picture movie actress and making a play for the great chairman. There was resentment that Mao had abandoned his well respected second wife, Ho Tzu-chen, who had borne him five children and was one of only 31 women who survived the legendary Long March. For a little over a year the Chinese Communist forces fled from Chiang Kai-shek's Nationalists to establish their base at Yenan. Almost 100,000 started the trek. They crossed innumerable rivers and mountain ranges, sometimes on such narrow mountain trails that men and beasts fell to their death. Something like a tenth of them arrived in Yenan. Yet Mao rejected the woman who had shared this agony with him.

This was a time of relative silence, so far as United States Government public statements were concerned. We were reluctant to comment on the chaos in China out of regard for the Chinese people. We did not want to say anything that might in any way be a disservice to them at this time of great trial for them. And it certainly was that. When I returned to Beijing after a 23-year absence I finally found a friend I had known in the old days. Noting his haggard look and the many lines in his face, I asked if he had suffered during the Cultural Revolution. His immediate, pained answer was, "Dr. Jenkins, *everyone* suffered during the Cultural Revolution."

I concluded a letter to a graduate student doing a paper

on China with the following in early 1968: "It seems likely that China in coming months, and perhaps even for several years, will continue in a state of some disruption. No one can say just what will follow, but I believe that China is passing a watershed heralding fundamental changes. I think there will be a trend toward an incentives economy (in line with trends in other communist states), although the system will doubtless be *labeled* communist for some time to come. Even a Maoist label, as symbol of a national cohesion that in truth does not exist, may be retained, while allegiance to many of Mao's policies will surely go by the way. He made some grave errors. As Machiavelli pointed out long ago, those who have the special knack to create a large organization seldom have the quite different—almost contrary—arts of administration and maintenance.

"It is less likely, but still possible, that revulsion to some of Mao's policies may bring about a regime of little continuity with the existing one. It is even less likely, though conceivable, that the military at some point may have enough of witnessing their country's travail and seek a solution crisper than the more likely course of gradual evolution through costly trial and error. This would be contrary to Maoist philosophy, which, while maintaining that political power grows out of the barrel of a gun, cautions that the Communist Party must at all times control the gun. I do not know anyone who claims with much conviction to know just what sort of China we will be faced with a few years from now. Much will depend upon such factors as the fate of the domestic power struggle and the success or failure of the "peoples' war" type of aggression and subversion in Southeast Asia. Other factors that could fundamentally affect the shape of China range from a denunciation of much of Maoism after his demise, to the probability of accelerated change in the rest of the communist world."

Again, I wrote to Jeff Parsons: "At some point the Middle Kingdom is going to get into gear, program itself to mesh with the modern world, and forge ahead. We may then have even more troubles, unless we have a concomitant social and political maturation on both sides enabling us to reduce the potential danger. This would mean facing up to some of China's real needs as a nation, when it gets under auspices that make such possible. This will not be easy for us. It will, however, be made easier by the gradual de-sexing of Communism worldwide, to which this present curious fracas should contribute handsomely."

(The "de-sexing" has happened in the '90s, breathtakingly.)

It seemed to me that it should be obvious to all that this was no time for us to try seriously to deal with the Chinese. Main themes undergirding the Cultural Revolution were anti-imperialism, anti-free enterprise, generally anti-Western values, and especially anti-Soviet Union and anti-America. Nevertheless, much of the public, including much of academia, which should have known better, were prodding us to do something about our supposedly neglected China policy, as though it were primarily the United States that was isolating China. The U.S. government certainly shared the concerns over the dangerous degree of isolation from the rest of the world of the mainland Chinese. That regrettable isolation, however, was chiefly self-imposed. It resulted from several causes, but perhaps most of all from Beijing's strong sense of ideological rectitude, from the messianic implications of that, from the consuming fear that outside ideas would make inroads on doctrinal purity (as they certainly would) and from the aggressive actions and words stemming from these considerations.

Many people have forgotten that we left both consular

and diplomatic personnel in China after the Communists took over, for some six months after the formal establishment of the Mao regime. This meant that in many areas of North China our officials were in Communist-ruled areas for over a year. They were withdrawn only when harassment made it impossible for them to stay with dignity. Furthermore, we gave no tangible support to the Nationalist Chinese on Taiwan until the Korean aggression in mid-1950. Up until then the Truman administration was seriously considering recognition of the Chinese Communist regime. We met officially at the ambassadorial level with the Chinese Communists over 130 times, in addition to meeting with them at conferences in Geneva. We proposed an exchange of journalists, and we unilaterally validated passports of American correspondents for travel to China. We indicated our willingness "unilaterally and without reciprocity" to see Chinese Communist newsmen enter the United States. There was no response. We gradually made relaxations on travel, trade and exchanges, with virtually no response from the Chinese. It was evident that in the 'devil's role' to which Mao assigned us, we served a useful purpose in his scheme of things at this time. In Chinese eyes we seemed to have been accorded the role of an 'enemy ally'—allied in the cause of maintaining Chinese revolutionary fervor! Indeed we began to wonder when, and whether, we would ever be released from Mao's inimical embrace. As mentioned earlier, we were pried loose from that sort of embrace courtesy of the Soviets, by their military buildup on the Chinese border, their invasion of Czechoslovakia, and the presumptuous Breznev Doctrine, designed to maintain the integrity of the communist bloc by force if necessary.

By the summer of 1971, therefore, for the first time since the outbreak of the Korean War in 1950 all lights were green for an approach to the Chinese. All Washington seemed to exhale at that gradual realization. The danger posed by a quarter of humanity under dogmatic and paranoiac leadership, that threw China into an agonizing siege of sickness with highly xenophobic manifestations, had long concerned much of the world. The chance to do something about it was a moment in history that had to be grasped and run with.

EIGHTEEN

The Kissinger Call

he road to Sino-American detente was a long one. From 1954 to 1970 Chinese and American ambassadors met for 134 sessions to discuss matters of mutual concern, first in Geneva and Prague, then in Warsaw. While assigned to the Embassy in Stockholm I traveled to Warsaw nineteen times as adviser in those talks. The encounters, held at an ornate former imperial hunting palace on the outskirts of Warsaw, were politely acrimonious, revolving around such issues as our participation in the Vietnam war, our support of the rival Government of the Republic of China on Taiwan, and Chinese support to revolutionary forces in Southeast Asia. Because of the relentlessly inimical stances taken by both China and the United States, each against the other, the talks over a period of some fifteen years were unproductive.

Finally, a little progress was made in the late 1960s, almost entirely at United States initiative. Even this was little more than a relaxation of travel restrictions and a gradual toning down of the anti-communist rhetoric in presidential utterances and in *Voice of America* broadcasts. About the turn of the decade some of the trade restrictions imposed because of the Korean war were gradually relaxed. When I was Lyndon Johnson's China watcher on the National Security Council staff, it was not until my third attempt that the president agreed to call the Beijing regime by its preferred name, the Peoples Republic of China, instead of calling it Red China, Communist China, the Mao regime or just the mainland regime, distinguishing it from the Free Chinese regime on the island of Taiwan.

In the last of the Warsaw meetings both sides finally indicated readiness for a higher level meeting. The Chinese were moved to this position primarily by the large Soviet military buildup on their border. The Nixon Doctrine, emphasizing a substantial U.S. disengagement from Asia, also helped make Sino-U.S. rapprochement possible for the Chinese. Unfortunately, however, the invasion of Cambodia in an attempt to knock out the Viet Cong Headquarters and disrupt supply lines caused the Chinese to break off the talks before the idea of a top level visit could be pursued.

Kissinger, at that time National Security Adviser to Nixon, astutely saw this break in the Warsaw talks as an opportunity to get the State Department out of the action and to assume control for the White House. With the cooperation of Pakistan, Romania and Norway, he established secret "back channel" communication with the Chinese— that is, channels not using the normal State Department codes and radiocommunication facilities, but employing the codes and other facilities of those countries.

Reassurances of the readiness to meet at a higher level in Beijing were again exchanged, but the proposition remained quiescent through most of the spring of 1971. Then, through the Pakistani channel, the Chinese reiterated willingness to receive a special envoy, whether Mr. Kissinger, the secretary of state, or the president himself.

During a publicly announced trip through Southeast and South Asia Kissinger feigned a stomach upset in Pakistan and pretended to retreat to the hills to recuperate. Instead he was taken to the military section of the Islamabad airport where he boarded a Pakistani plane with a Chinese crew. With three aides, Winston Lord, John Holdridge and Dick Smyser, plus two security men, on July 9, 1971 he landed at Beijing, to begin paving the way for a presidential trip to China. Secrecy this time made sense, and was not simply due to the Nixon-Kissinger fondness for secrecy per se. While Nixon's love of the dramatic and his desire to keep the State Department out of the act probably were at play, secrecy was justified on the basis of avoiding emotional debate in the media and in Congress on the pros and cons of the action. The public was made aware of the trip after the fact, when it was warmly, even excitedly, received in almost all quarters.

I could not have accompanied Kissinger on this trip because the media knew that my responsibilities were primarily with respect to Communist China and were aware that I had no responsibilities at that time for Southeast Asia, which was the ostensible destination for Kissinger's trip.

Kissinger, upon the announcement of his secret trip to Beijing, was catapulted into international prominence, to Nixon's dismay. Actually, neither gentleman has demonstrated fondness for seeing anyone else shine. Kissinger's desire to keep the opening to China under his control up to the time of the presidential trip, and to take major credit for

it, did not endear him either to Nixon or to Secretary of
State William Rogers. Furthermore, his inordinate love of
secrecy led to a diplomatic *faux pas* which was far more
serious than the discourtesy he tried to depict it as being.
He failed to inform Japan, an important ally, of our
approach to Beijing. Tokyo had consistently requested that
the Japanese leadership be apprised of any significant U.S.
movement toward China. It had been Secretary Rogers'
plan that Alex Johnson, former ambassador to Japan, be
sent to Tokyo to inform the Japanese of our approach to
China before public announcement of it. Nixon was at first
in agreement with that plan, but Kissinger convinced him
that leaks would occur.

Soon after the announcement of that journey to arrange
a presidential trip Kissinger called me over to the White
House. At that time I was director of the Office of Asian
Communist Affairs in the State Department, with responsibility for Communist Chinese, Korean and Mongolian
affairs. Some of my colleagues expressed surprise that I
wanted that job, after having been a senior inspector for the
State Department-Foreign Service, and having served on
the National Security Council Senior Staff, but I regarded
the job as a choice one. It entailed receiving the daily take
of intelligence reports from all available sources in
Washington and in the field, especially as related to
Chinese, Korean or Mongolian affairs. It was my responsibility to approve reports that made their way to our in-
house superiors or to other agencies. Many of those reports
contained key background information and appraisals that
helped to form the basis for major government policy. I
also made occasional trips to the Far East or to London,
Paris or Geneva on Far East matters. In Washington I
sometimes chaired inter-departmental meetings of representatives from State, Defense, Commerce, the Central

Intelligence Agency and other governmental organizations convened to create policy papers. From time to time I gave briefings on the Hill, at the United Nations or to the National Security Council staff. I met regularly with officials of the C. I. A., various White House requests had to be met, there were callers to receive, and lunches with newspeople or others of professional interest. Because of a widespread and growing interest in China, I did a great deal of public speaking around the country at universities, Foreign Affairs Councils and clubs, explaining Chinese developments in a domestic, regional and global context, and our policies with regard to them. For a time, indeed, at least within government, I gained a small reputation as "Mr. China."

I liked and admired Kissinger for his intellect, his wide knowledge, his delightful wit and his personal magnetism. At the same time, Kissinger's philosophy, like Nixon's, was too Machiavellian for my taste. I had already heard from some who knew him that he had a reputation for deviousness. His later career affirmed his addiction to secrecy and love of intrigue.

To my relief I did not note those proclivities in his dealings with the Chinese, except for the secrecy of the first quick trip. As perceptive as Kissinger is, he probably saw that, apart from any other considerations, one might as well deal straightforwardly with them, for they are too smart for one to indulge in the supposed delights of intrigue and get by with it. The Chinese can at the same time be disconcertingly perceptive, diplomatically deft and starkly telling in bringing the foreigner up short. For instance, if they suspect that a foreign guest is not what he declares himself to be, they have been known to change the true Chinese character for his surname on his dinner placecard to a character of derogatory meaning but similar pronunciation!

When I was ushered into Dr. Kissinger's office he greeted me immediately. "That's a good start," I said to myself. Sometimes persons of power in Washington, especially newcomers to the heady scene, would finish reading a paper on their desk before acknowledging a caller standing silently by. Presumably this was a puerile attempt to emphasize their importance.

Kissinger's handshake had just the right degree of firmness and duration to connote at the same time confidence, acceptance and friendliness. I immediately liked and was intrigued by this stocky, bespectacled ex-professor, of medium height, curly greyish-black hair, insouscient assurance and avuncular geniality, although I later learned that the assurance had a questionable foundation and the geniality could be turned off and on.

I then turned to acknowledge with exceptional pleasure a long-valued friend and colleague, John Holdridge, who had succeeded me on the National Security Council Senior Staff.

I was asked to have a seat. I noted with interest that Kissinger's office was grander and in a more prestigious location than that of his predecessor, Walt Rostow. I had been in Walt's office many times. It was in the basement of the White House, where Kissinger, too, had been located when he first became national security adviser to the president. His office now was a corner room on the ground floor of the White House, and near the Oval Office. The character of his office became symbolic to me. I wondered whether the upgraded status was due to the nature of Kissinger, to the nature of Nixon, or to a change in the nature of the job. I later decided it was all three. Kissinger gave the impression of being supremely self-confident in most situations because of his prodigious intellectual endowment and his facile way with words, and he had a 'presence' that seemed to assume, hence to attract, top-level treatment.

Nixon, on the other hand, while also well endowed intellectually, was a shy man, who attempted to camouflage his shyness by assuming an air of great importance. He was a man who seemed to need a loyal, strong confidant at hand, even while resenting that strength. Stationing Kissinger on the ground floor of the White House, in an office of attractive decor and not far from the president's office, appeared to be agreeable to the needs and natures of both men.

After brief initial pleasantries, Kissinger suddenly asked me, "What is your Foreign Service rank?"

"Class One."

"Do you know how that equates with military rankings?"

"I don't think in those terms."

Kissinger smiled. "I don't believe you do." Although I did not, I think Kissinger already knew the equivalency rank in the military; he was merely interested in knowing how important considerations of rank were to me. This seemed curiously to matter to him. Curiously, that is, until I was told later of an alleged incident when a Foreign Service officer expressed unwillingness to share a room with Dr. Kissinger on an official trip. The story goes that the man insisted his diplomatic rank entitled him to private quarters equivalent to those provided for a general. If the anecdote is true, it perhaps helps explain Kissinger's antipathy to the State Department, which, ironically, he would later head. Doubtless more important in explaining Kissinger's oft-expressed negative feelings about the State Department was a cue from his boss: the president was determined to run foreign policy from the White House rather than the State Department. This was not just an ego-driven preference, although there was surely a strong element of that. While the State Department, with its specialists in many fields, can offer invaluable counterweight to sometimes half thought-through White House ideas, too often it moves with glacial deliberation, and it is not known for innovation.

After asking about my equivalency status with respect to military rank, Kissinger turned his attention to John Holdridge, What is your Foreign Service rank, John?"

"Class Two," John answered. Kissinger nodded.

In this meeting with Dr. Kissinger he asked me nothing about China. I assumed he had been satisfied that I knew something about the subject from talking with people like Joseph Alsop, the renowned columnist, and John Fairbank, Harvard professor and recognized dean of academic China specialists, as well as with my colleagues in the State Department. I suspect it was primarily Joe who recommended me to Kissinger as one not only knowing something about China but also as one not obsessed with rank. I shall not hazard a guess as to which qualification was the more important.

Kissinger soon came to the reason I had been called to meet with him, continuing much as follows:

"The president is going to China. I am to prepare the way for his visit by going to China for discussions with Premier Chou En-lai on matters of concern to our two nations. I want you and your staff to prepare position papers, in utmost secrecy, for use in those meetings. Also, I have spoken with the concerned State Department officials and I have their agreement for you to go with me."

I would have been happy at the prospect of returning to China under almost any auspices after 23 years of enforced absence, during which time we had no formal diplomatic relations with the Mao regime. I was doubly happy to be going there with Kissinger on such significant trips—nominally, at least, as his senior adviser. Because of the secrecy surrounding the project, I was able to get only two members of my staff cleared to prepare a huge tome of "talking papers" for the upcoming negotiations. We could draw on all the resources of Washington, but we had to camouflage the reason for our requests, for a time even those directed to the Central Intelligence Agency. If we had worked in my office it would have been difficult to keep substantive matters secret from the rest of the staff. Accordingly, we were given an obscure suite on the seventh floor of the State Department, where papers were prepared some ten to twelve hours a day for a number of days. A paper was drawn up for every subject we could think of that could come up between the two sides. We gave the background and history of scores of topics, ranging from support of the Vietnam war, Soviet actions and policies, and the question of Free China on Taiwan, to trade possibilities and an exchange of journalists, students, and athletes. We outlined the probable Chinese position, the suggested position we should take, and often one or more fallback positions in case of need. The limits of our "falling back" were also indicated, such as our inability to meet the other side's desire that we abandon or appreciably lessen support for Taiwan.

The two members of my staff who were cleared along with me were my deputy, Bill Brown, and Roger Sullivan, who started out being my special assistant until someone observed that only Assistant Secretaries of State could have a special assistant. We couldn't think of another title for Roger, for that is what he was, so he became my uncapitalized special assistant, and everyone seemed content. In any event, they were two of the most brilliant Foreign

Service officers I have ever encountered. The knowledge, wisdom, foresight and thoroughness along with economy of expression embodied in those papers were impressive. Although I was responsible for the content of the final versions on which Kissinger relied almost exclusively in his negotiations with the Chinese, Bill and Roger produced the whole job with dispatch and assurance, with almost no substantive input from me. This was partly due to the fact that we had discussed most of these issues many times and thought much alike, but also because China was a subject of such interest, senior people all over Washington were after me over the phone or calling at my office (not at the obscure suite) for briefings or for appearances at this and that occasion, and I had no time except to read and approve the splendid and voluminous output of those two men. I was told that Kissinger had been heard to comment at the White House that the job was the best thing he had ever seen come out of the State Department.

Kissinger especially enjoined me not to let anyone at State, even the secretary, know that a draft of a proposed final communique for the later Nixon visit existed. I was able to make no mention of it for a long time, but one day not far from the date of the presidential trip I was in the office of Alex Johnson, Undersecretary of State for Political Affairs, on another matter, when he suddenly asked me whether anyone had prepared a draft final communique for the presidential visit. This presented a dilemma for me. I began to perspire. I could not lie to Alex, even under implicit instruction to do so. He had been a good friend for years, and I not only admired his ability and integrity, I also respected his judgment. Therefore, with an intentionally exaggerated show of discomfort I paused, sighed, fingered my tie, and said in a low voice, "It exists. It is a good one." I knew Alex well enough to know that he was sufficiently experienced in governmental affairs and savvy enough in any affairs, including the lamentable Kissinger-Rogers feud, not to pry further. He smiled, nodded, and dropped the matter.

Kissinger and Secretary of State Rogers did not work well together, to put it more charitably than the feud deserved. Kissinger did not like to share power—or secrets, which he saw as tools of power. Also, in part, he was simply reflecting Nixon's penchant for secrecy and his desire to keep State Department influence to a minimum. There were other reasons for secrecy, of course, including the practical one of keeping knowledge of the project to as few people as possible, so that leaks would not get to the Chinese or others before the negotiations.

For months the Kissinger-Rogers friction made it awkward for me. Rogers was my "home base" boss, and I came to have a high opinion of his judgement and of him as a truly decent and able gentleman. Still, with State approval I was on loan to the White House for this project, hence in effect under presidential orders, through Nixon's National Security Adviser. I had to reason that my contemporary primary allegiance was to the White House, since the president was Rogers' boss. I was not supposed to discuss preparation of the papers with any of my State Department colleagues or superiors. However, once the negotiating papers were completed, I thought it would not be proper for them to leave the State Department without the Secretary's seeing them. With some qualms, I decided to give a copy of the tome to Rogers as I sent one to Kissinger. I did not want to try to obtain Kissinger's permission, because I was afraid he would not give it, and I thought it would be too much of an insult for the Secretary not to see his subordinates' production. I had the temerity to stress the obvious to the secretary, by way of strong caveats as to its secrecy.

I knew it was coming. I held my breath when I next went into Kissinger's office. First thing, he asked, "Has anyone else seen the book of position papers?"

I struggled to inject into my response a flavor of 'certainly, what else?' I said matter-of-factly, "I have given a copy to the secretary, with cautions about how closely it is being held," I explained.

Kissinger's face registered both dismay and disapproval. I thought, there goes my chance of returning to China, or as a minimum there will be a strained relation between us. I spent a few anxious moments before Henry relaxed and said with a resigned smile, "Of course. You had to do that." I breathed easier. Kissinger asked, "What do you think he will do with it?"

"I'm sure his intention is to hold it closely. He has to go to New York, however, and he indicated he would take the book with him."

"That is not good," Kissinger said with finality.

"I didn't think it was my place to tell the secretary just *how* he was to hold the document closely," I explained. "Shall I attempt to retrieve it before he leaves?"

"No," Kissinger said, smiling more broadly, "I'll handle it in my own devious way."

The matter of the handling of the book was immediately eclipsed in my mind by concern about Kissinger's use of the term "devious." Here was a man with whom I was to travel and with whom I was to work pretty closely for a time. I wanted to know as accurately as possible what he was like. Even if he was at times devious, why would he in effect confirm the characteristic? Possibly his reference to such a trait was meant only as a would-be humorous, self-deprecatory gesture such as he had come to use, often effectively, to soften his arrogance. Still, it would seem to be at least an admission that he was aware of his reputation.

I reasoned that one would only make such an admission if one considered that deviousness was merely clever, and not reprehensible. That, it seemed to me, would in turn imply a view of the world very foreign to my own. It is possible that Kissinger's background and experiences in Germany would inevitably cause him to have a view of the world very different from mine. I recalled a conversation with my father that had been etched on my mind when I was fourteen.

Straight from school I went into my father's study and sprawled on the floor. Father sensed I had been wounded. After a few moments he quietly said, "You aren't yourself. Want to tell me why?"

"Bernard told a lie about me to my new girlfriend."

"How do you know?"

"Louise showed me the note he passed her in class. He said she should beware of me, because I had been naughty with other girls."

"You haven't been, have you?" Father asked.

"Of course not, but she doesn't know what to believe. I'll get even with Bernard somehow."

"Now, wait a minute, son, before you compound your problem. You've first got to find out why Bernard did such a thing—what it is in his background that would cause him to act like that. You must not just assume that he is a mean person. He may have a misguided need to hurt you because he has been hurt, or thinks he has suffered in some way." There was a long pause, while Father looked out the window. Then he resumed, "By the way, did your new girlfriend take much cultivating?"

"Not really. She seemed ready to be my friend. But now ..."

"Then couldn't jealousy be involved, because of your easy success with Louise?"

"Why should Bernard be jealous?" I asked. "His dad's rich. You know Mr. Schwarz, the jeweler. Bernard has a big allowance. He should have all the girl friends he wants."

"Have Bernard's classmates treated him well?" Father wanted to know.

"Some don't like him, and they sometimes show it."

Father looked at me quite a while. I became uncomfortable, but I had nothing else to say, and I sensed Father did. Finally, "Son, you can't help it, but you were born a WASP." He explained the term, saying it should be totally irrelevant, but unfortunately was not. "That means you have to be especially careful never, never to 'sting' anybody unintentionally. I know you would not do so consciously." Father lit his pipe, not looking at me, and asked, "Wouldn't it be more in your interest to set about making Bernard your friend? Then he wouldn't do things like that, and he might even try to correct what he has already done to you."

After a long, meditative pause, I said, "How do you 'set about' making him my friend?"

"Be *his* friend," was the staccato reply.

Within a month Bernard and I were inseparable, and would defend each other against all comers. Furthermore, he was dating Rachel, who, if anything, was even more attractive than my Louise, and the two girls were pals, too.

Thinking of my friend Bernard, I began to have some inkling as to why Kissinger was so defensive and why it is said that he sometimes found justification for means sometimes considered reprehensible, in the attempt to attain respectable ends. I have read that throughout his childhood in Nazi Germany he was taunted, belittled, and even attacked by his schoolmates because of his Jewish ethnic and religious heritage, and that he lost a number of close relatives in the Holocaust. I do not believe he has suc-

ceeded in erasing that era from his mind or his heart—
understandably.

In a way, the making of a self-professed enemy into
something of a friend would soon be tested by us with
respect to China. Of course the project before us was not so
simplistic. International power politics was very much at
issue. In any American policy, however, power politics
should not be the near-exclusive consideration. Despite the
supposed lessons from the clever old power games of a
Europe very different from the Europe of today, and fundamentally different from the America of any day, if some
sort of neo-Wilsonian idealism as a true and historical
strength-component of this country's approach to the world
is not taken into account in policy-making, then the policy
will not be realistic, for us. Of course at times the realistic
and idealistic components each may have to make conces-
sions to the other, but they usually can be mutually supportive as well. In the American context they must be, or
we deny a prime factor behind our historically demonstrated influence and power. I saw little indication of
Kissinger's cognizance of that, and it troubled me. With his
prodigious endowments, I believe he could have meant
more to his adopted country and to the world than he did.
He meant a great deal as it was, but I believe he also undermined a bit the foundations of our strength, which I feel he
never fully understood. I think every high public official
should periodically go through the foyer of the National
Archives Building and read the awesome documents there
laid out under glass, the documents that originally shaped
us and still impel us. It should be a requirement for assuming high office.

These thoughts went through my mind while Henry
thumbed through the tome I had sent over. I studied this
man. I wanted to become his friend, and not because he

was a notable public figure. He was just beginning to earn that status. Had he already achieved it, I doubt that those who worked with and under him would have been addressing him by his first name, and we all did. I wanted to be his friend because ever since I heard his speech at the National War College years earlier I sensed that I would enjoy his company as I had that of few people. That proved to be true.

Before the first detailed negotiating trip to China—not counting the secret trip to arrange a trip—I was called to Kissinger's office once more, when there was again no substantive mention of China. The gathering was in order to have press pictures taken that included Kissinger, John Holdridge, Winston Lord (assistant to Henry) and me. The subject of our discussion was primarily Lord's mother and her activities at the United Nations. I don't know what the resulting picture in Newsweek was meant to connote to the public, unless it was Kissinger deigning ostensibly to be briefed by a State Department official. The picture rather looked like I was doing that, but actually I was merely saying that I, too, thought Mrs. Lord was a remarkable woman. I was only momentarily puzzled by this strange meeting, for I had already come to the conclusion that such goings-on were vintage Kissinger. I tried to believe that the nearly-great man knew what he was doing. He appreciated the tome that my office had prepared, but he was too proud to elicit any appreciable *verbal* input from me. At the same time he seemed to want the public to believe that he was relying to an appropriate degree on State Department support. Of course I disliked the ruse, and was insulted by the patent nature of it, but I decided not to show how I felt, or to show insult if Kissinger thought I was naive enough not to see what he was up to.

Before we broke up the meeting Kissinger called in his

personal aide, a young Foreign Service officer by the name of Lawrence Eagleburger, and spoke to him in a belittling manner in asking him to bring in a certain document to show me. By way of "explaining" why he wanted to show me the document, he said in Eagleburger's presence, "We have no secrets from the State Department." I think I managed to keep a straight face. I was embarrassed by the impolite treatment in my presence of this fellow Foreign Service officer. Eagleburger responded with glum silence and went for the document.

I understand that Eagleburger had a physical breakdown on that assignment as aide to Kissinger, because of the latter's work demands and tantrums. However, thereafter he learned better than most of us how to deal with Kissinger without personal injury, and when Kissinger became Secretary of State, Eagleburger served as Undersecretary of State, the number two position in the Department and the highest rank achieved by a career diplomat up to that time. He topped that. When Secretary Baker moved over to the White House as Chief of Staff, to help Bush in his efforts to be reelected, Eagleburger became Acting Secretary of State, then Secretary. Eagleburger was well liked and respected at State, on the Hill and by the news media. Small wonder: as a man apparently totally self-possessed (content with his being) he had no need to strut, dissemble, prevaricate or toady. What attractive freedom he thus gave himself!

Kissinger's arrogance and fondness for demonstrating his power over others caused him to treat various members of his staff badly at times. I have known them to make demeaning gestures of a well-known and unequivocal nature in his direction behind his back. Understandably, these usually followed after Kissinger seemed especially to relish a just-dispensed insult or pointed slight.

Although I had never been the brunt of Kissinger's mis-treatment, it worried me, for arrogance and the psycholog-ically sadistic use of power are unfailing advertisements of weakness. The ego element in arrogance is blinding, and regardless of brain power, if one does not see clearly and in perspective one makes mistakes. I have seen the careers of too many people in Washington marred, or worse, mainly by arrogance. In my association with Kissinger I came to view him as of such value in the U.S. interest, at least in his handling of the U.S. opening to China, that I certainly wanted him to see clearly and to succeed.

For each of these negotiating trips to China Kissinger had quite an entourage with him. The plane Henry used was a clone of Air Force One, either of the twin planes being designated Air Force One only when the president was on it.

Kissinger was consistently thoughtful of me, except for an occurrence in the last moment I saw him before I retired from the Foreign Service—events not totally unre-lated. I shall describe that later. At the press picture-taking on departures, for instance, if I stood aside he would call me over to be by his side, for some purpose of his own. I suppose it was another gesture of reliance on the State Department. Also, in our two- or three-day layovers in Hawaii (one does not go into serious negotiations with jet lag) the entire top floor of the hotel for security reasons would be devoted to his party, unless he elected to stay at the private residence of some prominent person on the island, and I would have quarters close to his, or else a clone suite to his at the opposite end of the floor. I told him he was spoiling me, and confessed that I found it agreeable.

I had ambivalent feelings about the glee with which the world press, then and for some time to come, heaped praise on Kissinger. I thought he deserved generous recognition, but I saw trouble to come for him, due to the sometimes ridiculous extravagance of the praise. The media love to hoist its favorite of the moment onto as high a pedestal as possible, thus enhancing his newsworthiness. Unfortunately, when the media tire of a particular pet, or tire of the superlatives applied, or when it becomes evident that the hero has feet of clay, they seem to take equal satisfaction in denigrating him. Usually, some elaborate puffing up of their pet has presaged that act. I therefore expressed concern to my wife about the implications of the cover of an issue of *Time* magazine showing Kissinger in a Superman outfit. I liked Henry as an entertaining and intensely interesting friend, and I thought he was handling affairs with consummate skill in the area that I knew— China. I certainly did not think it would be in the nation's interest for the media to tire of him.

Actually, Kissinger remained in high favor with the public and the press far longer than most prominent public figures. However, the press was treating him more evenhandedly by the time I retired from the Foreign Service in mid-1974. Soon after my retirement the *Los Angeles Times* asked me to do a column concerning an imminent Kissinger trip to Beijing. After predicting what would be taken up and saying in effect that he would do and say all the right things, I added, "If he stumbles, he is more likely to stumble over himself than anything else, for very, very few men in history have been big enough to surmount the adulation with which he is handicapped." I did not want to see Kissinger stumble. I had no idea the column would be syndicated so widely. Friends sent me clippings from all over. Later, when I greeted the good doctor, then Secretary of State, at a reception at the State Department, I said (truthfully), "I've missed our association." And (facetiously), "I can't possibly imagine how you have gotten along without me." His response—I know not what it was meant to convey—was, "Not very well."

He was probably sincere in saying that he was not doing well, for by the mid-70s he had lost credibility in many quarters. Morality has never been his strongest suit. I have never enjoyed the association so much with a person about whom I had significant reservations. Despite his well publicized faults, I have found Henry to be always interesting and frequently entertaining.

NINETEEN

U. S. - China Rapprochement

hose of us who were to accompany Kissinger on the first fully substantive negotiating trip to Beijing gathered in the little street between the White House and the Executive Office Building, loaded our luggage into White House cars, and were driven to a military airport where the great blue, white and silver clone of Air Force One awaited. The press corps was out in force, taking pictures of the party from the cordoned off area.

There were some eighteen of us about to board, including John Holdridge, Winston Lord, several military, economic or other specialists, and two of Henry's secretaries, of requisite pulchritude, replete with typewriters and copy machine. The plane was an eye-popper, at least to this Georgia boy. Kissinger had a sitting room, a bedroom and bathroom with tub and shower. At the touch of a button the coffee table in the sitting room would rise to writing or dining height. I seem to recall that some wall appeared and disappeared on need, but I've forgotten what the need might have been. I do recall that the food was better than I have had on any other 'airline.' Every compartment of the plane was provided with electronic clocks showing three times: the time where we were at the moment, the time in Washington and the time at our destination. On my desk was a package of cigarettes with the presidential seal on it, stationery with a gold-embossed Air Force One letterhead, and a neat sign reading "Director Jenkins." I winced at the pomposity of that, but realized someone was just trying to be nice. Also on my desk was a phone that had a number of perplexing blue, white and yellow buttons. I was told I could be in touch with the White House at the touch of a button—a requirement of which I felt scant need. In fact, I didn't use the phone at all until on a later trip I called Martha from 35,000 feet above Alaska. I was assured it would not cost the taxpayer anything. The leased line (or rather, satellite channel, I should think) had to be open at all times, and in case of need my conversation would of course be summarily terminated.

HAK, an appellation that we often hung on Dr. Henry Alfred Kissinger, was in a jovial mood on the trip. His justly renowned wit was at its best. He roamed through the plane bestowing his charm on all. He was confident, I am sure, of his performance in coming events, and he was in charge—a combination designed to bring out the best in most of us. He saw me thumbing through my copy of the tome of negotiating papers that my office had prepared for him and asked if I was going to pontificate from it in Beijing. I replied, matter-of-factly, that as nearly as I could determine, I was going to do, or not do, exactly as he desired, for he was in charge. He smiled.

During the long voyage over the Pacific I tried to picture to what sort of China I was returning. In doing so, my former exhilaration at returning turned to sadness and even a bit of anxiety. I knew it would be very, very different from the China I had known and of which I had become so fond. I had known Communist regimes in eastern Europe, so I expected regimentation, drabness and resignation. I also expected a few impressive achievements in the intervening quarter-century, from Soviet tutelage and Chinese genius. I became saddened when I realized that there would not be the easy rapport between Americans and all classes of Chinese, a circumstance that I had valued most of all in the China of the late 1940s.

On landing at the Beijing airport we were met by appropriate officials from the Foreign Office and whisked into and through the city to the Government Guest House compound. I say "whisked," not because we were driven especially fast, but because the route was ours alone. At every cross-street in the city masses of pedestrians and bicyclists were collected behind a police cordon. We were driven in large, black, Chinese-made Red Flag limousines that were comfortable, silent and powerful. As was the custom in the Soviet Union, cars carrying officials were thinly curtained so that the passengers could see out fairly well, but people on the street could not see in. I asked if I could open my curtains, and was invited to do so.

At the airport and along the route into the city there were billboards with Mao sayings in large white characters on a red background, a couple of them curtly anti-American. By the time of the Nixon visit these had been taken down, and not many years later, after the chairman's death, commercial advertisements, many of them of Japanese and American products, appeared for the first time.

I was appalled at the architectural styles all along Ch'ang An Chieh, a street I had known well in the 1940s, during my first assignment in the Foreign Service. Now most of the buildings were unimaginative, ponderous structures of strong Soviet influence.

It was gratifying, however, to see that all Chinese in evidence were neatly and adequately, if drably, clothed, in dark blue or grey unisex trousers and what were called Mao jackets. Actually, the severe jackets, buttoned to the top, are Sun Yat-sen jackets, originated by that George Washington of China. I also noted that seemingly everyone had a bicycle. Not only that, but later, when it rained, virtually all of the sea of bicyclists sported a black plastic raincoat. That impressed this old China hand who had witnessed the deprivations of the old days, when such protection from the elements was seldom seen. We passed the old Forbidden City of imperial days, with the huge portrait of Mao Tse-tung above the southern entry to the palace grounds, facing Tienanmen Square. The entrance to Mao's quarters in the western part of the Forbidden City was pointed out. It was not excessively imposing, and there were but two guards at the red doorway.

What impressed me most strongly, however, as contrasted with the old China, was not fully to be explained visually. It was a matter of atmosphere, a sort of heavy societal aura: one of tension, of regimentation, of resentment, of resignation. It appeared in the faces of the silent crowds at the cross-streets. The Cultural Revolution was still going on.

In short, while I was exhilarated by the potential of the road to detente on which we had embarked in coming to China, I was at the same time inexpressibly disappointed and saddened by much of what I saw and sensed, especially later in the week when we had time to shop and to roam the streets a bit. I missed the carefree noises of the streets of old Peking.

We were housed in the Government Guest House compound in the western part of the city. It contained several yellow brick mansions randomly set in well kept grounds, with beds of flowers, shrubs, stately oaks, weeping willows, and a large lake with a colorful tea house. The residence in which we stayed was spacious and formal, with high ceilings and an imposing staircase leading from the reception hall to the second floor. The effect was reminiscent of many 1920s Florida boom hotels: austere, grand and comfortable.

The Great Hall, where we went to meet Premier Chou and other notables, consisted of rooms representing and decorated by the various provinces. There were also reception rooms, offices, a large theater and a colossal dining room, a vast expanse with no supporting columns. I am a layman in such matters, but that struck me as a remarkable architectural achievement, especially since the ceiling, at least the visible one, was not arched.

Premier Chou received us with dignity and reserved warmth. He was definitely not on any pedestal. I would say that his personal 'presence' took over the room, but it was more passive on his part than that. The room rather sought to be taken over by him. The set of his thick, black eyebrows strengthened his handsome features (he played feminine roles in plays as a young man). His voice was well modulated, a little high-pitched but vital. Here was a mild-mannered, immensely civilized, self-possessed gentleman. His reputation was that he could still be calmly ruthless, but only as a last resort, when conciliatory efforts failed to gain the goal.

We were introduced to some twelve other Chinese officials and led into a large reception room for tea, picture taking and get-acquainted conversation. The more senior people sat in overstuffed chairs arranged in a horseshoe shape, others in row seats to one side. I counted 51 people in the room, all of whom were in a photograph taken after the meeting, which appeared in newspapers around the world.

Before the Nixon trip we made three trips to China of a week each, preparing the way. Generally, it is not desirable that chiefs of state get together, especially for a highly publicized summit, until it is reasonably certain what will happen when they do—and the Nixon trip, at least every event or utterance of any interest that was not classified, was destined to be covered in the media in record-breaking detail. The Kissinger trips were therefore designed to explore points of disagreement and possibilities of agreement on a whole host of issues of mutual concern. Negotiations were conducted on these issues, subject to later presidential review.

During Kissinger's visits to China I sat on his right for the negotiations with Premier Chou En-lai, except for an occasional session. It may have been that Vietnam was the principal subject at those times. Kissinger must have known that for some three years I had not been in sympathy with our Vietnam policy. Walt Rostow may have told him. I did not think we understood well enough the psychological and philosophical drives that made the Viet Cong so fanatical. We were aware of, but did not pay enough attention to, the colonial antecedents to the problem and the fire-in-the-belly Vietnamese response to them. It was my conviction that, in our comfortable, affluent, then overwhelmingly powerful circumstance, we simply had not engaged in the exercise of trying to picture the inextinguishable, do-or-die rebellion that would be produced if our country had been run—virtually owned—by semi-well meaning, perhaps, but arrogant, comparatively superprosperous aliens.

We were also stuck with trying to support an inept and corrupt government in Saigon. The more we supported the South Vietnamese, the more dependent and the less effective, the more indolent and corrupt they became. There seems to be something about support tendered by a powerful friend like the United States that causes the recipients to relax their efforts, and often to spend their time and energy in feathering their own nests, resting in the false security of a powerful and concerned friend—a friend often seemingly more concerned than the recipients of the support.

I could not forget an incident on an orientation tour of Southeast Asia, when I was riding through the Vietnam countryside on a tour offered by our local chief of the Agency for International Development. We were driving behind a South Vietnamese government jeep in which was a captured and bound Viet Cong prisoner of war. The A.I.D. chief predicted that the South Vietnamese soldier would simply release the Viet Cong prisoner and not turn him in at his headquarters. Sure enough, a few minutes later the jeep slowed down and the prisoner, unbound, hopped out and ran across the fields, a free man. There was, of course, no pursuit, or semblance of one. The prisoner may have bought his freedom, but it is more likely that the South Vietnamese soldier released him because he was sympathetic to the Viet Cong.

I more and more regretted that Averell Harriman, then a roving ambassador in the new Kennedy administration, had stopped me from speaking out at a small meeting in the State Department on Vietnam policy about the psychological, philosophical, historical and political factors that so powerfully drove the Viet Cong. The meeting was designed to set the tone for Vietnam policy in the early days of the Kennedy administration. At that time I was Far East Planning Adviser for the State Department. I had spoken for only three or four minutes when Harriman interrupted me, saying, "Mr. Jenkins, this is a can-do administration. We don't have time for psychology and philosophy." I gulped, then muttered, "Then we will make a great many mistakes." However, in the resulting chorus of agreement with the 'can-do' Kennedy philosophy I think only Alex Johnson, who was seated beside me, heard my muttering. I wish I had said it louder, but it would have had no practical effect in the Camelot climate of the early Kennedy days.

After we had become actively involved militarily most authorities in Washington seemed primarily interested in the "body count" (the often misreported number of Viet Cong killed in action over a given period). I did not suspect that the body count was nearly as exaggerated as it turned out to be, although I once voiced some concern about that subject to General Maxwell Taylor, whose office was down the hall from mine. His reply was a shake of the head, which I could not interpret. I was repelled by the "body count" terminology itself and by the frightful number of lives and the amount of substance that the seemingly bottomless Vietnam pit continued to swallow up.

Furthermore, I did not believe that the possibility of a communist juggernaut rolling over Southeast Asia in the event we did not stem the tide in Vietnam was sufficiently likely to warrant the hideous expenditure of life and substance. The conditions for revolution were not nearly so ripe in other Southeast Asian countries as in Vietnam, and I thought the Chinese Communists were right in pointing out that ripe indigenous conditions were prerequisite to successful revolution.

I was also well aware of the difficulty of extricating ourselves from Vietnam with our national honor intact, but when the end finally came we did not accomplish that very convincingly, anyway. Of course that should not detract one whit from the honor of those who fought there.

Perhaps Kissinger, in having me otherwise occupied on a few occasions when he met with Chou, may have done so in part from not trusting me to keep my mouth shut on the subject of Vietnam, or at least to keep my face impassive. I was always careful to do so, except in U.S. Government inner circles. The closest I ever came to indicating publicly less than enthusiastic support for our Vietnam policy was in the spring of 1973, when in a speech at Emory University I said I thought we had entered the war "with honorable intent and monumental ignorance." I still think so.

There may, of course, have been more sensitive issues that Kissinger wanted kept strictly to himself. For whatever reason, at times he had me, and sometimes John Holdridge, negotiating with the assistant foreign minister on such matters as trade, educational, scientific and sports exchanges with the Chinese. Kissinger rightly concentrated on his major objective of creating a stable triangle of power among the Soviet Union, China and the United States, leaving lesser matters for Holdridge and me to explore. Nonetheless, these lesser matters were highly useful stones in building the Sino-American bridge of greater mutual understanding.

Mornings were often taken up with sightseeing. The Great Wall, of course, had to be seen. It is the largest construction project ever carried out on earth, the only man-made object visible with the naked eye from the moon. It stretches 1500 miles from east to west, and was originally designed to fend off the Huns from the northern border.

Parts of it date from the Fourth Century, B.C. In the Third Century, B.C., the Emperor Shih Huang-ti connected the disparate parts of the wall, which have been substantially rebuilt in recent times. The wall averages about 30 feet high, with towers rising to 40 feet. It is wide enough for five or six people to walk on it abreast.

Later, during the Nixon visit, a sight-seeing itinerary similar to that of the Kissinger visits was carried out, but with a far larger American and Chinese entourage. When a reporter asked the president what he thought of the Great Wall, he observed that it was a "great wall." (I was right behind him and heard this revelation.) The remark, which was duly reported back home, produced a momentary hush in the gathering on the wall. I was amused, but not sur-prised, that Marshall Green, the quick-witted assistant sec-retary for East Asian and Pacific Affairs in the State Department, jumped into the breach by saying to the Chinese interpreter, "Washington would be interested to know what the cost overrun was for this project." There was appropriate laughter. Actually, the true "cost overrun" consisted of the lives of numerous laborers who built the wall and are buried within it.

Back to the Kissinger visit. Photographs of us at the Great Wall appeared the next day in *The People's Daily* of Beijing, a nation-wide newspaper. After that the crowds that we encountered in sightseeing or shopping were more friendly. They 'got' the official message that such was per-mitted. They still did not welcome verbal exchange, how-ever.

On the other hand, it was a frustrating time for foreign, especially American, newsmen in Beijing. They thirsted for any tidbit of news of what was transpiring in the Kissinger-Chou negotiations, but their thirst could not be slaked. When accosted by them on our brief shopping tours

I finally tired of merely smiling and turning away, as we were supposed to do. I broke down, for several of the reporters were friends of mine, and I ventured, "I would really like to help you, but you know I can't." Even that daring, scarce opening of my mouth made the news back home! We were supposed to be so close-mouthed I half expected Henry to object to it, but he didn't.

In the little time we had to walk the streets I was puzzled by how silent the pedestrians were. They seemed bone-weary from the demands of the heavy-footed regime and especially from overlapping political campaigns in a society of incessant authoritarian exhortations.

Another sightseeing treat was a visit to the tombs of the emperors of the illustrious Ming dynasty, who ruled the country from 1368 to 1644, a period of native governing sandwiched between the Mongol dynasty and the Manchu dynasty. The Ming was one of the most stable periods in Chinese history. During the dynasty the Chinese extended their control into Burma and west, Mongolia and Takistan on the north and west, and Korea on the northeast. It was a time of notable artistic and literary achievement, and it saw the perfection of the civil service examination system, the manner of entrance into official ranks that lasted until 1911. That year marked the collapse of the Ch'ing dynasty, successor to the Ming, and in fact saw the end of imperial rule in China.

The cavernous tombs well reflected the glory that was Ming. Unfortunately, the priceless objects of artistry that the tombs must have once held have long since disappeared, through looting.

There was also a conducted tour of the Imperial Forbidden City and the Palace Museum. The spaciousness of the grounds and grandeur of the architecture are so photogenic, many major magazines have featured pictures and detailed articles thereon, so I shall not elaborate here. The museum, of course, contains some of the most priceless treasures in porcelain, lacquer and cloisonne vases, jade carvings, scroll paintings and other artistic creations to be found anywhere. In contrast, it also contains doubtless well-intentioned, but often gaudy or overly clever gifts given to the court by foreign dignitaries. One, for instance, was a wooden figure of a young man in casual dress who could actually smoke a genuine cigarette and blow out the smoke.

Afternoons were for the negotiations, though they were sometimes held at other times as well. They were usually held in one of the province rooms, often the Fukien room, in the Great Hall of the People. There would be twelve to fourteen people, half Chinese and half Americans, facing each other across the table. On the table were pads and pens, cigarettes and matches, and porcelain cups for green tea. In the practical Chinese fashion the cups had lids but no handles, so that one cannot fail to determine whether the drink is too hot to swallow. There probably were also bottles of orange pop, but I have a mental block to recognition of the overly sweet drink, which unfortunately was ubiquitous in China. The two principals, Kissinger and Chou, were flanked by their several aides, a scribe on either side, and an interpreter on the Chinese side only. Supposedly, Kissinger saw no need for an American interpreter, since both Holdridge and I understood Chinese. Besides, he surely did not want one of the State Department interpreters. So far as I have observed in international negotiations, even when both principals understand both languages, an interpreter will normally be engaged by each side, if only to give the principals time to think about what was just said and to phrase their own next utterances while the interpretation is going on.

Each session with Chou opened with pleasantries. It was typical of Chou En-lai's graciousness that in the first meeting he acknowledged each American at the table, indicating that he was aware of each person's expertise or past connections with China. In my case he noted that I had not only lived in Beijing, but also in Tientsin, where he had spent considerable time as a youth. Sometimes there was picture-taking, but we soon turned to business. Watching and listening to Chou En-lai and Henry Alfred Kissinger, high officials of two great nations that for so long had been in inimical confrontation—in no small part because they were dangerously ignorant of each other—now patiently informing and respectfully sparring across the green felt table, had to be one of the great shows of the 20th Century. Truly two of the most intelligent men to be found anywhere, each with a saving sense of humor, one with an engaging modesty and the other possessed of what at times, *mirabile dictu,* was an equally engaging arrogance. The latter was pretty well held in check on these occasions, however, for Chou En-lai's modesty did not invite a contrary display. In striking contrast to the Warsaw talks, the principals were carefully and politely listening to each other after almost a quarter century of hurled accusations by both sides. Now they were attempting to find common ground on which to build a safer, saner, mutually profitable relationship. Exciting, it was. And often so exquisitely performed by both principals it was at the same time an aesthetic experience.

In the first session each side gave its version of the history of the last century or so, with emphasis on the last 25 years. The two versions were not exactly congruent, but they were so absorbing that a couple of times I found that I had left my mouth open as I listened. The exchange afforded a unique opportunity for each side to understand why the other thought as it did, on issues ranging from war and peace to colonialism and 'peoples wars.' It is not surprising that the two views of the recent histories of Korea and of Vietnam differed fundamentally. Each side saw what it was doing, or had done, in both countries as its duty in its self interest, and each side thought it was also acting in the interest of the world. We saw our efforts as assisting those who gave clear indication they did not want to assume the communist yoke. The Chinese saw our intervention as inexcusable meddling, too near to Chinese territory for comfort. At times the historical review was presented with such unrestrained candor I could hardly believe what I was hearing. After all, I was much more used to hearing the stylized, venomous froth of the Chinese-American Warsaw talks.

A number of misunderstandings were cleared up in the formal discussions with the Chinese. One important one involved a sheer mistranslation of a phrase in one of Nixon's speeches. The president had said that we intended to be second to none in our strength, whereas the Chinese translation implied that we sought, through overwhelming strength, world hegemony and domination! One wonders how much the translator was injecting his own prejudices. Anyway, the exhilarating realization was that prejudices—on both sides, really—over the course of the three pre-presidential substantive visits began to fall away, like the not-so-slow melting of a forbidding glacier. Throughout the talks there was a notable absence of diplomatic doubletalk. The candor was always refreshing, sometimes startling. Nothing was swept under the rug. Some differences were baldly, if politely, stated and readily labeled as real, but possibly not insurmountable. Other differences simply dissolved through better understanding. We complained about Chinese aid to subversive rebel forces, principally in

Southeast Asia. The Chinese side could not convincingly deny such support, for the evidence was conclusive. Yet Chinese officials had frequently said that China "did not believe in exporting its revolution." That did not mean, Chou hastened to explain, that the Chinese were unconcerned about revolutionary developments in other countries. He not only held that the Chinese revolution was not being exported, he insisted that it could not be, since revolution must follow naturally from local contradictions within a given country. We pointed out that even so, that was not consistent with their claim that China did not interfere in the affairs of another country. Chou replied in effect that the Chinese could live with such inconsistency. I was reminded of Emerson's saying that "a foolish consistency is the hobgoblin of small minds." In any event, clearly we were not dealing with small minds.

Once when Kissinger had me negotiating with the assistant foreign minister on scientific, educational, technical, journalistic and sports exchanges, I presented at some length a carefully prepared package of a number of such possibilities for consideration. My Chinese opposite number accepted the package with coolness, even unconcern, "for further study." I was neither surprised nor disconcerted by this superior, off-handed, semi-rejection of a thoughtful and detailed—actually a very friendly—package of suggestions for closer association. Considering more than a century of what the Chinese justifiably viewed as ignominy at the hands of the arrogant and exploitative West, it was not surprising that in the New China the attempt would be made to put us in the role of supplicant.

I was then expected to present a number of suggestions regarding trade. In reaching for that packet of my papers, I mentioned that it contained numerous suggestions for possible trade relations. The Chinese negotiator promptly said several times, arrogantly and peremptorily, "We are not interested in that subject, not at all interested." He had spent time as a model in New York when he was a young man, and there were in fact traces of the classical facial features of his youth remaining. He evidently considered himself to be an authority on our country and the character of our people. He seemed to believe that Americans were such economic animals that I would be obliged by back-home pressure to return with attractive agreements on trade, if necessary at the expense of begging, if not groveling, for them. Although I certainly had been expected to present the trade package, I had no intention of presenting it in any such context, so I simply said, "In the event of your disinterest, I suggest we proceed to the next item on the agenda." I then solicited and received a nod of agreement from Holdridge, and exhaled when Kissinger later also agreed with my tactic. That evening at the banquet the Chinese "specialist" on America was red-faced and flustered. Evidently Chou had roundly reprimanded him. The two sides were soon in serious and profitable, mutually respectful, trade negotiations.

In the next negotiations my opposite number, not surprisingly, was a different Assistant Foreign Minister, Chang Wen-chin, a soft-spoken, able and pleasant gentleman who later was Ambassador to the United States. He reminded me that we had known each other in Tientsin soon after the "liberation" (Communist victory), but that we could not at that time be friends. The ex-model America specialist, I was told, had been dispatched as Ambassador to Mexico. I was sorry. I rather liked him, and sympathized for him in his would-be patriotic blunder, but I, too, had my country's dignity in mind.

As I looked across the dinner table at Premier Chou I reflected on the growing mutual admiration between

Kissinger and Chou. Even in the initial secret trip Chou En-lai had impressed Kissinger. It was obvious that the admiration was returned. It occurred to me that each gentleman probably seldom, if ever before, had encountered a fully worthy opponent. After the first session with Chou, Kissinger had said to Holdridge and me, shaking his head in admiration, "We are dealing in the big league with these people." He had, of course, dealt in the biggest of leagues. He indicated he much preferred dealing with the Chinese than with the Soviets. "With these people you know when you are getting somewhere," he said. I wondered whether it occurred to him that the reason was precisely that, contrary to ancient Chinese reputation, these people were more open than devious in their dealings—at least in the light of their present needs.

I think all of us were impressed by the caliber of the Chinese with whom we were dealing. One day in the lounge provided for our times of relaxation several of us fell to characterizing the Chinese people. That is an audacious thing to do with respect to a vast country with a 5,000-year history then in the turmoil of the Great Cultural Revolution, but we came to substantial agreement on the following points:

First, we considered that the Chinese, not only those with whom we were dealing, were uncommonly intelligent. We conceded that while the anthropologists and sociologists insist that there is no ethnic corner on intelligence, the Chinese seemed to us to be something of an exception to the rule. Certainly, a remarkable percentage of Chinese students going to the States for study are straight-A students. For my part, I can remember only one rather stupid Chinese whom I encountered in all my eight years in China (including Taiwan and Hong Kong).

Second, we considered the Chinese to be almost patho-

logically energetic—when motivated. Witness fabulous
Hong Kong, largely built by the Chinese with the British
furnishing the law and order and only a part of the man-
agerial expertise. Witness the economic miracles of
Singapore and Taiwan. Communism was clearly not com-
parably motivating.

Third, we recognized the obvious: the Chinese are a
proud people, and it behooves one to remember that fact in
dealing with them. A case can readily be made to justify
Chinese pride. For centuries China was by most measure-
ments the most advanced nation on earth. China had a
highly civilized culture at a time when our European ances-
tors were tossing bones over their shoulders at the dinner
table for the dogs' delectation. Furthermore, two centuries
before Christ the Chinese created a form of centralized
government that the West did not achieve for almost two
millennia later. In the Confucian tradition government was
to act according to ethical principles based on learning
rather than on divine revelation or aristocratic inheritance.
Never mind that the learning eventually became rote and
sterile. Initially it was an impressive step ahead. There was
a belief in the perfectibility of human nature by scholarship
and ethical precepts. Princes should rule by example rather
than fiat. Much like Mao's brand of communism, however, Confucianism was more appropriate for a sedentary,
agricultural life rather than for commerce, industry, and a
gearing into the requirements of international intercourse.
Both have been steadily eroded as China has, with great
discomfort, reluctantly yet intentionally begun to succumb
to the realities of modern institutionalization, urbanization,
domicile mobility, informational glut, and interdependence
to the point of transnationalization. Ancient China today
has been sucked into the rushet of modernity from which it
is unlikely to emerge.

In speaking of Chinese pride I was reminded of an evening of beer-induced conviviality spent with a Chinese-American graduate student at the University of Chicago. We had become close friends. We had been speaking of American folkways and mores, when I said, "Pao-an, you seem so much at home here, did you have no cultural shock on first coming to America?"

"Oh, no. My family had been 'Westernized' for two-and-a-half generations, and I grew up in Shanghai, a sophisticated industrial city. Here it's more of the same, only better." We spoke of other things, then he returned to the subject. "Come to think of it, there is one thing I didn't think I would be able to stomach when I first came. Here at the university after the athletic period, when we all go to the showers, I have to shower with a whole roomful of fellow students who are mostly Caucasians, and there are no partitions. It's not a matter of modesty, of course, it's a matter of sheer revulsion! (He put his hand on my arm to soften his next words.) "You hairy apes!" he said. "To us Easterners it simply means we've been out of the trees a lot longer than you have!" Very possibly true.

Fourth, we decided that the Chinese, the traditional ones at least, were possessed of a different sort of logic than ours, and that, too, must be taken into account. Traditional Chinese logic seems to employ the rather subjective criterion of "the fitness of things," a far cry from our more mechanical Aristotelian syllogistic logic of major premise, minor premise, followed by the inevitable conclusion. One may state to a traditional Chinese a major premise, the associated minor premise, and have him agree to both, then grandly state the inevitable conclusion, only to have him respond with finality, "But it isn't fitting, (or appropriate, or convenient.)" Chinese logic is associated with a sense of balance. If one does a traditional Chinese a

284   Country, Conscience And Caviar

favor, he is almost in pain until he can return the favor (redress the imbalance). On the other hand, if one does a Chinese a disfavor, it is well to batten down the hatches, for the storm is coming.

At that point in our discussion Henry burst into the room and called to me, "Mix me a martini, Al." I turned to go to the credenza to do so, but he called out from across the room, "Never mind. I don't want it. I just wanted to see if you would do it." What a question! Of course I would do it. It would never occur to me not to make a martini for *any* friend who asked me to, particularly for one who may have just come from negotiations a deux or at least from serious, solo cogitations. Kissinger seemed strangely to need further assurance that I was not one of those haughty stuffed shirts, who he erroneously thought peopled the State Department-Foreign Service.

While we had little time to use the lounge, mealtimes were relaxed and unhurried, the meals sumptuous and delectable. In the early evening there were banquets in the Great Hall of the People. There would be fourteen Chinese and Americans at the main table and four or five satellite tables of ten people each, to accommodate the rest of the party and an equivalent number of Chinese. All the tables were round, according to Chinese custom.

Each meal of the day was a wondrous production. The best of Chinese food is unbelievably labor-intensive. Breakfasts and luncheons were normally at the Guest House, with only the American group at two large, round tables. At breakfast I once suggested to Henry that in view of the thoughtful planning and considerable effort in preparing our meals he might want to ask the chef to come to the dining room to receive our praise and thanks. He thought it an excellent idea, but upon my inquiring through the server, we were told that it would be better to express our thanks upon departure at the end of the week, when all the servants would be lined up in the foyer. I think the main chef was probably not fittingly clothed when we asked for him. I was reminded of the experience years ago of our Consul General's wife, Mrs. Myers, when one hot summer's day she insisted on inspecting her kitchen unannounced. She thought it odd that her head chef backed around in showing her the kitchen, until he forgot and turned around, at which point it became evident that his only garment was a frontal apron.

After the evening meal there was usually entertainment, be it a musical, truly wondrous acrobatics and juggling, or various sports in a spectacular new arena with a floor that could fold away electrically to reveal an ice rink. At performances we witnessed, the arena was always filled with Chinese, evidently produced on call or at least by careful prearrangement. They were in colorful dress, grouped by colors into sections, so that in the distance the banks of seats opposite us resembled a formal flower garden.

The musicals were the only form of entertainment that was rather hard to take. In late 1966, in the early stages of the Cultural Revolution, Chiang Ching had been named cultural consultant to the Political Department of the Chinese Army. That was her first official position. From it she held sway over the musical productions.

o   o   o

While returning home from our third visit a flash message was received in flight that Beijing at last had succeeded in gaining a seat in the United Nations at the expense of the Government of the Republic of China on Formosa. Henry strode up the aisle of the plane toward me with the telegram in hand, shaking his head and shedding a few crocodile tears at this event, implying that it distressed him. I knew that it did not, but supposed that he wanted me to mention his 'distress' to colleagues in the State Department, who had virtually made a career of keeping the Chinese Communists out of the United Nations, in order to keep Free China in. I can't believe that he thought I was that naive, but who knows? I was not amused. I was not even grieved at the announcement myself, although I was well aware that the preponderant sentiment in the Department of State was against admission of the Mao regime into the U.N. For my part, I thought it was past time for a quarter of humankind to have representation in a body designed to knit the world more amicably together, even at the highly unfortunate cost of Free China's losing its seat. I felt that way despite my recognition of the relative virtues of Free China as compared to the cynicism and sheer unworkability of the Communist system on the mainland, and despite my friendship with, and in many ways admiration of, Chiang Ching-kuo, then president of the Republic of China on Taiwan. Several years earlier I had conducted Chiang around the United States on a five-week tour. Naturally I said nothing to Secretary Rogers or to anyone else about Kissinger's non-existent distress.

While schedules were similar for each of the three weeks we spent in China in preparation for the Nixon week, there were occasional deviations, such as overnighting at Anchorage, Alaska, in returning from our third trip. The one-day delay was because it was deemed unseemly for Kissinger to arrive in the States from China on the very day that Free China lost its seat in the United Nations to the Communist Peoples Republic of China.

At breakfast in Anchorage the next morning I was seated at a table for two with Kissinger, when he said, "I have just received an invitation to attend festivities on 'Alfred Jenkins Day in Georgia'." (Governor Jimmy Carter had issued a proclamation to that effect for May 12.) Kissinger paused, noting my non-reaction. I already knew he was being invited, against my judgment. The planners of the event were well-intentioned, but I thought even sending Kissinger the invitation was presumptuous. They could not realize in Atlanta the shell of prestige with which many high Washington dignitaries coated themselves.

"I'm going," he added. "You are a credit to your state." I knew he had no idea of doing anything of the sort, hence my passive reaction to begin with. Volunteering that he was going to attend was a curious thing for him to do—not the best example of his humor. It was something of an insult for him to think I would believe him. I could not conceive of his attending any event designed to laud someone else.

Moments later, while I was pondering his intent in making the patently false declaration, I suddenly heard him saying that someone had observed that he was "the second most powerful man on earth." That made me fear for his balance, and that bothered me considerably. It bothered me because I thought only an insecure person, not centered in his being, would repeat such a remark about himself. An insecure person easily allows ego to get in the way of judgment, no matter how brilliant or how patriotically dedicated the man is. If the man is a public servant, that's troubling.

Although my assessment of Kissinger's personal qualities is mixed, I have valued and do value his friendship because of those qualities that are admirable and enjoyable. The press and various biographers have reviewed almost *ad nauseam* Kissinger's alleged deficiencies and worse, including his sometime cavalier attitude with respect to morality (the "duplicitous" and "devious" tags, his secrecy and intrigue-prone addictions) even while, often as an afterthought, delineating his remarkable assets in intellect, in negotiating talents and in personal charm when it is turned on.

I thought Kissinger did his part in the China opening brilliantly—with style, consummate diplomatic skill and, I believe, with unvarying straightforwardness. Fortunately, it is primarily in that context that I have had the pleasure of knowing him. Whatever may be said of the gentleman, I have never experienced a moment of boredom in his presence.

One evening Chou En-lai honored us with a small, intimate dinner in an area of the old Forbidden City where a number of the top officials resided. I do not recall any American present besides Henry and me, except Holdridge, but that may have been because in the relaxed mood I fear that Henry and I shamelessly monopolized the conversation with Chou. I thought it a particularly agreeable affair (perhaps for that reason), with much talk qualifying as banter. At one point Kissinger's previous connection with Harvard was mentioned. I solemnly explained to the premier, to Henry's amusement, that Harvard was "a pretty good school: we at Emory, in fact, refer to it as the Emory of the North." (Emory is actually widely known as the Harvard of the South.) Chou played along, nodding with equal solemnity.

One morning in returning to the States from one of the trips, when we had worked on the plane much of the night dictating papers to hand to the president on arrival in Washington, I said to Kissinger, "I hope to go home to bed as soon as we land. When will I see you again?" His answer was revelatory of Nixon's make-up: "Well, I don't know, Al. I am to have dinner with the president tonight. If after dinner he shows that film "Patton" to his guests one more time, I shall shoot myself."

The nature and special characteristics of both gentlemen have been so thoroughly, not to say mercilessly, dissected by psychohistorians and some others of closer and longer association than mine that I am not disposed to engage as exhaustively as I might in that international sport. I shall observe, however, that I never expected to meet a prominent man who was more complex than Lyndon Johnson, but Nixon was. I say "was" partly because since the time I knew him in very limited personal contact but to a great degree vicariously through mutual friends, I have gained the impression that today he is more in possession of himself and is somewhat less complex. In his present role of outspoken elder statesman he evinces much less of the hazards of egocentrism and the weaknesses of arrogance. His rehabilitation in the public eye since Watergate and resignation from his high office has been remarkable, and I believe his role as elder statesman has proven to be of value to the country.

Nevertheless, the relationship between Kissinger and Nixon has always intrigued me. For a long time they were indispensable to each other in serving their professional and at times personal needs, and in doing so they often served the country with distinction. Yet it is clear that neither gentleman harbored an unstinted admiration for the other. An article in Newsweek of September 7, 1992 spoke of Kissinger's readiness to use obsequious language in speaking directly to his patrons, and evidently sometimes in speaking to others about them. The article went on to say that when Kissinger first met Pat Nixon he "praised her husband lavishly." Mrs. Nixon's response was refreshing: "Haven't you seen through him yet?" she asked.

Kissinger sang a different tune behind the president's

back. I have heard him speak of Nixon in witheringly dep-
recatory terms, and I also find credible an assertion in the
same *Newsweek* article that Nixon complained that
Kissinger needed to seek psychological help. Are such the
wages of a combination of power, arrogance, and self-
doubt, along with outstanding ability? Add a bit of egoma-
nia and you have dangerously unstabilizing frustration
when the ego is thwarted. One sighs and reflects on the
relative simplicity of an Eisenhower, yet in a way I found
that frustrating, too, because reportedly he would play
bridge on the plane instead of reading my memos. I
admired Eisenhower in some ways, but when the assistant
secretary offered me a picture of him for my office, I took
it on trial for a week, propping it up on my bookcase in
front of me. I gave it up, because periodically it disturbed
my work by yelling "fore" at me. Eisenhower was so preoccupied with golf and bridge that one often heard, during
his presidency, "Such-and-such would not have happened
if Eisenhower were still alive." Nevertheless, with the
notable exception of the McCarthy massacres too long tolerated, the country ran fairly well in those days, and
Eisenhower left us with some good advice: beware of the
military-industrial complex.

On returning from our third trip I did not get to go home
to bed as planned. Instead, I was asked to proceed forthwith
to the State Department to assist in the briefing of the press.
That would again be my fate when we returned from the
president's week in China. I had to back up the State
Department spokesperson in discussing the Shanghai communique. I think it may have been at that session when a
newsman asked the spokesperson, "Despite the Shanghai
communique, isn't our China policy left rather ambigu-
ous?" The spokesperson's answer in a burst of brilliance
was, as I recall, my favorite of all momentous quotes: "Yes,

we have to preserve ambiguity in the interest of clarity."

I went home and thought about that one. I concluded that the spokesperson was not speaking Washington gobbledegook, but was being absolutely accurate. We had serious obligations to the Chinese authorities and people on either side of the Taiwan Strait, across which each side bristled at the other. Accordingly, there was ambiguity simply built into the China tangle from our perspective, and if our policy had not reflected that ambiguity it would not have been clear.

After these several Kissinger trips of a week each, the ground had been adequately prepared for the presidential one. Those eight days, by common assent, was clearly "the greatest show on earth" at the time. Naturally, I was eagerly looking forward to participating in that historic event.

TWENTY

The
Halting
Inner
Journey

had mixed feelings about the attention I
received in the media at this time in my life.
Apparently as a result of it Martha and I were
invited to a number of so-called jet-set parties
in Washington and New York, one of which
was close to being a Concorde set party. I suppose I was invited as sort of quasi-VIP decoration.

We had not been strangers to the "upper crust," partly
because soon after we bought a house on "O" street in
Georgetown we landed in the "Green Book," as the social
register in Washington is known. I imagine that was at the
instigation of Molly Thayer, society columnist for the
Washington Post, a brilliant, witty, somewhat noisy but not
quite profane riot. Molly's garden abutted ours in the rear
of our houses, and we had been good friends ever since
she used to visit Ambassador Wadsworth in Jidda, whom

she planned to marry.

Martha and I were used to endless dinners and receptions mostly within diplomatic circles, but these jet-set affairs were flashier. More of the women were more ostentatiously and often more provocatively dressed than I was used to, and they tended to be doused with expensive perfume and a great deal of it. More men wore contemporarily avant-garde velvet suits and floppy do-dads on their shoes, and showed more variety in tonsorial preference than is found in the staid diplomatic circuit. One of them, an interior decorator, toward the end of one evening confided to me that he had decorated his own interior-exterior with a caduceus tattooed in his groin. That party was in New York. As yet a semi-Methodist, I was semi-shocked.

The guests at these parties were often amusing or attractive or both. As I looked around at them, I decided that wealth, particularly old wealth, tends to produce a high percentage of attractive people physically, sartorially—yes, olfactorily—and in the social graces; higher, certainly, than does penury or even modestly affluent circumstance.

At one party in Georgetown, after spending an agreeable time conversing with a bouquet of excessively fragrant ladies, absorbing remarks from witty to penetrating to off-puttingly strutting, I stood in a corner and took in the scene. It was attractive, but in a too-insistent way for lengthy exposure. On an impulse I bolted the party long before it would begin to die, walked the two blocks to my house and plopped down in the library with my feet up. Martha was at this time briefly in Pennsylvania with our two children, Sara and Stephen.

As the son of a prominent Methodist minister I had been reared in very comfortable yet somewhat limited material circumstance. I confess that much of my life I have been attracted to posh environments and financially privileged people. For one reason or another I have been thrown with such people a great deal, not to have had wealth myself of such proportion. These 'privileged' people included certain members of father's congregations, families of fraternity brothers at Emory, some of my Foreign Service colleagues and other friends met in diplomatic life at home and abroad, hosts and hostesses in connection with my public speaking tours, and friends in my retirement area on the Oregon coast.

I decided that having great wealth was not reprehensible, unless it was gained by ignoble means or used for ignoble purposes. Wealth does not seem to fit the characteristics of a zero-sum game, wherein if the rich get richer the poor of necessity must get poorer. Wealth is more a matter of creation than it is a divvying up of a finite quantity. Then what bothered me about these parties? The best I could come up with was that too many of these people seemed to me to be posturing and parading in varying degree—that is, not entirely sincere in what they were advertising as their true being. That, to me, far from validating the supreme self-confidence with which they tried to permeate the atmosphere, was a proclamation of self-doubt. Self-confident people do not posture or parade.

Suddenly a vision of the most vivacious, 'attractive' and perfume-drenched lady at the party came before me. She reminded me of the remark of a wealthy, would-be bewitching matron, overheard at a Paris soiree: "—but, sir, I would not be *natural* if I were not affected!"

I leaned back in my chair and my eyes fell on the Green Book on an upper shelf of the library. I was amused when data on the family was being requested for inclusion in it and we were asked whether we did not have a second address. As a matter of fact, we did have a country home in the Virginia Blue Ridge mountains. The children were listed as being at a private school at that time. So we sounded spiffy enough, I suppose, though that was not our objective. I thumbed through the register, wondering if some entries boasted three addresses, which, according to Oscar Wilde's *The Importance of Being Ernest* inspires uncommon confidence. I smiled, recalling that our children referred to the Green Book as "the area's leading humor publication." That was unfair, but was revelatory of the democratic training to which they had been subjected by Martha and me at the dinner table. Unfair, because as I thumbed through the book my eyes rested on the names of some of the most admirable people I had ever known. At the same time, occasionally my eyes rested on people who, perhaps erroneously, I regarded as largely poof and tinsel. Often decorative poof and tinsel, granted.

I fell asleep in the reclining chair. Two or three hours later I awoke rested, so I poured a brandy and just stayed there, thinking. I realized that for some years I had scarcely given thought to things that truly matter—questions that plagued me as a child and youth concerning life, the nature of the cosmos and of man and what makes both tick. And the latter tick best.

Was my career making me into a surface person with respect to life's core issues? That possibility shook me. What sort of man had I become, and what sort did I want to have become at the end of my Foreign Service career? More senior and 'powerful?' Hardly. That prospect had considerably less appeal for me, now that I had seen far more of the senior and powerful than was true earlier in my career.

As I observed the Washington scene, what troubled me was that there is something about power that tends to isolate the holder of it. If there is not true greatness in the holder of power, in that isolation it is easy for him to come to believe that the power can with impunity be used irresponsibly. *Such use of power, of course, soon diminishes the power,* thus further removing the powerholder from the subjects of his now weakened power. It seems that this vicious turn is true in interpersonal relationships, just as it is in domestic or international affairs.

Was I in the wrong career for maximum personal growth in this life? I had never thought so. Despite its imperfections I believed deeply in my country, and tried to serve both it and my conscience. In my attempts to serve my conscience I had not often encountered a problem because of my country's requirements, but accepting the official policy on Vietnam war was certainly one. Inwardly I agreed with my sixteen year-old son, Stephen, and his friends in their voluble opposition to the war, but was hesitant to indicate as much even to Stephen. I certainly did not agree with the youngsters who tore down the American flag in front of the State Department. They were only pulling down a symbol, but I viewed that symbol as representing such precious rights and stands that its desecration affected me profoundly. So much so, that I could not get my breath in trying to express to my son the pain I felt on viewing that desecration from my office window. This was while fires were burning all over Washington one day in 1968 in the anti-Vietnam demonstrations. I said I did not think those youths had any idea what they were doing. Stephen listened in silence, but I think he understood. I had opposed the war partly *because* of what that flag symbolized to me.

One evening when I was agonizing over Vietnam, Martha finally had enough. She conceded that her life was filled with the children, guest lists and menus and not with country-versus-conscience dilemmas, with which she could not fully relate. Still, she said softly but firmly,

"Alfred, stop wringing your hands over this. Be thankful that in our country you can speak your mind within government councils without landing in jail. Quit stewing." I did. I did outwardly, but I continued to fret inwardly.

Here I was approaching the peak years of my career, and I found more emptiness than I had expected. There was fulfillment, too, of course; and I was well aware of the tremendous import, for us and for the world, of the attempt for rapprochement with China.

I think what produced the feeling of emptiness was the conviction that I was not dealing with fundamentals. Diplomacy and negotiation are necessary, and often productive of great benefits—for a time. But as I saw history in the making—and in the undoing—those benefits tended to erode over time, to conform less to the agreed words at the conference table, helpful as they may have been, but gradually to conform more and more to the level of understanding and support of the masses of *people* involved. The fundamentals seemed to center around the understanding, the awareness, the level of consciousness of individuals.

I loved the Foreign Service, although in three more years I would decide it was time to leave it. That very evening I had a premonition of that decision. If I left the Foreign Service, my main occupational focus in life, what would I do with my life? For one thing, I would spend more time with my wife and children. Beyond that, I could not see clearly. I did resolve to return in earnest to life's "core issues."

Meanwhile, I sought to do what I could under the circumstances about my neglected inner life. First, I began to meditate regularly. I studied several approaches to the art, both Western and Eastern, and adopted an amalgam that was my own. Although I had known two or three, it never occurred to me to "surrender" to a guru, for I disapproved philosophically of such an ostensible abdication of personal responsibility. Second, I did a combination of yogi exercises and Western calisthenics. Thirdly, I cleaned up my diet as best I could in the life I had to lead. I consider all three activities very much interrelated, abetting each other. I found these activities to be a welcome boost indeed during this demanding time of my life.

Chief contributor in this regard at that time was my association with Maharishi Mahesh Yogi, and the teachings in his "Science of Creative Intelligence." That association and the related teachings have influenced my later life considerably.

One morning I accepted a pamphlet from a fetching young lady on the George Washington University non-campus in Washington telling of an introductory lecture on Transcendental Meditation. I attended it, I fear, as sort of a lark, hoping to be amused, or at least bemused. The lecture was given by Jerry Jarvis, perhaps the closest person to Maharishi at that time. I later came to know Jerry well, and I admired him. I found myself listening to Jerry in that introductory lecture at first detachedly, then attentively, then respectfully. A hard sell, such as many self-improvement schemes employ, would have sent me packing home early on. Jerry's soft sell, however, hooked me. His approach essentially was, "We think we have something of value here. If you think you would like to hear more, we'll accommodate you." I was initiated into TM, as was my family. I was immediately put off by the Sanscrit mumbling in the initiation ceremony, and the symbolism of the rites, which seemed a bit pretentious. I wanted to know what was being said in an unknown tongue, and to whom it was addressed. However, the basic teaching leading to stress reduction made a great deal of sense to me. As I practiced the technique, I have to say—to my surprise—that I felt nothing short of gratitude for the teaching. Furthermore, I certainly did not expect the Beatles guru to satisfy me intellectually, but he did so. His lecturing at a two-week retreat in Maine was one of the most thrilling intellectual feasts I have ever experienced, and I have been privileged to experience quite a number.

The teaching and practice benefitted me physically, and inspired me to want to grow spiritually. To be totally honest, I found, again to my surprise, nourishing spiritual food in the movement at that time that I have seldom found in organized religion. Yet I was discomfited by what I supposed to be the Hindu aspects on the fringe and the quasi-religious overtones, while hearing protests that TM was not a religion. Genuflection, in my understanding, has been associated either with religion or with royalty, and royalty was not involved. As an American, I do not associate it with teachers. Nevertheless, in the quiet, dignified and honest early years of the TM movement I had little trouble in gaining my consent to lecture gratis on behalf of that movement all over the country, and I appeared on both nation-wide and local TV talk shows on its behalf. For five years I even served on the Board of Trustees of Maharishi International University (a very creditable, and fully accredited, institution) and served as its chairman for three years.

I left the movement when it became more flamboyant, making what charitably can only be viewed as premature claims, and appearing to be more money-conscious than my taste could accommodate. Nevertheless, the teaching is valuable, and Maharishi is a remarkable man. I spent two months with him at his hotel in Arosa, Switzerland, and saw him on numerous other occasions. I am as grateful for what he has meant to me as I am disturbed by certain trends in his movement.

At any rate, as I get older, I am more attracted to simplicity in spiritual matters than I am to rites, dogmas and trappings of any sort, even to the ecclesiastical trappings from which I once derived aesthetic enjoyment. Today, I find them a distraction.

The three activities mentioned above (meditation, exercise and improved diet) in combination proved to be an economical way to increase energy, to clarify the mind, and in general to further the inner growth about which I was concerned. I felt stress-free, calm and alert when the day finally came that I would leave for China on assignment.

I remember earnestly wishing that my friend, Dr. Kissinger, would practice these three arts, from which I thought he would derive profound benefits, and I thought through him the country might even profit the more. Certainly his staff would profit from the effect on their boss. However, I smiled in trying to picture his meditating and laughed aloud in trying to picture his doing yoga, although if I strained I could picture his curbing his appetite for Chinese food. Somewhat.

Twenty-One

The Week
That Changed
The World

n the morning of Thursday, February 17, 1972, the President and Mrs. Nixon and their entourage boarded Air Force One, recently named "The Spirit of '76," for an historic mission that the President said was on behalf of all mankind. We arrived in Beijing in the morning of the following Monday (Sunday night in Washington). Nixon was the first United States President ever to set foot on Chinese soil. This was also the first time that an American president had negotiated on the soil of a nation with which the United States did not have diplomatic relations.

There was an invitation for such a trip no less than 27 years earlier. In secret talks with American diplomats in the winter of 1944-45 Mao Tse-tung had suggested that Chinese Communist leaders and the American president meet. Even then the Chinese wanted to avoid heavy reliance on the Soviets. However, the approach was rebuffed by the Roosevelt and Truman administrations.

The subsequent communist military conquest of the mainland and Mao's signing in Moscow of a treaty of mutual assistance with the Soviets raised a loud and persistent cry in the United States of "Who Lost China?" This gave the unscrupulous Senator Joe McCarthy of the House Unamerican Activities Committee the opportunity to carry on before a national TV audience a witch hunt against a number of officials in the State Department, based on totally unsubstantiated charges. In the sordid atmosphere of the time one could 'incriminate' oneself by merely having observed that the Chinese Communists had been more active and effective in fighting the Japanese than the Nationalists (true), or by having advocated at least keeping a dialogue open with the side seen as the eventual winner in the coming all-out Chinese civil war (not bad advice, and certainly not subversive).

The 30-year treaty signed by Mao with the Soviets, largely a result of the American snub, lasted only ten years. An outstandingly able Foreign Service Officer and victim of McCarthy, John Stewart Service, who was born in China of missionary parents and was fluent in the language, maintained throughout that Mao really wanted not Soviet, but American help in the economic development of China. Not until 1972 did Mao begin to get it.

President Nixon's long-unsullied record as an anticommunist fighter enabled him to approach the Chinese Communist regime in political safety and with widespread public approval. While as late as 1960 he had warned against being soft on the "international criminals" in Beijing, in 1967 he wrote in *Foreign Affairs* that China should not remain forever isolated from American contact. Noting the large Soviet military buildup on the Chinese border, Nixon was probably the first to envision the possibility, and the advisability, of a rapprochement with the regime in Beijing. It is to the credit of both him and Kissinger that they came to view an approach to China as a means of a new balance of power relationship that would lead to a more stable world, and would not only tend to preserve American prestige, but would engage our efforts positively in the coming post-Vietnam era. They also foresaw the vital need for reinspiriting the American psyche, through positive developments, in the era following the less than face-saving exit from Vietnam.

In early 1971 Chinese readiness to countenance an approach to the United States stemmed from several considerations. While in the early 60s they had suffered severe economic reverses, with the result that in Warsaw they would not negotiate from weakness, the Chinese were faring considerably better in the late 60s. They could face negotiations with the United States with confidence, and they had reason to attempt it. They were alarmed by the recent massive buildup of Soviet military forces on their northern border and the several Soviet-Chinese military engagements of a limited extent that had taken place there.

Furthermore, the Chinese were deeply concerned about the implications of the Soviet invasion of Czechoslovakia in August 1968 and the subsequent Brezhnev Doctrine, which threatened Soviet intervention if any Communist nation dared to go its own way.

While the chief concern was the Soviet threat on the northern border, the Chinese were also much troubled by the U.S. military presence in Vietnam and our support of the Government of the Republic of China on Taiwan, which vowed to retake the mainland.

The Chinese wanted to discuss all of these issues with

the American authorities. They evidently felt that cautious rapprochement with the United States would be something of a safety measure, and might in time demonstrate positive benefits in matters other than security.

For years the Chinese had depicted the United States as the very embodiment of evil, as "occupying" Taiwan and having a military presence on the Chinese doorstep in Vietnam, a fellow Communist nation with which the Chinese claimed to be "as close as the lips and teeth." The stance of the United States had been uniquely valuable in terms of Maoist propaganda at home and abroad, causing some sinologues to question whether Mao would be willing "to release us from his inimical embrace."

For our part, the president had decided that an approach to the People's Republic of China would be advantageous in the complex Soviet equation, might prove to be profitable in trade and perhaps in other fields, would gain widespread domestic and international approval by reducing regional and global tensions, would satisfy the growing cry for some movement in our allegedly stagnant China policy, and would correct the anomaly of a great nation with global interests having no significant relations with, and suffering under insufficient knowledge about, a quarter of humankind. It must also have crossed the president's mind that if his visit to Beijing could be carried off in style, and if it were successful in its objective, his chances of being reelected to a second term would be enhanced.

During the 50s we could not approach the Chinese because of the bitter legacy of the Korean war and the shameful Joe McCarthy period, when we could not think of touching anything labeled Communist. By the turn of the decade, however, these considerations had faded. After McCarthy's ignominious decline we gradually seemed to realize that we were a strong nation with long proven institutions that were likely to withstand a bit of Communist association, wherein our influence would likely be more potent for good than theirs would be destructive. Also, many of us had mused about the interesting possibilities inherent in a 'bourgeois bacteria' invasion of China. We made a couple of conciliatory gestures at Warsaw, such as an exchange of newsmen, but by that time, it was the Chinese who would not approach us. They would not negotiate from their weakened position in that period.

By late spring 1971, however, all signals were "go" for a Chinese-American reconciliation to whatever degree might prove feasible and desirable. The first public indication of a thaw in the long frigid relations between China and the United States was an invitation from a Chinese table tennis team for the American table tennis team to visit China. Both were participating in a tournament in Tokyo. The invitation took the American public, and even American officialdom, by surprise. Bill Cunningham, an officer in our Embassy in Tokyo, at Ambassador Armin Meyers' request, phoned me at five o'clock in the morning Washington time to tell me of the invitation. Word of it was soon all over the media, for it was of paramount newsworthiness. Bill later told me that a Chinese on the American desk of the Foreign Office in Beijing had said that while Chou En-lai at first opposed the invitation, Chairman Mao himself had said it should be extended. There was later a reciprocal visit of a Chinese team to the United States.

Meanwhile, Kissinger's back-channel communications produced a firm invitation for a high level visit that resulted in Henry's secret trip to Beijing in July 1971. There followed the three more substantive Kissinger trips, and finally the president's trip.

o   o   o

There were no crowds of Chinese to greet the president and his entourage when we stepped onto Chinese soil. Premier Chou En-lai and some forty lesser officials were on hand. The Chinese army band played our national anthem in creditable tempo, and there was a crack honor guard of several hundred soldiers, sailors and airmen, each contingent composed of personnel of the same height, as uniform as the Rockettes of Radio City. No foreign diplomats were invited for the occasion. The reception must have been a trifle disappointing to the president, despite the astounding, emotional event of our national anthem blaring forth on the Chinese Communist tarmac!

Soon after arrival at the Government Guest House, however, the satisfaction level picked up. Chou asked whether the president and Kissinger would be good enough to join him in visiting in the home of the almost deified Chairman Mao. Unbelievably, the United States secretary of state was not included in that call on the chairman! Still, that hour with Mao evidently set the stage for a highly successful eight days of growing mutual understanding. The mood at the banquet given by Chou that evening in the Great Hall of the people (in the grand dining room that seats 5,000) was almost euphoric. At dinner the band played numerous old American favorites, not only "America the Beautiful", but unexpected ones such as "Turkey in the Straw." Following dinner Chou and Nixon gave warm toasts from the podium, then wandered from table to table toasting in fiery *mao tai*. The reciprocal banquet later given by Nixon was similarly upbeat, the *mao-tai* possibly contributing to the even more effusive toasts. I noted that one enterprising newswoman pocketed the president's chopsticks after he left the table.

As we left the dining room the chief of protocol pointed

out my old friend, General Fu Tso-yi, who had been so kind to me in Kalgan during my first time in China. He was so emaciated I would not have recognized him.

Although I was present with the presidential couple and their extensive entourage through most of the week's discussions and negotiations, banquets, sightseeing and travels, the week has been so extensively chronicled in writing as well as in surely the most detailed TV news extravaganza of all time, I see no need to dwell at length on it here. I shall include only a few personal experiences or observations during the eight Nixon days in China.

A number of additional reservations on the Chinese side were satisfied during the week. For instance, the Chinese expressed hesitancy about the exchange agreements because they thought all Communists had to be fingerprinted on entry into the United States. The hesitancy was understandable, because in the old days when a peasant needed to agree formally to a document with the landlord, since he could not write his name, the agreement was sealed with his fingerprint—hence the 'downward' connotation of the act in the Chinese mind.

William Rogers, our then secretary of state, was sitting next to me at the table—or rather I was sitting next to him—and he asked if that requirement was still in effect. Before I could answer, the able and alert Foreign Service Political Officer, Nick Platt, said he thought that was no longer true. As I recall it, even though he was certain the fingerprinting requirement had been lifted, he said in effect, "Let's make assurance doubly sure." He went outside the room where a white telephone had been installed that, upon the receiver being lifted, automatically rang the White House switchboard. Nick asked to be connected with the State Department Operations Center. The officer on duty there roused some poor State Department official in Chevy

Chase at three o'clock in the morning Washington time and asked whether Communists on entering the United States had to be fingerprinted. The answer, doubtless with a few choice expletives deleted, came back, "No." The point is that the answer was received in less than four minutes from the time it was asked at the table. The Chinese later bought two earth satellite stations. I do not remember the exact timing of the purchase, but I am inclined to think Nick's salesmanship was involved in the Chinese decision.

So far as I could see, the entire visit went off without a hitch. It should have. We were all given a large notebook and a pocket replica of it, containing a literally minute-by-minute scenario for the full eight days. The arrangements had been thrashed out with the Chinese by an advance party from the White House some days before.

Mrs. Nixon was superb. She did and said everything right. For each occasion she dressed most attractively and appropriately in view of the ultrapuritanical nature of the Cultural Revolution era. She clearly won the Chinese with her warmth and her ready smile. She had carefully done her homework. One of the four thick loose-leaf notebooks that my office had prepared for the trip was for Mrs. Nixon. Very much in character, once when a few of us were gathered at intermission during the performance of *The Red Detachment of Women,* she took the trouble to thank me for her notebook, and said she thought it was interesting that Madame Chiang Kai-shek attended the college where my father was president, and had been in my parents' home a good deal as a young lady. Mrs. Nixon said, "Go over and tell Dick that; I don't think he knows." I didn't do so, for the president seemed to be in earnest conversation, but it was typical of this likable First Lady that she used her husband's first name in speaking with us. I thought she was a gracious, modest, strong and wise woman. The outpouring of expressions of respect and affection at the time of her recent death attested that most Americans thought so, too.

My conversation with Mrs. Nixon reminded me of an evening in 1960 when I was watching a late-night re-run of the Kennedy-Nixon presidential campaign debates. A neighbor, seeing my light still on, came over to chat. He had spent a "wasted" evening with acquaintances and admitted he had tried to buffer himself from the boredom with generous libations. When the debates ended I thought my friend had fallen asleep, but suddenly he raised his head and said, "You know, we are close friends of the Nixons. That's especially the case with Pat and my wife. We love Pat. She is a sweet, caring and honest woman ..." (long pause—deep breath) "... but I wouldn't trust Dick Nixon as far as I could toss your sofa." I didn't want to hear that. I thought it evident that Nixon was bested in the debates, but even if he lost the election I thought his determination and ambition meant that we would see more of him, as did mutual friends who knew him better than I did. When my friend left I lay on the sofa and reviewed the evening. I told myself that while alcohol could at times act as a truth serum, at times it could also elicit nonsense.

o   o   o

The last two evenings in Shanghai were strenuous for the senior level in hammering out the final communique. It was an ingenious document, safeguarding the position of The Nationalist Government on Taiwan as well as could have been done and at the same time delineating sufficient common ground on which to build a new relationship with the quarter of humanity on the mainland of China.

The communique was agreed upon in Shanghai in the small morning hours before our departure from China. I believe it was after the agreement had finally been reached that Secretary Rogers was good enough to invite me to go with him to the president's suite for a sort of celebration chat. The only ones present at that time were the president, Rogers, Bob Haldeman (White House chief of staff) and me.

Naturally I appreciated the privilege of partaking in that poignant moment. I first met Mr. Nixon when he was vice president and about to make a journey through East Asia. He came to the State Department for briefings, and spent a while in my office. I seem to picture him perched on the corner of my desk, asking very incisive questions. He was modest and engaging and evinced broad knowledge of the area he was to visit. I was impressed. I was even more impressed when on his return I heard his account of his trip as given to the National War College class. He spoke with easy fluency for an hour and a quarter without notes, showing keen perception and occasional wit, then fielded questions just as brilliantly.

On this final very late evening in Shanghai, however, as he, I thought, strutted in his silk lounging robe with his big cigar, his erstwhile superb command of the English language was not in evidence. It was preempted by a stream of profanity that appeared to me to serve no purpose, and to be unskillfully, even awkwardly, used. Of course he had just brought off in high style one of the great coups of all time in international relations, so perhaps he should be forgiven for a bit of preening. I find it less easy to forgive him for insulting the English language when he was capable of using it thoughtfully and masterfully in celebration of a uniquely historic moment. Despite the cigar and the profanity, or rather because of them, he struck me as trying to camouflage an inherently very shy man, shy to the point of having a blaring inferiority complex.

After initial acknowledgement the president completely ignored me, but I was only momentarily put off by his curious discourtesy. I knew he had the reputation for being uncomfortable when he had to deal one-on-one, or nearly so, as in this case, with someone he did not know very well. I'm told that is why at the White House he dealt almost exclusively with a very few members of his staff, dealing with the rest through those few. On the other hand he was very gracious in written attention. During a half-hour stopover he spent at Stockholm's Arlanda airport in the early 60s I went out to greet him (at the time I was Ambassador Jeff Parson's deputy in Stockholm). Nixon later penned a very generous note to Jeff commending my handling of his stopover, including his press conference. Also, following his week in China he sent me a laudatory letter concerning my contribution to the whole process of the opening to China.

Having lost interest in the dialogue (very nearly a profane monologue) to which I was subjected, I fell to contemplating Bob Haldeman, who was sitting on the sofa to my right. I sized him up all wrong. With his spiky crew cut, set jaw, determinedly unfraternal air, I pictured him in a pickup truck with sawed off shotgun and ... no, not a Confederate flag. In those days he was not known for his joviality. He seemed cold, unapproachable, hard. What was the sobriquet accorded him? "Great Stone Face?" Since then I have seen him on TV when he was smiling, dressed in a well tailored dark blue suit and red tie, the combination psychologists have deemed best designed to create a good impression. He was articulate, had an impressive vocabulary, was perceptive in discussing complex issues, and altogether projected intelligence and even warmth. I suppose he previously had a job at the White House where a stone face enhanced his service to the president in terms the latter required. Or to some extent perhaps he was a victim of

"White Houseitis," a malady alarmingly widespread at 1600 Pennsylvania Avenue.

o   o   o

Before we left Shanghai Premier Chou En-lai demonstrated once more his thoughtful and gracious manner in personal dealings, one-on-one or otherwise. Typical was his unannounced call on Secretary Rogers the morning of our departure from Shanghai—a courtesy not required by protocol. I believe Chou saw that in this whole show Kissinger had upstaged the secretary of state to a degree that caused the premier to want to accord Rogers special attention. I believe Chou liked Rogers, as did everyone I ever heard of who knew him, except Kissinger, and I think Kissinger's dislike was for professional, not personal reasons.

As always, Chou charmed us all in that visit with his dignified but friendly, urbane, suave manners, designed to compliment those present. He managed to pay some little attention to each person present. This was a special man, much beloved by the Chinese and many others.

Later, when I went to the Chinese Embassy in Washington to sign the condolence book at the time of Chou's death and to pause for a few moments of silence before his black-draped picture, seeing how moved the Chinese lined up on either side of the picture were (a number were red-eyed), I confess my own eyes watered a bit. That certainly did not happen when, a few months later, I signed the book at Mao's death. Nor did I note any of the Embassy officials having difficulty maintaining their composure. Despite extravagant publicly expressed adulation, Mao was not widely respected or revered in his later years. His many political campaigns to insure conformity and increase production through a combination of exhortation and threat were in general not successful, and he was blamed for perpetrating the madness and destruction of the Great Cultural Revolution.

As for Nixon's opening to China, there was virtually universal approbation of the move. His week in China was indeed a week that changed the world, just as he characterized it. It helped break the logjam in disarmament negotiations with the Soviets, and probably contributed in time, and in ways difficult to document clearly, to both perestroika and glasnost in the Soviet Union, to its later disunion, and assuredly to trends in China itself toward free enterprise. Nixon and Kissinger, in agreement that the practical approach to international affairs was on a basis of balance of power politics, managed to secularize the Communist problem, ridding it of much of its almost religious crusade character displayed in the days of Secretary Dulles. That was a salutary change. The balance of power effected among the Soviet Union, China and the United States made for a markedly improved security climate and opened the way for more peaceful bilateral dealings among all three. A Sino-Soviet rapprochement of any significance, however, since they were heretics in each other's eyes in the Communist religion and not mere infidels like us, had to wait some 15 years. Gradually, both trade and cultural ties were expanded, scholars in great numbers were exchanged and each addressed the other's nationals once more as "comrade," but Moscow's strategic objectives, to contain China by military power and to pry it loose from both United States and Japanese influence and cooperation, persisted for some time.

o   o   o

At a dinner party at our house soon after the president's week in China, and in response to a question of Joe

Alsop's, I said that I thought Nixon had "done the right thing, at the right time, in the right way." Martha, in an unabashed volley of spouse-support said, "Yes. He did it your way!" That was an unconscionable exaggeration, but the kernel of truth, at least, was that it was done in just the way I thought it should have been done, and in large measure on the basis of papers emanating from my office, for which I took ultimate responsibility.

The whole opening-to-China show was glamorous, fascinating, and deeply significant for the entire world. In relaxing in my library late one night soon afterward I was belatedly startled that I had actually participated in the opening to China to the degree that I had been so privileged. However, I found myself dwelling not so much on the drama of the process, as on what I had been enabled to see of interpersonal relations at the top level of government, and the modus operandi at that level. I admired the ability, the generous endowment of talent of numerous people at the top in Washington, but I was discouraged and depressed by the bickering, the callous climbing and the dissembling in high places. I had never pictured that there would be so much human frailty among our leaders charged with great responsibility, for I had not previously been much exposed to the political scene at close range. I had been in the career service, which is largely buffered from politics. It is only when one gets senior enough to need to deal with top elected and appointed officials that the political scene appreciably impinges. Too, much of my career had been spent overseas.

Of course I was exhilarated by the events in which I had participated, but just as much, perhaps even more, I was saddened. The Washington scene presented for me a maddening mixture of admiration and distaste. I was relieved to learn that soon I would be leaving that scene, with a small entourage, to set up the United States Liaison Office in Beijing—predecessor to the United States Embassy that followed several years later, on the establishment of full diplomatic relations.

TWENTY-TWO

But One
Stomach
To Give

t's actually happening!" I kept saying to myself on the 22-mile train ride from Hong Kong to the Chinese border. I was not only returning to China, thus living out a dream of nearly a quarter-century, I was returning in a manner and for a purpose of which I would not have dared dream a short while earlier. When I saw the half-squatting Associated Press photographer taking a picture of me, followed by the small entourage that was to help me set up the U.S. Liaison Office in Beijing, I immodestly thought, "He's going to make his paper a little money, syndicating that," for I was the first American official to cross into China on permanent assignment in 23 years, and the only United States Foreign Service officer to serve on the mainland of China under both the old regime of Chiang Kai-shek and the new regime of Mao Tse-tung.

When transferring to a Chinese train at the border in those days, one detrained and walked across the border at Lo-wu. The picture of me walking across the border, brief-case in hand, followed by security officials, an administrative officer, a political officer, a secretary and one or two others, appeared in the New York Times of April 6, 1973, and in many of the major newspapers throughout the world.

Kissinger had several times said that the plan was for me to be the first United States ambassador to China on resumption of relations. As it turned out, however, the Chinese wanted to send to the United States the most senior ambassador in their entire foreign service—the only ambassador who was also a member of the Central Committee of the Communist Party. Nixon in turn called on the services of our most senior diplomat, David Bruce, who had been ambassador to England, France and Germany. Sending Bruce to Beijing was a brilliant move on the part of the president, and a great compliment to the Chinese. Both Bruce and Chou En-lai were seventy-five years old and both spoke fluent French. They got along very well indeed. If I experienced any disappointment, it was fleeting, for the opportunity of working with the revered David Bruce as his senior deputy was highly appealing. Besides, I had already had an assignment with ambassadorial rank equivalent, and had been offered ambassadorships to two countries where the prospect either did not appeal or would not have utilized my particular training and experience. I wanted to be in China.

For most practical purposes the Liaison Office served as an Embassy. The nomenclature was in keeping with the agonizingly incremental steps we took in moving from a quarter-century of animosity to full diplomatic relations with the People's Republic of China—incremental partly because of Chinese Communist non-response, but also out of deference to the Government of the Republic of China on Taiwan.

In early April 1973 I found myself in Hong Kong giving a briefing to a roomful of newsmen on the coming establishment of facilities for a U.S. diplomatic presence in Beijing. In answer to their questions I was discomfited to realize how often my answer had to be "That has not yet been determined," or "The Chinese have not indicated," or "I do not know." In the typical Chinese Communist way of doing things, one learned what next steps were possible just in time to take them. This was, I believe, by way of keeping the foreigner under careful control—an objective understandable in the light of the history of the preceding century.

On landing in Beijing my party and I were cordially welcomed by appropriate level Foreign Office officials, and also by a number of foreign ambassadors posted in Beijing. When later I expressed appreciation to one of the ambassadors for the courtesy, his reply was, "Well, we viewed your coming as an uncommonly welcome event: we reasoned that you would soon be followed by a good American doctor, a good American auto mechanic and John Wayne. Don't forget us when you show the Duke."

We were housed in the old Peking Hotel, the best quarters of the sort available at that time. A long stay there would not have been joyous, except at mealtime, but it was satisfactory. What was not satisfactory were the office quarters first assigned to us by the Chinese. They were on one floor of a seven-story building in the diplomatic quarter known as San Li T'un. At first opportunity I explained to the head of the Diplomatic Services Bureau that the assigned office quarters, even as a temporary arrangement pending the building of new quarters, would not be adequate "for purposes and activities for which I am confident the premier would wish to provide." I felt a little guilty using the premier's name, but it seemed the best way to get anything done in China that needed doing. It was known that I had reason to know a good deal about what the premier did envision in our relationship, even though in fact I didn't know very clearly what that was on this particular subject. My feeling of guilt was soon handily expunged when I was told that a half-built embassy compound intended for another country would be modified and shifted to us, and its completion expedited. The Bureau meant it. Bright lights were installed all around the site and workmen swarmed over the site 24 hours a day, one hundred strong, so I was told, on each of three shifts.

I soon inspected the finished building and found it perfect for our purposes at that time. Ambassador Bruce had said he wanted a modest presence for some time, so we did not need a huge building. Everything turned out to our liking, including the subsequent use of the originally assigned office quarters. Those quarters were two apartments in a building designed as residences for ambassadors and their families. When the offices went into the newly built compound, Ambassador and Mrs. Bruce occupied one of the apartments in that building until their residence in the Liaison Office compound was completed. Martha and I inherited their apartment when they moved. When the other Deputy Chief of Mission, John Holdridge, arrived, he and his family occupied the other apartment at San Li T'un.

There was something of an anomaly in our having two Deputy Chiefs of Mission. The Sunday supplement, *Parade* magazine, in its *Personality Parade's* fact-and-gossip column had it that there was a big hassle between the State Department and the White House as to who would be the deputy, so there had to be two. If so, I knew nothing of the sort, and I never sensed any awkwardness between John and me. It is true that Dr. Kissinger and Secretary Rogers were something less than devoted to each other, but when it did not work out that I was to be the first ambassador, (had I been, I assume John was to have been my deputy), I feel certain that the president and Kissinger very kindly dubbed us both as deputies.

The experienced and wise Ambassador Bruce did right in keeping a low profile in our early days of resumed service in the Middle Kingdom. In line with his wishes, I recall being disturbed when I heard the Department was intending to send as his vehicle, a Chrysler Imperial limousine. In the first place it was too big, and in the second place the name was not right for us in a communist country. "Chrysler" is fine, but "Imperial?" Someone was asleep. It was changed to a Chrysler New Yorker, which was just right in size and in nomenclature.

Life in the Peking Hotel was awkward from the security standpoint. I assumed that the conversations among my small staff and me were heard and recorded on the floor above, from where after the work day a small group of cadre with little black briefcases emerged. That did not particularly trouble me, for the entire arrangements in the rapprochement between our two countries had been so forthright that I was more often grateful than otherwise that I could assume our conversation, usually centering on needs, got to the appropriate authorities via the ceiling. Almost any country would have taken advantage of the easy setup to listen in on the conversations of another country's officials at a time like this. It must have been an especially important listening post for the Chinese, who until very recently, at least, seemed convinced that we were bent on their destruction. I purposely enunciated clearly a number of comments of a friendly nature that I was happy to have recorded. If I sent a message to the Department in code, I wrote it down without speaking it.

My conviction that we had a devoted audience of Chinese cadre seemed to be confirmed one chilly April day. It seems the hotel's steam heat was habitually cut off each year on April 15th, regardless of the weather. I announced to the ceiling that I was cold, and a couple of my cohorts agreed volubly. Some twenty minutes later the radiators started to knock, and we had heat until balmy weather arrived, irrespective of the calendar. I extend my thanks to the People's Republic of China.

We did send a number of messages to the Department in code, involving various developments in setting up the Mission. Without the usual code machines this was a laborious process. When we went to the dining room the two security men had to carry two large canvas bags of code equipment and documents to and from meals. Also, pretty soon three Marine guards arrived to join us. We therefore had by far the largest contingent in the dining room of any of the foreign diplomats still staying in the hotel. Our security antics and the size of our group made us stand out peculiarly, but the several diplomats of other countries who were still residing in the hotel were kind enough not to gawk or comment.

Almost everything involving China was special and uniquely viewed in the States at that time. When I went back to the Department on consultation I was told by Departmental code clerks that the first telegram signed JENKINS from Beijing, captioned "Beijing No. 1," had been framed and put on the wall in the code room.

There were countless details involved in setting up the Mission, but most of them were easily surmountable if the right Chinese official was contacted. The word seems to have gotten around that full cooperation was to be extended. This was publicly indicated one beautiful Sunday, the first day in a long time that the famous Western Hills had been open to the public. Vice Foreign Minister Ch'iao Kuan-hua invited me to an excursion to the Western Hills. We had a pleasant luncheon a deux, at which we discussed a number of matters not exactly secret, except for a historical item or two, but also not for public consumption. What was evidently for public consumption was the indication that the American presence was not only accepted, but sanctioned. After lunch Ch'iao and I strolled through the crowds laughing and talking as though we were old friends—a scene obviously engineered by Ch'iao for official purposes. As a matter of fact, we were indeed friends, having previously enjoyed a particularly agreeable dinner and evening at Secretary Rogers' apartment in New York, along with one very affable George Bush, then our Ambassador to the United Nations.

After a few weeks Ambassador and Mrs. Bruce, John Holdridge and a number of other members of the Mission arrived. Getting to know both Bruces was a joy. Evangeline Bruce was elegant, charming and a warm friend. David was just as wise, able and personable as his reputation had it. At 76 he was more than equal to the responsibilities. His only concession to his maturity was a reluctance to take on early morning duties. Accordingly, John and I alternated in holding the staff meeting each morning, and many decisions fell to us, always subject to the ambassador's veto. I do not recall that he ever was moved to exercise it. What I do recall with satisfaction is the smoothness with which two deputies operated. I had a very high respect for John's ability, and on his part he was slightly deferential in recognition of my being *primus inter pares*. He later went on to be ambassador to Singapore.

More Marine guards came. I was relaxed about that, on the assumption that my caution had been honored: that in view of the history of American Marines in China it was essential that, although they were in civilian dress, they should clearly be identified to the authorities as Marines, for their identity would surely become known. The Chinese with whom I talked in the Foreign Office thought they had not been so identified. Perhaps at least the premier knew. I believed that with the courtesy of proper identification our desire for Marine guards at the Mission would be understandable and their presence tolerated, provided they acted with decorum. Every other U.S. diplomatic Mission in the world that I knew of had Marine guards.

Before long the understandable pride of the Marines caused the Pentagon, or State, or somebody back home, illadvisedly to authorize their serving in Beijing in uniform. They had been in civilian clothes up to that time. I held my breath. I had cautioned against that. It is possible that even that could have been stomached by the Chinese in the early heyday of our resumed relations, though I doubt it. In any event, the uniforms and the added offense of loud parties at the Marines' quarters prompted the Chinese authorities to ask them to leave. They were replaced by civilian guards, at considerably more expense to the American taxpayer.

During the year and a half that I served in the Liaison Office in Beijing I can't say that Martha and I were very happy. The associations among the office personnel were certainly gratifying, and the work of the Mission was interesting, often intensely so. I found setting up the office challenging and rewarding, and I enjoyed knowing a number of the officials with whom I dealt. However, it was not a happy time for the Chinese people, and we were so fond of China and the Chinese, that made us unhappy.

Life for the Chinese was both drab and filled with an underlying anxiety. Everyone belonged to some sort of societal unit, and had to attend political indoctrination meetings that by all accounts were deemed to be too frequent and too boring. Everyone had to do calisthenics with his unit at the sound of a broadcast bugle at some very early hour.

What was truly remarkable is that so far as I observed in Beijing or Tientsin there were only two feminine hairstyles, presumably for the bulk of half a billion women throughout the country: braids if you were young, box-bobbed if older. Anything else was considered to be too alluring in ultrapuritanical Communist China during the Cultural Revolution. Incidentally, I noted only two hairstyles for men also: very short, or subcutaneous.

Slogans were everywhere. The country seemed to be ruled by a combination of exhortation and fear. I saw an enormous petrochemical plant outside Beijing that was almost entirely controlled from one large room with countless switches, buttons and levers. Neatly printed over many of these controls was a Mao saying, roughly the equivalent of "Up and at 'em!" "You can do it!' "Pull up your socks!" Rather like having over your shaving mirror "Every day in every way I am getting better and better." Such, eventually, palls.

At this time it was claimed that there was no unemployment in China. That appeared to be substantially true, for almost everyone had a government-assigned task. There was, however, ludicrous underemployment. One often had the impression that clerks were shoulder-to-shoulder behind the counters.

Once Martha asked the Diplomatic Services Bureau, our umbilical cord to existence in Beijing, for a cleaning woman. The Bureau sent eight cleaning women. They mostly drank tea and looked out the window. Martha had to finish the job properly after their two-day stay. The point is that there was no alternative cleaning establishment down the street that would offer to do the job better, cheaper and quicker. No competition.

If I had ever lost my faith in private enterprise and competition (and I have not) I should have had it abundantly restored from staying in Eastern European hotels, where the Communist government owned everything and the staffs acted accordingly—as did the repair people. I once stayed in a room in one of the two best hotels in the capital city of an East European country that well illustrates the point.

The ceiling light, a round fluorescent atrocity, would not go off. I punched the button both ways, nothing happened. I had to lie and stare at that thing all night. Furthermore, the bedroom curtains wouldn't close. The draw cord had broken, someone had tied a square knot in it that would not go through the pulley. I was on the first floor European style, so I had little privacy. My suspicious mind made me wonder if the authorities hoped to have compromising pictures taken of me, but I was totally alone. Still, I did try to smile as much as possible.

My razor plug would not stay in the wall receptacle, but would jump back out on its own. To keep it in I had to put a foot against it halfway up the wall, then turn 180 degrees to shave in the mirror. If I had not been into yoga for eleven years, I would not have gotten shaved.

There was no stopper in the tub, and no shower. I sent the driver out to buy a stopper. He came back two hours later, saying there wasn't a stopper to be had in that great capital city. It was not in the five-year plan.

In the closet the thread to hold the wooden part of the hangers to the metal hook had worn, so that the only way I could keep my clothes up was to put a shoe in a jacket pocket and hang things askew, so that the friction would keep the hangers intact. If I forgot and sat down too suddenly on my bed, however, all my clothes would fall down in the closet.

On departure I said to the assistant manager, "Really, you should charge an amusement tax for staying in that room!"

Long live competition and free enterprise!

o   o   o

Apparently almost everyone in Beijing had a bicycle. There were seas of bicycles on Ch'ang An Chieh Boulevard, the faces of the silent riders sober, if not glum.

Small wonder. The populace had long since learned that it behooved one to follow the current official line on any given subject, generally the one given in the People's Daily editorials. The problem was that the line could change overnight with seeming contempt for either logic or consistency. That was not all. Not only could it change suddenly, it could change retroactively! Even that was not the full extent of the problem. The line as embodied in the editorials was often couched in such Delphic phraseology that it could be interpreted in more than one way. If one were lucky enough to interpret it correctly at a given time, since policy changes could be applied retroactively, it could mean that a month later it could be declared to have been incorrect for that earlier period when it was at that time deemed to be correct!

That sort of thing can become a bit disconcerting after a while. Inconsistency, illogic and unpredictability of authority were eroding the society. It seems that the human nervous system is built to withstand occasional severe stresses, but even moderate stress, for instance, from unpredictability, if ever-present, can be disastrously debilitating.

In fact, the policy path of the regime has been so tortuous, so uncertain and costly, even the leadership must have become bewildered and frustrated. The Great Cultural Revolution itself would seem to be born of Mao's frustration. The preceding movement labeled the *Great Leap Forward,* as well as the *Hundred Flowers Campaign,* for the most part had both failed of their objectives. The former was supposed to industrialize the country almost overnight (a typical effort, "backyard furnaces" to produce steel!), but the quality of produce was unusable. The *Hundred Flowers Campaign* was to invite criticism of the regime, ostensibly to aid in reforms, but it brought forth such an avalanche of criticism from the unwary that it had to be turned off. Many of the unwary lived to be sorry they had spoken up.

During the Cultural Revolution a major casualty was art in its many forms—and that in a people long renowned for exceptional, in some media unique, artistic achievement. Such is the penalty exacted by a doctrinaire straightjacket. For instance, during the Cultural Revolution, when personal aggrandizement was tabu, it was actually claimed that musical compositions were composed by committees. Upon hearing them, one was seldom moved to question the claim.

When after the Nixon trip cultural exchanges between China and the United States were initiated, Eugene Ormandy brought the famous Philadelphia Orchestra to China. He agreed to afford orchestral accompaniment to an embarrassingly pretentious piece called *The Yellow River Concerto,* allegedly composed by a Chinese Communist committee. As digital calisthenics it was impressive, almost defying human execution, but I doubted it was art.

At intermission a half dozen of us were gathered in a little room with Madame Mao, who was still at large then and was our hostess for the evening. Once when she was engaged in conversation with others, someone leaned toward Ormandy and said, "Mr. Ormandy, that *Yellow River Concerto* was trash, wasn't it?" Ormandy cocked his head to one side, thought for a moment and responded quietly, "Bad trash." I record this because I do not consider that it denigrates the inherently artistic Chinese people at all. It only insults the perpetrators of the Cultural Revolution, whom the Chinese have long since roundly denounced.

It was the wrong time for Martha and me to be in a country of which we were once so fond. Accordingly, we sat down one evening after watching a local TV program so politicized it almost served as an emetic, and decided we had enough. I decided to retire from the Foreign Service. Having loved China and things Chinese for most of my life, I never dreamed that I would want of my own accord to leave China prematurely, but I did. Added to the distaste for the situation described above was Kissinger's breach of hoary practice in failing to brief me on his conversations with the Chinese during a visit he paid to Beijing as Secretary of State. I was to be charge d'affaires for the ensuing two weeks, since Bruce was going to Tokyo. In the next two or three days almost every non-communist ambassador in Beijing called at my office in full and natural expectation of being briefed, at least in general declassified terms, about some of the substance covered during Kissinger's visit. To their astonishment and my keen embarrassment, in effect I had to confess ignorance. I have no idea what they reported to their Foreign Offices, but that they felt constrained to make some sort of prompt report following the Secretary's visit I have no doubt. That was not in the U.S. interest, nor was it in accord with unde-viating practice in diplomacy, so far as I ever heard or cer-tainly had before experienced in the Service. I could not believe that the Secretary of State would do such a thing, either in ignorance of virtually inviolable Foreign Service custom or as some sort of petty personal put-down for some unknown reason.

Furthermore, the governmental climate back home was increasingly disturbing. The Watergate revelations came just before I was assigned to Beijing to set up the Liaison Office for Bruce's formal opening, and I first heard of phone tapping of honorable colleagues which bespoke of White House paranoia to a degree I liked to believe was distinctly unAmerican. True, the Kissinger-Nixon com-bine built salutary new relationships with both Russia and China—no small achievement, even though world political developments facilitated the achievement. Even from afar, however, from what I heard and read, the arrogant, closed system of the White House was not securing, and could not secure, the sustained domestic support that in any system, but particularly in ours, spells the difference between suc-cess and ultimate self-destruction. I, myself, was troubled and unsure of what I was trying my very best to support.

There was another semi-humorous but still serious consideration leading to my early retirement from the Service. Martha went for paper and pencil and dealt in numbers for some minutes. Finally, she said, "Honey, according to my figuring, in our career we have attended somewhere between seven thousand and nine thousand diplomatic dinners, luncheons and receptions!"

At that I stood up, slid my fingers below the top button of my jacket and gravely orated, "I regret that I have but one stomach to give to my country." I sighed, fell back into my seat and said, "Let's go home."

At that Martha smiled contentedly and went to her jewelry box, returning with two sheets of folded notepaper. She said, "I found this about five years ago in a book in your library. You probably haven't opened the book since you were studying Chinese at the University of Chicago. I thought this interesting and put it aside. You should read it."

I had not seen the notes since they were handed me, according to the date on them, on April 14, 1943. On that evening thirty years ago I had taken my friend, Mary, to a fine Russian restaurant in downtown Chicago. A "counselor" was going from table to table, telling people about their past, present and future, and advising them—according to her reading—concerning their strong and weak points. The counselor spent an inordinately long time with me, then said she wanted to go get paper and leave her notes with me for me to read later. I paid little attention to the notes, because I had very limited faith in astrology, numerology and tarot readings. However, in 1974 in Beijing I was astounded to read in the notes, among other things: "You should go either into advertising or diplomacy, because you can convince almost anyone of almost anything, a faculty handy in both pursuits. If you go into advertising, you will become immensely wealthy. If you go into diplomacy, you will become immensely fulfilled. If in diplomacy, you would rise to quite senior levels, but not to the very top, for two reasons. First, because in later career you would deal sufficiently with the top to make the top unattractive to you. Second, you have an irresistible urge to puncture pomposity, and that will not be popular with some of your superiors."

When I looked up, Martha said, "That counselor had to be psychic. You cannot deny the validity of either prediction relative to your diplomatic career."

"True."

On returning to the States we first settled in Bryn Mawr, on the Philadelphia mainline, because to return to our Georgetown house would almost inescapably put us back into the undesired Washington *crise de foie* circuit. Even Bryn Mawr was more social than suited our taste at that time, so we retreated to our week-end home in the Virginia Blue Ridge Mountains, tripled its size, installed an indoor swimming pool, a sauna, a pool table (to entertain house guests so I could go into a corner to read), and, I thought, enough electric and electronic gadgetry to delight my soul in retirement.

Not so. For four or five years I lectured on China around the country, indeed around the world, from Singapore to Stockholm.

Twenty-Three

The Tao
Of The Peace
Process, From
Negotiation
To Meditation

uring my years as a globe-trotting speaker, I had time to reflect on the future and how we must approach it to develop a peaceful and prosperous world. For centuries one of humankind's most avidly pursued goals has been world peace. It has been pursued relentlessly, but for the most part in vain.

One has to wonder why there has not been more success, when efforts to assure world peace have been so persistent. Tom Hughes, as President of the Carnegie Endowment for International Peace, once observed: "There is always researching for peace: and we live in the most research-ridden era in history. There is always traveling for peace: and we are part of the most over-traveled generation ever. There is publishing for peace: and we live in the most publication-surfeited society of all. There is conferring for peace: and hundreds of respectable devotees worldwide devote some of the best years of their lives repeating themselves to one another at one conference after another." Yet the world is not peaceful.

I, myself, have researched, traveled and spoken for peace. I have met many of the same earnest faces at conferences on five continents, who offer the same earnest pleas to each other in hopes it will do some good in the cause of world peace. Perhaps it does, a bit. It is better to speak and dream of a peaceful world than not to do so, for we tend to gravitate toward that on which we consistently focus our attention, and unpeaceful visions are flashed at us quite enough.

Traditional approaches to world peace must still be followed, though they have proven to end short of the goal. Such efforts as summit meetings, the United Nations, arbitration boards and the like help, but demonstrably not enough. I have done a fair amount of international negotiating, and have been an adviser in still more. I have often seen agreements reached, only to see their effect dissipate—seldom because of perverse or dishonorable leaders, but seemingly from a lack of sufficient understanding and support on the part of the public that the agreements are meant to serve.

As well-intentioned as these efforts are, they do not tackle the root cause of the problem. One of the several reasons I retired early from diplomatic service was frustration at the limited effectiveness of traditional approaches to international security.

During my assignments in Washington I have seen policies laboriously fashioned through interdepartmental meetings, a few of which I have been privileged to chair, that were often exciting due to the expertise, the wisdom, the sheer human concern that went into them via the specialists' contributions. Often an excellent policy package, in world interest as well as in United States interest, would then be sent to the White House for approval. As appropriate, the Congress would be brought in, and the 'domestic considerations' (not necessarily so labeled) would be larded into the foreign affairs package. Then, sometimes the package would come back to the State Department-Foreign Service for implementation significantly altered, or even essentially reversed. The White House and the Congress are not to be blamed. If only to get reelected, presumably they were reflecting as best they could the composite will of their constituency: the indifference, the greed, the charity, the understanding, the stupidity, the wisdom, the love and the hate of you, me and our neighbors. Granted, the will of pressure groups is often the form that the will of the people takes, but pressure groups in our country are so multifarious, presenting so many different interests, the result may be a more accurate reflection of grass roots intent than that afforded by any other system yet devised, at least for a large, heterogeneous country. The trouble is that the grass roots intent may be based in large part on ignorance, greed, religious fanaticism, xenophobia, or some other form of myopia. Of course it is also based on understanding, charity, tolerance and love. It's an amalgam.

No leadership can for long rise appreciably above the understanding and support of its constituents. As a result, year in and year out we get just about the kind of governmental performance we deserve—sometimes a bit better, sometimes a bit worse. But over the long haul it reflects alarmingly well the composite will, understanding and level of awareness, the level of consciousness, of each of us in the 50 states. Something like that is also true of other governments, in widely varying degree.

It is not a flattering reality, but ultimately you and I and our brothers and sisters around the world, through *individual* contribution in thought, word and deed are collectively responsible for the dangerous tensions existing on earth. Our thinking on this problem usually has not encompassed the concept of ultimately *personalized* responsibility. We prefer to luxuriate in the appealing fiction that virtually all blame should rest on the rascals in city council, or in the governor's office, or in the grasping powers that be in Washington, Moscow, Peking or Pretoria. Taking personal responsibility for what life presents to the individual frightens the weak. They want freedom, not the inseparable other side of the coin: responsibility. True freedom means the freedom of responsibly to make a thousand choices a day, great and small; and the global sum of those choices pretty much determines the way the world works—or fails to work.

Presumably, freedom of choice, arising from the play of conscience as distinct from the non-choices of instinct, is a relatively late, crowning gift of agonizing eons of evolution. Many, probably most of us, are still afraid of it. We run about anxiously scanning the horizon for some altar or authority, be it secular or sacred (or merely sacerdotal), on which to lay this recent, too-troubling gift of conscience-directed freedom of choice. We are afraid to fan the divine spark within our breasts, lest it burn, or lest it reveal the startling creator deep within our silence. Rather, "Tell me what to think, and I will think as I should." Hardly. Tell me what to think, and then I am unlikely to think at all.

It seems that anything like a *definitive* answer to the problem of world peace does not lie in electing beneficent power figures or in saying the right things at negotiating tables, as desirable as both may be. The ultimate solution seems overwhelmingly related to the status of the human condition that we all collectively create and unceasingly recreate. It is built of the quality of the living and yearning and thinking of the John Does and the Mary Smiths, no less. How, then, do we get John Doe and Mary Smith to forsake paltry pastimes, debilitating pleasures and petty prejudices, to say nothing of envy, greed and dishonesty, which, all for the lack of the great solvent, charity, result in excessive and unwholesome individual and societal stress and strain, which impairs perception, which then causes misunderstanding, which breeds mistrust, which results in fear, which in frustration breaks out in crime and vio- lence—in family, nation and world?

In other words, how do we bring about a condition wherein right action, in integrity of conscience and clarity of vision, is habitual—the norm? Not to the desired extent, it seems from historical evidence, by being given a list of dos and don'ts by government, church, guru or daddy. To a degree, we may have profited by the concern and offer- ings of all of these, but inadequately. Effective guidance has to be not a casuistic list, or the pronouncements of an authority, but something more generic, basic, and self- earned. Our parents, priests, teachers and politicians can tell us what right action is until they drop, but right action seems seldom to come from mere intellectual acceptance. The great administrator of our lives is our consciousness, and it administers precisely according to the level of its development—its careful culturing.

Our era presents us with opportunities commensurate with the dangers we have created. Everything is speeded up today, and there is hope that such a circumstance includes our very evolution into a new level of awareness of reality, of universal law, worthy of the human potential. The physiology and psyche of humans are developing new powers; or maybe we are discovering how to bring out long-latent powers. Just review the scientific journals, if you want to be inspired. We may be on the point of producing the fully human man and woman in sufficient numbers to make a fundamental difference in the human circumstance, for science and spiritual concerns (as distinct from dogmas-in-concrete) are becoming mutually supportive. We are beginning to heal the terrible, terrible wound inflicted on our civilization when the Pope in the 13th Century turned down Roger Bacon's plea that religion embrace science instead of bristling and spitting at it. For centuries science bristled back; but today science and at least the less dogmatic spiritual interests are becoming reconciled. *There simply is no question that spiritual thought can be scientifically respectable these days.*

Science and spirituality are discovering more and more common ground and actually becoming mutually supportive. This is especially true with respect to physics. Using its own methods and postulates and trying bravely to stay within its own province, for some time now physics has found itself, despite itself, outside itself—in the province of metaphysics. We are discovering after all that we live in a universe, and not a duoverse.

Our culture will be in deeper and deeper trouble if it fails to bring remnants of the old belief system into consonance with scientific belief systems, such as we have in physics, psychology and biology, all part of God's province. Neither an individual nor a society can function well and long without a reasonably cohered concept as to the nature of reality and what that implies for living.

True, church attendance has held up fairly well. Most people, it seems, are willing to indulge in the old familiar hymns, the content of which they no longer believe—but for how long? Probably many reason that lacking anything better readily at hand, it is in the interest of society to cling to an outmoded, discredited belief system than to have no belief system at all, and it probably is. The disturbing fact is that we yet have no cohesive, culture-wide alternative with allowable differences to meet differing needs, but all resting on the lowest common denominator of scientific respectability.

The remarkable growth of interest in other religions, in non-dogmatic spiritual practices and even in self-help programs devoid of any religious content has progressed far beyond the fad stage. The interest has lasted and grown partly because the offerings of many of the main stream denominations are either outmoded or anemic. Church attendance is partly sustained because most of us want an affiliation that will insure a memorial service when we pass on. Also, some of us attend to hear a well-educated minister express himself so delightfully. Church attendance may therefore constitute more of an aesthetic than a religious experience. Sometimes the content of the sermon is respectable when the ritual and hymnology are not.

If religion is to survive healthily, to guide us to better ways of living and to help us to view rightly the nature of reality with understanding, today it must approach human understanding in terms of reason, not in terms of fanciful, would-be authoritative, gigantic leaps of faith. Theology made a great mistake in setting itself apart from science, for theology clearly has had the worst of the bargain in that estrangement. By becoming a very special study among many specialties it lost its rightful universality. If God is the chief subject of theology, as the very word would imply, and God is omnipresent, that is, in all things, then scientific descriptions are describing God, and the rightful province of both science and theology is universal. But they must get along cooperatively. If not, theology will more and more be the loser, not science. Einstein and a good many other giants managed to recognize the inseparability of the two quite amicably in their personal convictions.

If the scope of science does not adequately embrace considerations of morality, and if religion often insults our scientific sensibilities, how do we raise the quality of our consciousness so as to know our spiritual essence, to enhance our relationship with the Creator, while honoring intellectual respectability? We all know, really! Emerson has chided us, saying, "Mankind needs not so much to be informed, as to be reminded." The many paths to spiritual growth, or merely to "self-improvement" if you wish, in the last analysis say one thing: you have to go within. The Kingdom is within. We are sovereign there, perhaps more so than we desire! But the mind must be stilled. We are told, "In the beginning was the word." And in the beginning of the beginning was the unspoken thought, which some insist is far more powerful than the spoken word. And *before* the beginning of the beginning was the silence, where all things are born.

The real secret, it seems, is regularity—in prayer, in meditation, in whatever form of spiritual centering and culturing is suitable to the temperament and level of understanding of the individual. Again, what we consistently put our attention on is what we eventually create. Since societies and nations are composed of individuals, it seems that an individual culturing peace within himself, divesting himself of fear, hatred and cynicism is actually, actively working toward world peace! Peace begins with the individual, and is a relative matter within the individual. In the depths of my rather hard-bitten, knocked-about being, I have come to believe that such is of more lasting effect than the fruits of the negotiating table.

"But I have a job, a spouse, children to rear, golf to be played; how can I find time for regular attempts to culture my consciousness through meditation and prayer?" A Japanese told me how:

When I was eighteen I spent a summer on the shore of Lake Erie. On returning from a pre-dawn swim I recognized in the hotel garden Dr. Kagawa, a then famous Christian writer, lecturer and counselor. I introduced myself and asked, "What are you doing up so early?"

He smiled and replied, "I get up at this hour every morning, to write poetry and have my hour of meditation."

"But I know something of your extremely busy schedule, constantly traveling, lecturing, counseling, writing at least 20 books. Surely you don't mean you spend a whole hour every day in meditation and prayer," I protested.

He laughed softly. "Well, on days when I see that I have more to do than seems humanly possible, then I find it necessary to spend two hours in meditation and prayer."

"What do you mean?

"It is my effort-saver, for where there is no contradiction there is no waste."

When I returned home I told Father of the encounter. His comment:

"Of course. Daily realignment not only gets rid of wasteful contradictions, it tends to slough off other totally useless, encumbering baggage, like self-importance. Only then can one begin to know the exquisite exhilaration of freedom."

No time to partake of our most effective sustenance? It makes no sense.

One simply needs to know that every thought is prayer and every prayer is answered, if it is not canceled out by oppositive thoughts. If through the conscious mind the subconscious is programmed confusedly, life will be, must be, confusing. If we say, "I wish that would happen, but I know it won't," then the law works ineffectively on that issue, or not at all. It is concentrated, channelized thought, prayer and meditation, when habitual and one-pointed, that cannot help but have prodigious results, for that is the law. We get that which we steadily hold before the mind's eye. The law of attraction does not work only when we want it to work. There is no escape from it. We can apply it on purpose or submit to it passively, but there is no denying it, because thoughts have inevitably resulting actualities.

All of these factors impinge on each other, abet each other, and go to make us what we are. Aristotle rightly said, "We are what we repeatedly do." And we do what we repeatedly think. Meditative and prayerful attention on the character of our thoughts can make us whatever we wish to be. Such is our limitless potential. Truly, we have a power that is the gift of a God whose law is love. We destroy ourselves by denying it, or honor and feed the divinity within us by going within, communing with that divinity, then accepting its influence in every facet of our lives. Louise Hay has beautifully reminded us, " We are one with the power that created us and that power has given us the power to create our circumstance." That is done through the all-powerful subconscious continuum of which our individual subconscious partakes, and proceeds to make real that which has been imprinted upon it.

Despite the sometimes magnificent effort of our leaders, in this curiously interknit world, woven with forces partially (if not mostly) unseen, it seems that the followers often overwhelm the efforts of the leaders. The consciousness of the individual in a constituency has to be raised before there will be right functioning of the group, whether family, nation, or world. Effective leadership requires enlightened followership. Centuries of prodigious effort tell us there simply does not seem to be a promising shortcut.

Twenty-Four

Afterword
Summa
Cum
Difficultate

hile traveling on speaking tours I pondered at length my conviction that the achievements of diplomatic maneuvering in foreign affairs too often and too soon tended to lose their validity and import. Of course that can happen because of changed circumstances that make the agreements no longer appropriate. However, as I have indicated, I believe that often it is in good measure because of either a lack of understanding or a conscious withholding of support on the part of the masses of people involved.

That is oversimplification, of course. Many factors may be at play in sabotaging agreements made at the negotiating table, from personal aggrandizement to corporate greed. I still believe a major problem is incomplete public education and awareness—full perception. Preferably, in my next occupation I wanted to find something having to do with that basic level of underpinnings on which foreign policies must ultimately rest: the level of the individual's perception and awareness.

I considered a number of possible late occupations. Several friends suggested that I get into acting, since they claimed the ham in me was constantly coming out. Admittedly, I had been possessed of drama fever since the productions in my garage as a child. Also, once when I was in Paris for a conference I had enjoyed a brief but, if I may say so, successful appearance on the stage of the Follies Bergeres, no less. For years I had heard of the famed musical and flesh extravaganza, so when on a stroll I came upon the theater, I started in my fractured, or at least cracked, French to buy a ticket, indicating a place in the rear of the house, where the seats were not yet X-ed out. A light, I later understood, turned on in the pretty little head of the ticket lady, who said in French, "But, sir, I have just had a ticket turned in, for center isle, second row. Would you like it?" In my Georgia naivete I said *"Bien sur, Madame, et merci beaucoup."* Of course it turned out to be the hot seat. During the seventh extravagant scene a charming, fortunately petite, chanteuse came down, sat in my lap, and with the spotlight on us sang into one of my protruding ears. I remember wondering anxiously how much my budding diplomatic career would be tarnished, or worse, if I were recognized. The lovely lady arose after endless moments, and I exhaled, having long enough under the unsolicited circumstances inhaled her overly applied Parisian bouquet.

I thought I had done quite enough for Franco-American *amitié* for one evening, but apparently not. During the eleventh extravagant scene a truly ravishing and, I fear, femininely authoritative chanteuse came down, took me by the hand and invited me to ascend the stage. I strongly demurred, but she literally dragged me into the isle, and *her* Parisian scent weakened me. Once on stage I relaxed. Facing three thousand people has always relaxed me and released the ham in me. I love it.

"Wat ees your name?" she wanted to know. (This was the traditional scene in more or less English for the benefit of as much as one-third of the audience.)

I was in no mood to speak English when I knew my French to be so entertaining in its imperfections. *"Jean,"* I lied. *"Mais mes amies les plus intimes m'appellent Jacques."*

"Hi, Jack," she coquetted. Noting my Georgia accent in French, she inquired, "And wair ees y'all's 'ome?"

"Atlanta, Gawjah, honey chile." The audience cheered, either because there were hundreds there from Georgia or because Vivian Leigh and Clark Gable's *Gone With the Wind* was still fresh.

In turn, I asked, "And wat ees your name?"

"Marie, Monsieur."

"It should be Angette."

She batted her long, false eyelashes and asked if I wanted to dance with one of the chorus girls. I headed for the lissome lass I had cast my eyes on all night. Fortunately, the orchestra played a samba, so I was able to display the artistry resulting from my 400 hours of lessons with the unbelievable red-head at the Arthur Murray studio in D.C. The audience expressed boisterous appreciation.

That over without stumbling prostrate, I heard the gorgeous chanteuse, with what I thought was excessive suddenness, considering the brevity of our acquaintance (I was still a Methodist), call from the other side of the stage, "Kom keess me."

Although I had often spoken before large audiences, I had never before been asked to execute the Jenkins kiss before three thousand people, and I'd as soon not be asked to do so again, even when a captivating, very buxom blond is the recipient. I was in a quandary as to how seriously to kiss this vision before me, so near. I neither wanted to disappoint the audience, nor certainly the blonde, nor appear excessively licentious. I didn't know how to ask this babe for guidance. But since I had just been to dinner and ordered a filet mignon "a point," when she asked me to keess her, without thinking, I said "A quel point?" At that I bestowed a keess that I thought unmistakably had southern flair, yet escaped lechery—the delicate balance that we southerners have long perfected.

So help me, in my question to her I thought I was simply asking "How far do I go?" The French audience, however, long practiced in the double entendre, which is a national pastime, brought down the house. I was quickly handed a bottle of cognac and dismissed, but not before the chanteuse pointed to my receding form and said to the audience, *"Pas mal,* not at all bad!" so I guess my only stage performance as an adult was not a disaster.

Still, as I pondered next steps on the deck of our Virginia house, I decided the present state of deterioration of my physiognomy made acting an unpromising prospect.

One evening for dinner I invited the son of friends of ours to the Metropolitan Club in Washington, to celebrate his graduation from chiropractic college. Driving him home I said I had tired of traveling and lecturing and I now had to find something else worthwhile to do. He said, "Why don't you become a chiropractor?" I laughed.

When I got home, however, I couldn't think of a good reason not to become a chiropractor, so I did. The idea appealed to me precisely because it was so different from anything I had ever done. I reasoned that even if I decided not to practice after graduation I would learn a lot, for I had heard that chiropractic graduate school level training these days meant five extremely demanding years. It could be done in four if one went year-round, but that would be ill-advised. During my training a few young men in their 20s dropped out. If I had been twenty I am quite sure I would have, too, but in my late 60s it wouldn't look good. I obtained my Doctor of Chiropractic degree a month before I was 70, and for four years had an active practice at the classy Marketplace at Salishan, two minutes from my residence in Salishan Hills on the central Oregon coast.

My shifting gears from diplomacy to chiropractic appears to have been widely regarded as a peculiar feat. It does not strike me that way at all. As much as I had found diplomacy fulfilling, I wanted to tackle something that was closer to bettering the individuals who collectively support diplomatic efforts—or fail to do so. Knowing that body, mind and spirit all affect each other, chiropractic appealed to me even in the line of my spiritual and philosophical interests, for I was not attracted to religion or esoteric teachings as a profession. Furthermore, chiropractic eschewed drugs and was non-invasive. I liked that.

I think the shift in occupation was in character, because of my overall belief as to the nature of reality. I reasoned in this sequence:

The thing I would like most to see on earth is world peace.

That will not happen until nation-states, or the successor to them (for they are becoming obsolete), have matured beyond their present level of understanding, accepting that the law of cause and effect is inescapable, operable in *every* circumstance. Like individuals, nations must reap what they sow. Unfortunately, the reaping is too often recognized as, happily, likely to come due during the next administration.

With all its many faults, I believe America still holds promise of achieving a significantly higher level of collective knowledge, understanding and awareness—awareness that every thought or act produces results for which responsibility has to be taken. Hence the quiet passion I attempted to hold for U.S. diplomatic efforts and for my own career responsibilities.

However, no country is going to have fully effective government in domestic matters or in foreign affairs, until it has a more fully aware citizenry to sustain it. That is why no government has yet been able fully to meet the needs of its citizens, despite the innumerable forms of government attempted throughout world history. The more basic problem is that no citizenry has yet been able to meet the needs of its government! Government, regardless of its form, even if totalitarian, is ultimately empowered by and takes on the composite nature of its individual citizens, collectively.

The level of awareness of the individual citizen in turn depends on the level of his or her combined physical, mental, emotional and spiritual make-up. These elements of one's nature are so inextricably interrelated, one can advance relatively toward a higher understanding and awareness by improving the quality of any one of them— but the ideal is to improve all, of course.

In my practice I used a non-force form of chiropractic with a holistic approach to the human condition. I did all I knew how to do in contributing primarily to better physical health in the community, through lecturing as well as in my office practice. Furthermore, since all facets of the human being are so wondrously interrelated and interdependent, I hope my effort contributed in its way to better mental, emotional and spiritual conditions as well. At any rate, if one is in physical pain, it is difficult for one's mental and emotional life to prosper, and usually difficult to forget self enough to grow spiritually, as well.

Still, I imagine few diplomats become chiropractors. At least not at age 70. Perhaps that oddity intrigued the National College of Chiropractic into giving me an unexpectedly warm welcome. Thus I matriculated *magna cum laude,* even if I graduated *summa cum difficultate* five years later.

My 'maturity' was peremptorily tagged on my first day on campus, when a charming little four-year old lady accosted me on my path, slung her blonde curls back, put her hands on her haunches, and looking up at me with knitted brow inquired, "Are you an old man?

I learned later that her parents had been in the dormitory for four years, so she had probably seen an old man only in picture books.

Somehow I was loath to acknowledge the fact with a simple "Yes." I replied, "I can say without fear of contradiction that I qualify chronologically, at least."

"Umph!" she umphed. I am not sure how much I had enlightened her, but she skipped happily away, apparently satisfied with her own appraisal.

There were trials. In interminable, late-afternoon hours in anatomy lab, I thought if I did not soon get out of my lungs the suffocating, stinging formaldehyde fumes billowing from that vindictive cadaver, I would expire before I could become God's gift to suffering humanity. As soon as I viewed the hulk assigned to my group of six students I decided he had been a master sergeant. Even in his ponderous, hard-blubbery post-mortem rigor he seemed to dare us to cross him. He did not have the gentle aspect of a Phi Beta Kappa, and the clogged condition of his arteries betokened a heavy beef-eater and an accomplished beer guzzler, a life style possibly further affirmed by our discovery of an implanted pace-maker. As a former enlisted man I knew a master sergeant when I saw one. I wielded my scalpel with flair, slicing away with retributive gusto. At the same time I found myself daydreaming of the placidly paced, civilized evenings of urbane conversation in the diplomatic circuit. I even thought a little more lovingly of the damaging gourmet food. I learned, however, that while I was dissecting The Hulk it was not in the best interest of constitutional continence to daydream of the pâté de fois gras or even of the caviar. The chilled vodka was another matter.

Maybe I went back to school despite its trials because the ghost of Aunt Annie told me to get a fifth degree. Since Methodists tend to emphasize education (and therefore become closet Unitarians in droves), perhaps the urge persists in meta-Methodists. While the precipitating event leading to chiropractic training, as I have indicated, was taking the son of friends of ours to dinner, there was more substantive reason than that. I had become more and more interested in the natural approach to health and in the elementary importance of prevention. I found validity in the prediction attributed to Thomas A. Edison: "The doctor of the future will give no medicine, but will interest his patients in the care of the human frame, in diet, and in the cause and prevention of disease." There was a third reason, which sounds a bit mushy, but is nonetheless true. I considered that the world had been uncommonly good to me, and I wanted to find some medium through which to pay it back a bit. True, I had not had a staggering financial income, though I had usually been far more than comfortable; I had, however, enjoyed at almost every stage of my life a staggering psychic income. I found my practice an ideal way to say thanks to society.

I had, and have, great respect for many things that the medical profession is able to do, especially in control of communicable diseases and in life-saving measures in crises. Doubtless there are times when we need drugs or surgery, and sophisticated machinery. A hospital with a good, practical record of effective patient care is an invaluable community asset, and should be supported. I have advised my patients to support the one nearby.

I came to believe, however, that the over-reliance on drugs and surgery in our country is a national disgrace. We spend more per capita by far than any other country on what are accepted as health measures, yet we are one of the sickest of the "have" nations—probably *the* sickest. (Just ask the World Health Organization.) Obviously, something is badly wrong. Apart from AIDS, the degenerative diseases: arthritis, diabetes, heart attacks, strokes, cancer—are what are killing us off in droves today. Obesity is epidemic, and the list of ailments that are more likely to appear if one is overweight seems to grow each year. Drugs and surgery have not made an impressive overall record in preventing or curing these maladies. A lecturer I once heard put it this way: "We have been carefully schooled to believe that what is wrong with our bodies is a deficiency of toxic chemicals and too many organs!" We have not received enlightened schooling.

There are as many levels of wellness as there are of illness, and no definitive line can be drawn between the two. Far more attention should be paid to wellness and its causes than to illness and its causes, if we want to be well and stay well. Perhaps we have things upside down. In the old days in China one paid his doctor as long as he was well, and stopped paying him when he became ill. We can safely conclude that the system was conducive to an uncommonly caring attitude on the part of the physician. Such a simple arrangement might be ridiculous in the modern context, but with a little ingenuity some comparable, if more complicated, insurance schemes might turn the medical profession—and its symbiotic drug industry—around. We might at long last think seriously of preventive medicine, incalculably reduce suffering and deaths along with the astronomical costs of our current mainline health care system.

For 30, 40, 50 years we live the affluent "good life," the effects of which cumulatively kill; then, when we have symptoms that finally become intolerable, we go to a physician of whatever ilk, and say, "Fix me up." Which, being interpreted, generally means, "Give me a 'pain killer' to cover up the cause of my malady while easing my pain, or, if you really think you should, take out the offending organ." Often the surgeon really thinks he should, for that is what he is trained to do impressively well, and we all like very much to do what we do well.

The body is an incredibly complex phenomenon, subject to all sorts of intellectual, emotional, spiritual and "material" influences, seldom pacified by having a few chemicals poured into it, or, except *in extremis,* having some organ subtracted from it. Ponder a description by Alfreda Oliver, author of books on modern scientific findings: "We deludedly think we know the body physical so well. But the body exists in and consists of a vast complex of ethereal activities; it exists in a great storm of vibrations, undulations, vortices, and flying particles so minute as to be little more than symbols of mathematics. The true nature of the human being is composed of this tenuous, free-flying, etheric substance, which is also the nature of the universe itself."

We gain some idea of the irrefutable validity of the

holistic approach to health—to enliven the patient, not just attack the symptoms, for symptoms are nature's way of trying to tell us something important.

Thus, the sensible next step up from dependence on a cover-up pain killer would be to concentrate on correcting the cause of the disease, rather than leaving the disease to fester and grow under the cover-up. The next giant step above that would be to guide the patient vastly to raise the level of his immune system and to rid his body of long-stored toxins, not only at the alimentary canal level, but at the cellular level, so that the disease would have a less inviting environment for devilment, and a good chance of fading away and not returning.

Provided the patient has not been so mercilessly dosed with chemicals that his damaged immune system leaves little with which to work, I believe there is no incurable disease, including AIDS. I know full well, however, that there are determinedly incurable patients. There is a vast difference.

Almost everyone knows the basics for good health: adequate and appropriate exercise, adequate rest, good nutrition, moderate sunshine, good breathing, a good conscience and a royal refusal to be burdened with the past. More important yet is a passionate love of and dedication to the moment's activity. From talks with hundreds of patients in my office I am led to believe that boredom kills as many people as bullets. Also, rapidly increasing numbers of people are beginning to realize the elementary importance of proper body, especially osseus, alignment, so that neither neural nor vascular supply is impeded. Then only can the organs have a chance to function optimally.

The patient will be best served only when chiropractors, naturopaths, homeopaths, acupuncturists, physical therapists, the allopathic prescription-doctors, drug producers and surgeons all cooperate in proportion as the condition of the patient indicates. Strides have been made in this direction in the past few years, but there are miles to go.

One-on-one treatment methods with demonstrable results from one's efforts is very different from the efforts in diplomacy, which may affect millions in more or less degree, but which are more diffuse and ultimately for the most part impersonal. On the other hand, when a patient comes into the office literally crying from pain and leaves crying with gratitude, that is incomparable payment. Recently I had a tourist more than half seriously try to get me to move to Seattle, claiming she was free of severe pain for the first time in three years. And hers was no isolated case. In short, during my practice, when I returned home at night, I was usually more content with the day just spent than at any other time in my entire life—and I have spent some pretty satisfactory days in other pursuits.

I spent four years of fulfilling chiropractic practice with my dear wife in my office as receptionist, secretary and unparalleled practitioner of goodwill artistry, to say nothing of her being my chief sustainer. One evening we attended two parties, and several people remarked how lovely she was. She seemed so healthy, so beautiful and vibrant. The morning after the two parties she took her usual three-mile fast walk and did the usual number of laps in the pool at the Lodge, I am sure. Then she went into the sauna, lay down on a bench, went to sleep, and did not wake up. There was no struggle at all. Her family has a history of genetic heart problems. We had many exciting plans for the future, when I would gain my consent to give up my beloved practice. I gave it up sooner than expected, for I did not want to continue without Martha. I had lost my life mate of 46 wonderful years, and my best friend.

Epilogue

Salishan Hills, Central Oregon Coast. September 1993.

t this point in my life, at least in my more surface existence, I feel a separation from much with which formerly I have been linked: from my roots in the Southland; geographically, from all my relatives except my daughter; from valued friends in the east; from the adrenaline-loosening demands of former careers; from broad and meaningful responsibilities. The Pacific's expanse separates me from still-beloved China. And the void most difficult to accept on the surface level is the separation from my dear wife.

Yet I try to live less and less on that surface level. I cannot say that I have solved those questions of the nature of God, of man and of cosmic law that troubled me as a child and youth. I am not at all sure they are subject to 'solution.'

than solved, explained or defined.

In any event, these questions trouble me less than they did when I was a youth struggling to be me. I have long since become me, through trial and error, success and failure, love and meditation. I think I have learned a few things to avoid with care, and many things to cultivate with passion.

I have learned bits, I believe, from diverse environments and varied pursuits. First, from times on my father's farms: the health and joy that reside in simplicity; the headiness of fresh air; the contentment from vigorous exercise; utter trust in wonderful neighbors and devotion to them. From being a teacher and educational administrator: the incomparable excitement of watching young, fast-growing minds; the cool-warm innocence of children, versus the challenging and absorbing complexities of faculty; the cost of having been taught certain fears; the penalties and potentials of becoming adult. From military intelligence service at the Pentagon: not a great deal of lasting value except a fascination with China. From 28 years in diplomacy: more than I can possibly say, but perhaps most of all that a negative, suspicious view of the world and a positive, approving view of the world both invite self-fulfilling prophesies. From lecturing around the world: that to be paid well for what you most love doing is very agreeable. From four years of chiropractic practice: a great deal about sickness, wellness, the advertising-engendered, atrocious, standard American diet, and much to love in human nature. From 46 wonderful years of marriage: that a close relationship, if it is to be successful, takes a great deal of attention and consideration—and that it can be worth far, far more than the costs.

I have indeed learned that in international affairs, in boardrooms, classrooms and bedrooms, amicable and full communication is the key to understanding, and hence to satisfaction, to happiness, to communal effort and fulfillment.

Considering the variety and complexity of people, places and events with whom and with which I have endeavored to accommodate, work, enjoy and cope, I have come to a somewhat surprising conclusion. I believe that the laws of life are simple: we get what we put out, and we create our circumstance in accordance with what we truly believe to be the nature of reality. While I believe the laws of life are simple, the living by them may not be easy, largely because of the extreme difficulty we have in believing that life can be approached in simplicity.

Each of us sees through his own private prism—presented, perhaps, by genes, but then ground and reground according to his differing thoughts, actions and life experiences. I have friends whom I admire and respect, whose prisms will surely tell them that the above and much in the last two chapters constitute arrant nonsense. Never mind. I have simply stated where I have landed in my eighth decade.

Once again, as I end my story, my father's dignified, warm image comes before me, saying, "Son, always remember, in all ways, *de gustibus non disputandum est* (concerning tastes, let there be no dispute). Father knew about prisms. He tried to show me both their reality and their inestimable value. For that, I have had reason to be grateful at every stage of my life. If we all came to recognize, accept and value the inescapable reality of varying prisms, our essential oneness beyond them might become more apparent and a peaceful world at last conceivable. We would recognize not only our interconnectedness with all beings, but our interconnectedness with all things, and ultimately with all thoughts and all actions. The human experiment would have taken one of its rare, quantum leaps, comparable in magnitude to the origin of consciousness itself.

To order additional copies or to send a gift of:

Country, Conscience And Caviar

A Diplomat's Journey In The Company Of History

Please send _____ copies at $19.95 each, plus $4 shipping and handling for the first book, $2.50 for each additional book in the same order.

[ ] Check   [ ] Money Order   [ ] Visa   [ ] MasterCard

Card # _____ Exp. Date_____

Signature _____

Name_____

Company/Organization _____

Street Address _____

City/State/Zip _____

Please advise if recipient and mailing address are different from above. Surface shipping may take three to four weeks.

Please return this order form with payment to:

BookPartners
P.O. Box 922
Wilsonville, Oregon 97070

For credit card orders call: 1-800-468-1994